To
Carson—
Thanks for joining me
on this journey. I hope you
enjoy the saga.
Best always!
Mark.

The Forger's Apprentice

Life With The World's Most Notorious Artist

by

Mark Forgy

ISBN: 1470193086
ISBN 13: 9781470193089

To Elmyr and Alice

Part One

In the summer of 1969 college was little more than a bulletproof vest giving me a deferment from the draft and Vietnam. The previous year saw hope and sanity burn on the funeral pyres of Martin Luther King and Robert Kennedy. Chicago's Democratic Convention captured the mood of the country: tear gas, riot police, batons beating protesters, and organized resistance. American society had not been as divided since the Civil War. By April of '69 more than thirty-three-thousand bodies in black zippered bags came home from the Tropic of Hell. I knew I wouldn't let myself be inducted or induced "to just sign up and get it over with," as my father urged me to do. It was an immoral war, indefensible and unwinnable, I thought. Drugs and the spirit of rebellion carried me and millions more in their currents. Rather than going to beautiful Southeast Asia, I elected to go to Europe. It would be an escape from my flirtation with higher learning, although the consequences of my decision would change my life in ways I could not have imagined.

On the Spanish Mediterranean island of Ibiza, I discovered a refuge friendly to the '60s counterculture. There, I met an artist named Elmyr (pronounced el-MEER). "De Hory," his family name, he declared "is *Hungarian*." The inflection in his voice elevated the ordinary to extraordinary, as in "I would like a *steak*," lending a piece of meat the uniqueness of a jellyfish soufflé. He had an impresario's flair about him I came to accept as normal, and this infectious enthusiasm was apparent to anyone around him. His appearance, like his manner, was best appreciated in a mirror, or the eyes of an adoring audience. "People," he told me, "will always judge you by their first impression, so it is important that you look your best and make a favorable impression." He imparted such pronouncements as though reading them off a stone tablet. It was therefore unsurprising that his silver hair was neatly parted, and often by the tortoiseshell comb he always kept in the pocket of his crisply creased pants. Shirts made from Egyptian cotton, cashmere sweaters, wool suits tailored by the same hands as those made by appointment to some member of the British royal family, and polished leather shoes—preferably Italian—all had their assigned places in his drawers or bedroom closet. Refinements such as these went with the polished silver, rows of books, and the paintings and sculptures that graced his hilltop villa, all part of the careful stagecraft intended to impress others. The charm, ready smile, and the twinkle his brown eyes unleashed reflexively made him a human magnet—attracting his victims who, succumbing to an irresistible allure, welcomed their fate. I, like so many others in his company, fell under his spell.

I sensed something special about Elmyr when I spotted him the first day I arrived on the island. It was a sun-filled autumn morning when the ship docked in the port of Ibiza town. Towering above the clustered white stucco buildings, like irregular, vertically stacked dominoes, the sand-colored ramparts of the Old City suggested this small island had been a once-important landmark along an ancient seafaring trade route between the Balearic Islands and the Mediterranean coast. Leaning over the rail, I watched as two men pushed a mobile stairway next to the ship while two others looped thick ropes around steel-knob hitching posts. It was Sunday, the first of November, and though still warm, the crowds of summer had vanished. I noticed Elmyr standing alone on the quay; he wore a cardigan sweater, open-collar shirt with an ascot, and Hollywood sunglasses. Inspecting this new brigade of hippies who disembarked, he searched our faces, looking for one familiar to him. I approached him and asked if he spoke English. He smiled. "Like they do in Kansas City!" he responded, although his accent was something other than

Midwestern. I then asked if he could recommend any hotels. He pointed to a narrow cobbled street. "You'll find several inexpensive *pensions* in that direction," he said. I thanked him and left. When I discovered nothing available, I resigned myself to another night sleeping on a beach. That evening, after weaving in and out of some portside bars, I ran into Elmyr again. "Did you have any luck finding a place?" he asked. I told him no. He said "Well, I have a guest room in my house you're welcome to use, if you like." It was a spontaneous offer, I thought, one I couldn't refuse. My overnight stay drifted into days, then a week. I tried to make myself useful, offering to help with whatever needed to be done during that time. He then asked if I cared to stay on, working as his assistant. His home had a swimming pool, a housekeeper he'd fashioned into an amazing cook, and Elmyr was generous and entertaining. There was no down side that I could see. Nor could I guess the secrets in Elmyr's past. All I knew was that he disappeared into his studio each morning and that I wasn't supposed to bother him during that time. Curiosity only once prompted me to ask what might warrant knocking on that door. He glared at me as though I'd forgotten my mother's name, turned without replying, entered his sanctum, and closed the door.

My chores around his house entailed helping out at his frequent parties, keeping his garden weed-free, cleaning the pool, driving for him, and secretarial duties, helping with his correspondence; his English vocabulary was larger than mine, but his handwriting looked as cryptic as a doctor's prescription. I also had a slightly better grasp of punctuation. There was no heavy lifting, just mostly indulging a need I recognized—companionship. Here was a man who was lonely despite the flurry of social activity surrounding him. Within a few weeks of our meeting, he told me that if I wanted to live in Europe, I needed to speak two or *three* languages. He then enrolled me at the local Alliance Française for private French lessons.

He recommended books he deemed essential. He urged me to read Balzac, Dostoyevsky, and Thomas Mann, along with art books, biographies, and history—everything that would give me a well-rounded education. Yet it was daily life that provided the most remarkable learning experiences of all, and meeting Prosky made clear the chasm between the life I had known and what it had become.

While it would have been easy to dismiss Prosky as an archetypal thug, I tried to avoid that impulse of first impressions, one Elmyr indulged with a nonchalance he learned from a lifetime of habit. I wanted to be more generous in my assessment of others. Still, it was hard not to notice that Prosky's nose had been at odds with others' points of view more than once, and how his early-man features stretched over Bigfoot's chassis. Underneath his black leather jacket and half-buttoned shirt, shocks of black chest hair intertwined with gold chains. A neat shave line encircled the base of his neck, where the forest began. He possessed the coarseness of a wood rasp, but he and Elmyr shared an interest in art and money, and both were Hungarian. Moreover, Prosky could sell you cold dishwater and make you feel good about buying it.

One day I glimpsed, from the second-floor window of Elmyr's home, Prosky's black Mercedes convertible with its red leather seats. A talc of off-road dust dulled the car's sheen. He parked in the shade of the house, got out, and walked up the stone steps to the front door. The steel doorknocker announced his unexpected call. His six-year old daughter waited with his Doberman pinscher in the car. (Elmyr quipped, "in case the dog got hungry.")

On this occasion Prosky brought him an auction catalog from Sotheby's in Geneva. Inside, he proudly pointed out a painting featured in its sale of twentieth-century art, a scene of Nice in southern France. Palm trees lined the harbor and street-lamped promenade; swaths of pinks, blues, and greens were backdrops for people, buildings, and horse-drawn carriages. What was unusual about this painting was the signature in the lower right-hand corner of the canvas. Elmyr and I examined the reproduced picture and instantly recognized it as one he had done a few months before. Only now, it bore the name not of Elmyr, but of the French artist Raoul Dufy.

For more than twenty years, Elmyr made a career of creating fake masterpieces—not only Dufys but also many better-known impressionist and postimpressionist artists. His long trail of chicanery earned him the title of the "world's greatest art forger," a label that always made him wince, as he believed it demeaned his dignity. However, the specter of those years and evading the consequences of his illegal activities still troubled him. Every knock at the door might be an Interpol agent and a moment of reckoning. Furthermore, he was weary of constantly looking over his shoulder to see if a Damoclean sword was waiting to fall. Now he was trying to emancipate himself from his past and establish a reputation as a fine artist in his own right, but Prosky, among others, was more interested in passing off his fakes as originals—again. That was where the *big* money was, and people knew Elmyr's reputation as an easy mark.

Despite his efforts to sell his own work, people still wanted his Picassos, Matisses, Modiglianis, and Renoirs. He also understood the likelihood of others trying to profit from his talent, but did not have the stamina or will to *police* their intentions. I recall how his suntan could not disguise the blood loss in his pallor that afternoon as he gazed in silent déjà vu at the catalog's Dufy. Its pages trembled in his hands. Prosky remained oblivious of the growing storm in Elmyr's face. Instead, unable to contain his joy, Prosky began moving with the gaiety and weightlessness of a marionette. His little secret burst. "It fetched thirty-five-thousand dollars," he chortled.

Visibly upset at the surprise news, Elmyr went off on a tirade in Hungarian. His stiffened forefinger bounced repeatedly off Prosky's sternum, backing up a man whose shadow easily swallowed him. Moving with not-seen-before speed, he began frisking Prosky in a ticklish way. Elmyr's hands darted into Prosky's trouser pockets one after the other like a striking serpent, emerging with fists full of cash. Then, pushing him into an easy chair, lifted one of his legs like a professional wrestler, and removed his shoe and sock to reveal a neatly folded wad of money, repeating the surprise move with his other leg. Disarmed by Elmyr's slapstick assault, Prosky lay supine in paroxysms of laughter; tears trickled down his cheeks while his naked feet rested on a small table in front of his chair. Their comic ballet ended as abruptly as it began.

The booty from his money-yielding piñata lay on the floor: Swedish kroner, dollars, and Swiss francs. Collecting them on his hands and knees did little to salvage Elmyr's dignity, but the glint in his eyes signaled his triumph. No matter how long removed from the antics of these two men, the memory remains imperishable. At the time, I didn't know if this spectacle was typical of gypsy bargaining techniques, but was happy it became an entertaining ritual each time they did business. Fernand Legros, Elmyr's former dealer, had not acted as brazenly as

Prosky had. In essence, he declared to Elmyr, "See, I can exploit you and there is nothing you can do about it."

My life by this time had evolved into an otherworldly existence that in its strangeness often seemed LSD-inspired. I know the sort of dance of the two silverbacks I witnessed that afternoon would never occur back in Minnesota. Outrageous behavior like that would be grist for Sunday's sermon and community indignation. However, this small island of Ibiza was a universe away from a quiet life that often comforts Midwesterners. "Don't draw attention to yourself," was a constant reminder from my parents. In Elmyr's world humility had its place—say, reposing in a casket. In his mind, it was a vapid attribute, like the word *nice*, which I quickly dropped from my vocabulary after using it once in his presence to describe someone. Elmyr had looked annoyed, shooting back, "What do you mean, nice? He wouldn't *pee* on your dining room table?"—an image forever linked to that word. His response was less a rebuff than a catalyst realigning my view of a world order, one that conformed more to his oft-repeated adage: *kalt odor heiss, aber nicht warm*—cold or hot but not warm—meaning he had little tolerance for anything in half measure. "Nice" was therefore tepid and uninteresting.

It was clearer to Elmyr than to me that my job was migrating into other areas I hadn't anticipated. Elmyr was becoming my mentor, before I knew what a mentor was. I only later realized his willingness to provide an open door to an unknown world carried with it other expectations.

One evening, we sat reading in his café-au-lait leather chairs. Beethoven's triple piano concerto accompanied our winter night ritual. Olive wood burned on the stone hearth fireplace behind us. A furrowed *V* above the bridge of his nose signaled the gravity of his thoughts. "Is something bothering you?" I asked. He was reading a biography of one of his favorite painters, Caravaggio, a brawling, precocious genius with an unerring compass for finding trouble. The sway between success and sorrow was a persistent pattern in Elmyr's own life. The tribulations of the great artist and inventor of the dramatic use of light and dark called *chiaroscuro*, possibly dredged up memories he tried to suppress. Elmyr, like Caravaggio, had been a fugitive from the law, his talent underappreciateated and at odds with prevailing tastes, and both men forced to bear the risks of being homosexual. "This is disturbing. His life was so hard," he breathed with the spent energy of a marathoner. Neither artist was a stranger to poor choices and their lamentable consequences. Elmyr was about to share with me one mistake that changed his life.

"I appreciate your help around here, and your company. I'm glad you're interested in other things, not hanging out at the bars, and that you want to learn about art and languages. You also know about my past and my association with Fernand Legros. I know there is nothing Legros would like better than to see me dead." This made sense, as no one else could incriminate Legros as Elmyr could, knowing he personally handed off hundreds of his artworks to Legros. These were secrets he would rather see Elmyr take to the grave.

I then began to grasp the drift of our evening's chat. I could see my role expanding. Beyond chauffeuring, garden and pool chores, and secretarial duties, it seemed my job description would now include… bodyguard! Just then I wondered if this would entail a weapon of some sort. What might that be? A knife? I'd surely cut myself. A gun? Oh, I once found my brother's small handgun and shot three holes in the apartment wall before figuring out how the safety worked. Elmyr may have thought my presence as a witness was deterrent enough to thwart any assassination attempt on his life, although the logic of this rationale remained elusive. If Elmyr were in harm's way, I could offer the resistance of a turnstile. This was a leap of misplaced confidence since any snarling lapdog would back me down in a fight. Given my willowy physique, most observers would probably mistake me for one of those underfed, melon-eyed urchins on the verge of tears, immortalized on velvet by equally famished artists. Visions wallpapered my imagination of some baboon-jawed thug, with a finger's breadth between his eyebrows and hairline, repeatedly smacking a tire iron into his other hand. Despite a mental picture of our lifeless bodies stuffed in a steamer trunk, my fondness for Elmyr made me sputter, "I'll do whatever I can to help."

The morbid notion of our gangland-style murders was a striking contrast to the life I had come to accept as normal. For me, life in his villa, La Falaise, was an enchanted existence. Nor could I see any signs of the danger he feared that evening. To the contrary, he appeared enveloped in adulation from friends, a bad-boy media darling in the world's press, newly conferred folk hero and giant killer for exposing the fallibility of art experts.

On the other hand, the experts' embarrassment still glowed red. This was apparent from an article about Elmyr appearing in *Life* magazine early in 1970. Their Paris bureau chief, Rudolph Chelminski, came to interview Elmyr. During his three-day visit, he and Elmyr seemed to establish an immediate rapport. Within two weeks of Chelminski's departure, he sent Elmyr a draft of his article. It was a sympathetic view of the artist. When it appeared in print, its tone was substantially different, suggesting Elmyr was an amateur, a "dilettante." Chelminski wrote him an apology, stating he couldn't account for the changes but would find out why it bore no semblance to the piece he submitted. Elmyr later discovered it went to one of the senior editors of the magazine who was connected to the Annenburg family of Philadelphia. Their art collection and reputation epitomized those deeply rooted interests that could not support any praise of a man they viewed as the Antichrist. Therefore, it was as counterintuitive for anyone with stakes in the art establishment to say anything complimentary about Elmyr, as it would be to throw salt in an open wound.

Despite Elmyr's yearning for approval, he knew he would always have his detractors. While this backlash possessed a sting, it amused him to be riding a swell of notoriety. Since his history was now out in the open, he thought, perhaps his life of stealth and deception was finally past. People wanted to meet this "famously infamous" man, as he newly described himself, always with a smile and ring of irony.

The pace of entertaining at La Falaise accelerated, and he reveled in the attention of those around him. I now better understood Elmyr's whirling social life was as essential as oxygen to him, and that it also had as much to do with his aversion to being alone as it did with his naturally friendly disposition. I came to believe that my company and that of others was his remedy for the sense of abandonment that plagued him from childhood. He made no distinction between solitude and loneliness. Either left him unplugged, feeling isolated. When I went to visit friends, his face assumed the look of a child lost at the mall. I knew this ever-present need for companionship was the portal that allowed me into his world, but it also dismantled the judgment filter that allows one a self-preservation instinct. The absence of this defense mechanism let the barbarians through the gate at will, and I could not always protect him from repeated pillaging of his unwary nature. How did he remain impenetrable to the lessons of misplaced trust? Furthermore, how could a man be guileless and consistently cunning enough to fool others at the same time? These contradictions made this new father figure in my life a daily source of wonder and endearment. I came to believe those close to him, whose friendships he clutched with a terrier-like tenacity, felt the same depth of love for him.

In many ways it felt like an out-of-body experience to simultaneously participate in and witness my own conscientiousness-raising transformation. Elmyr became the guru overseeing my education. He found an eager pupil in me, one ready to accept his tutelage and absorb the knowledge that seemed to gush from him. I often felt like the sorcerer's apprentice, attending a private academy, privy to arcane bits of information whose usefulness or purpose were not immediately apparent but would give me the social graces of aristocrats. It was, after all, this rarefied world of the landed gentry in which he demonstrated an obsessive interest and claimed his own genesis. Furthermore, his skill at negotiating the thinnest limbs of obscure family trees with the deftness of a ring-tailed lemur was mystifying. Pointing out the significance of incestuous alliances, marriages, and titles of people I had never heard of, nor cared to, he shared these facts as though they were as meaningful and important as knowing the alphabet.

I recall standing before Rafael's portrait of Pope Julius II in London's National Gallery, with Elmyr expounding on the painterly qualities of the picture. His enthusiasm then seemed to increase as he explained the sitter's genealogical connection to a noble Italian family Elmyr counted among his friends. "Julius the second was a Della Rovere, duke of Urbino." He continued, "The Della Rovere family actually produced two popes, Sixtus IV, who had the Sistine Chapel built, and then his nephew, Julius II, who commissioned Michelangelo to paint the ceiling." History, art, literature, everything had its place on a living tapestry, and he loved knowing how all the threads were connected. Sharing his knowledge came easily, and it was through these private lessons that education assumed a dimension it never possessed in my formal schooling, all for my benefit.

Stories flowed endlessly. He recounted his adventures and hardships. I marveled at his endurance. From the comfort of those leather easy chairs his life unfolded before me, narrated in Alistair Cooke erudition

9

for his audience of one. Lest I lend some mythic proportion to his anecdotes, he was quick to dismiss this inclination. I once said in response to his tale, "You're so wise." He shrugged, adding, "If that were true, I wouldn't have made so many stupid mistakes." Unfortunately, the clarity of hindsight had a short shelf life for him.

La Falaise was much more than a cultural sanctuary. It was the School of Elmyr. There, he showed me the love a father shows a son, a bond and depth of commitment I never knew with my own father. He taught me that relationships were the foundation of true happiness. Consequently, the love and trust he invested in others were his greatest source of validation and vulnerability. While he was eager to give me a unique education, and provided me a safe harbor, I became his sentinel, wanting to protect him from those who might take advantage of him. Somehow, I eased into this role, not in the daunting way of some no-neck bouncer, but more the ear-whispering counselor, simply because I could spot the sharks' fins surfacing before he did. It was odd, an unlikely responsibility for a twenty-year-old from the Midwest, to advise someone worldly, a couple of generations removed from me. The difference, I think, was that he came to rely on my observer's perspective. Moreover, experience showed him that sound judgment did not come easily to him and that the insights of his own self-awareness were of limited value.

In retrospect, the odder life became in Elmyr's world, the more normal it seemed. My own evolution resulted from his showering influence on me, which was most apparent when I returned to the States after living in Europe for a year. I wore ascots, talked about wine, dropped names unknown to most. My friends viewed me as they would a nudist at a Baptist bible camp: stunned and surprised. They could barely understand my new British accent. The doctrine of Lutheran humility drummed into me in my youth vanished completely. I knew I couldn't remain long in Minnesota. I had to return to the island, breathe the salubrious air of Ibiza, and regroup once more with my inner snob. After two weeks, everyone probably awaited my departure with the same relief as the end of a cholera epidemic. To my mind, the reason for the newly noticed disparity between us was simple. They weren't growing, and I was. This wasn't true, of course, but our life paths *were* diverging. Looking back, it was unsurprising how much I had become Elmyr's alter ego or that I was oblivious of my transformation. I suppose it was akin to the "Stockholm syndrome," only being held captive in a Swiss finishing school. Twelve months earlier, this metamorphosis would have been unimaginable. However, if one subscribes to the idea that there is no such thing as happenstance, and that everything occurs for a reason and by design, then I am comfortable calling this chapter in my life —destiny. And telling the entire saga as I experienced it is part of that destiny.

Elmyr's Story

Anyone would notice the meager size of Elmyr's bedroom, where his bed hugged a corner of the room. "I had to have it specially made because it would have been too big and partially blocked the doorway to the bathroom," he explained. A narrow pathway separated the end of the bed and a dresser opposite. I can visualize his autocratic German architect, Irwin Brauner, a student of the Bauhaus school of design, arguing that it only needed to accommodate a bed to *sleep on*. So, why make it bigger? Bauhaus minimalist theories of design were immutable and often a landscape for battle when Elmyr suggested changes he thought might make his home more suited to his liking. Off the bedroom there was a sitting room that he used as his studio, with a view overlooking a bay. Here, finished or partially completed canvases leaned against the walls. Two palettes and tubes of oil paints rested on a table beside the color-splattered easel. This was where he created his art.

No room in the house, except the kitchen, was devoid of artwork. Oils, gouaches, watercolors, pencil, and pen and ink drawings in Elmyr's own style were displayed, as well as a collection representing

Ibiza's sizable colony of artists. Their styles ranged from figurative to contemporary abstract art. Facing his bed hung a gouache by one of the island's resident painters. It was a turbulent watercolor of horses and riders in reds, browns, and ochre. When I questioned him about the artist, he said, "It's by a Dutch painter, Leiss...very talented. He lived here for some time, but ultimately died of a heroin overdose. It was sad. He died so young." It may sound cliché, but at that time in my life I hadn't yet heard a story of an artist whose life was *not* measured in mile markers of tragedy. Around that time Elmyr gave me a copy of Benvenuto Cellini's autobiography to read. It, too, was full of storm clouds, perpetually raining on a trend-bucking iconoclast. What else should I have suspected from Elmyr's own stories? Still, on his bedroom dresser underneath the Leiss was a framed family photo. It suggested a time in his life before war, loss of innocence, and a career of artful deception.

Elmyr, shown as a young boy, dressed in summer white, stands behind his seated mother and aunt. "There was a large country house behind that row of trees," he told me. All the adults are elegant, with serious demeanors. Elmyr, perhaps due to his childhood exuberance, smiles amid the sobriety of his family members. His mother casts a distracted, melancholy gaze, almost prescient of their impending sadness and devastation. I can't forget how his upbeat mood quickly changed when I said to him, "Tell me about this photograph." His expression turned wistful, his tone somber, recalling a distant, bittersweet time. From that solitary photo, no one could guess Elmyr's destiny.

"It was at my grandmother's summer home," he began. "She was a very cultured woman, very elegant, and I remember that she collected some drawings I had done at the age of six or seven that she thought good enough to frame. She was intelligent and knowledgeable about art and knew exactly what was good or bad. This was my earliest recollection of anyone thinking my artwork worthy of displaying, although I was mildly surprised when I did see them on the walls in her home." Although I'm not certain what effect this gesture of family pride had on him—it may have been memorable as an isolated demonstration of approval.

Elmyr, with his mother and aunt – circa 1916

His family stared back at me from a bygone era. Another group photo showed ladies in plumed hats, pearls, lace-frilled dresses, men in round-collared shirts, tiepins, mustaches, and slicked hair, all in rigid poses. This image attested to what I learned from our fireside chats, suggesting that he came from a background of means and social status. Still, I was more eager to climb aboard his train of thought than he was to travel again across that terrain of haunting remembrances. At times, I had to coax these souvenirs, as I suspected there was no shortage of psychic scar tissue associated with his past, so I felt I was sometimes prying off a bandage on an unhealed wound.

I knew he was born to a life of prestige and wealth in Budapest in 1906, in the twilight of Central Europe's Austro Hungarian Empire. No one in his family or in the rest of Europe had any reason to believe their lives of privilege would not assume the same predictable continuity as the Danube's muddy waters. That blush of cherubic innocence disappeared with the assassinations of the Archduke Franz Ferdinand and his wife by a disgruntled anarchist in Sarajevo, Bosnia on June 28, 1914. His nihilistic snit catapulted the continent (and far-off parts of the globe) into a bloody morass of war that heralded the demise of a way of life captured in those early family photos.

As a child, he felt the love he wanted from his mother was never forthcoming. Instead, that emotion radiated from his wet nurse and surrogate mother, a servant in his family's employ, he told me. They enjoyed the warmth and bond his maternal parent seemed incapable of showing. His diplomat father spent long periods away from home, according to Elmyr, posted to various embassies throughout Europe, which also suggested a distance in his parent's marriage not only measured in kilometers.

"My mother was a very beautiful woman, and I remember that she was always surrounded by men," he said. "My parents were having a party one night. I watched from behind the stair balusters, but for some reason I wanted to go downstairs to my mother. I was probably four or five years old at the time. I ran to her and wanted to kiss her, but, telling me that I would disturb her makeup, she turned her head away." There is no way of measuring the ramification of his rejection. It may be just coincidental that the desire for validation and love that I witnessed seemed to be an unending quest throughout his life. What his parents could not offer him in demonstrative affection they substituted with material comfort. This bourgeois inclination and indulgence also featured prominently in his worldview and casual acceptance of a privileged lifestyle.

By the time the Armistice of 1918 concluded, Europe was a ghost of its former glory. The monuments to hubris and folly were seemingly endless fields of grave markers, which in a macabre way resembled a surreal crop sewn and harvested by the grim reaper. This moment was also the death knell of centuries'-old empires, and with their demise, new countries and borders emerged. Elmyr's well-to-do family lost substantial land holdings in Transylvania, now located in newly established Romania.

Gaunt and pale faces of this lost generation reflected the tireless and ever-inventive obsession with their own self-destruction. Edvard Munch's eerie figure featured in *The Scream* might have best captured the revulsion to Europe's nightmare. To prove Voltaire's insight into human nature when he said that history never repeats itself but people always do, a little more than twenty years would elapse before the Second World War would try to eclipse the madness and calamity of the previous one. Despite the staggering shock of war that left an entire world reeling, dazed, and with a profound sense of despair, those who had not succumbed to its devastation and misery attempted to reclaim their lives and normalcy. Elmyr's family was perhaps more fortunate than many. His mother came from a long established line of Jewish bankers from Szeged, Hungary's second-largest city after Budapest. Despite their diminished fortune by the four-year-long cataclysm, they retained the means to live comfortably amid a drastically changed Europe.

It was easy to see in Elmyr's face and hear in his voice the personal pain of living through the disintegration of a life he had known and memories that would not let him forget. It was an unusual occurrence when he recounted these souvenirs, and he would not dwell on them. It was up to me to thread together this oral history. These intimate snapshots of his life were vivid, poignant, like something reluctantly revealed within a clenched fist when slowly relaxed. The texture, detail, flavor, odors of a faded epoch filled my senses and allowed me to understand him better, his past and present heartache.

This ability to make his stories and insights come alive is what I remember most when I accompanied him to many of the great art museums of Europe. I just stood back, listened, and watched. Entering a gallery, he looked around, leading me to a painting he thought significant. His arms gathered momentum as he conducted a symphony—retracing the brush strokes in a visual staccato, andante, allegro, or adagio—then asking me to come closer to examine some detail, as though peaking through a knothole to reveal something remarkable. These visits animated my education. When, for instance, we stood in the Prado before a painting of Hieronymus Bosch, *The Garden of Earthly Delights*, depicting the torments of hell, he had a special talent of translating the artist's peculiarly tortured visions in an earthy way. "Mark," he would command, "come look at this, you see the detail of these creatures. You can easily see how Dali was influenced by him and borrowed ideas for his work, that *phantasmagoria* of surrealism." Bosch's religiously inspired depiction of hell, I surmised, was perhaps less gruesome than the reality of war with which Elmyr was too well acquainted. The painting's horrific nature, however, resonated with his personal recollections of cruelty, death, crushed innocence, and human frailty.

His visceral upset was again apparent when viewing Goya's visually compelling series of etchings, *The Horrors of War*. They were at once a hypnotic and disturbing testimony to man's inhumanity to man. We viewed this important part of the Prado's great collection on every visit to the museum. Goya's visions are haunting, yet his masterly draftsmanship is riveting. Elmyr showed me how a savage subject matter can be both repellent and something that lifts the soul. We might otherwise have fled this splendid gallery for the preponderance of images of Christ enduring crucifixion.

Elmyr made frequent trips to Madrid, partly because he had friends there, partly because it was the nearest European capital offering those refinements he enjoyed—good restaurants, upscale department stores, nightclubs, his favorite art supply store, Macaron, and the Prado. It was an easy cure for island fever, that sense of sameness that sets in among residents living in a relatively confined area. Not as chronic as for those inhabitants of Devil's Island, I imagine, but still giving one the desire to get away. I understood this restlessness. In Minnesota we called it "cabin fever." After being holed up all winter, inside, with uncommunicative

Norwegians, and eating colorless food spoiled by too many spices, like salt or pepper, you'd just want a change of scenery.

I found it exciting to see those masterpieces from Elmyr's art books, up close at the Prado. Today, as I look through some of his sketchbooks, populated with people, it is easy to see his fascination with their faces. He said to me once while leafing through a book on Modigliani, the artist whose style I thought Elmyr captured best in his illicit mimicry, "You know Modigliani painted only a handful of landscapes in his life." He also was a people painter, a searcher of souls. "If you look at Rembrandt's portraits, the humanity of his sitters pours out," he declared. Elmyr also succeeded in mapping out psychic depth in the topography of those faces. He demonstrated penetrating insight of others in his art, but outside his medium, he was clueless. I remain unable to explain that disconnect. Unfortunately, it didn't occur to me to say to him, "If you really want to understand a person, get to their core, do their portrait." It would have provided him the most effective border patrol imaginable.

Nevertheless, we returned to the Prado's collection of Flemish and Dutch art, the life-size, mid-Renaissance portraits, especially Albrecht Dürer's self-portrait as a young man. Painted in 1498, Dürer, like his contemporary Michelangelo, who created his Pieta a year later, reminds us that talent occasionally justifies egotism. Wavy tresses rest on his shoulders; he strikes a foppish pose of self-possessed confidence. This talented dandy glares back at us, inviting praise for his sartorial splendor and awesome skill. Elmyr told me, "Dürer once met the great Venetian painter Giovanni Bellini. He asked Dürer how he achieved such fine detail in his work, if he painted with one-bristled brushes. Standing in the Italian's studio, Dürer grabbed the nearest brush and said 'With one of these.' "

Whenever we examined the works of the great masters there—Velasquez, Rubens, Goya, and others—especially their graphic work, I saw a similarity between their drawings and Elmyr's. It was the result of a time-honored tradition, little changed for five hundred years. All these artists through the centuries received similar training, following techniques common to figurative art. "Drawing," Elmyr said, "is the foundation of everything." And he was opening my eyes. I was learning to see what he was teaching me, beginning to understand principles of draftsmanship, design, composition, color—the foundations of his world—enabling me to better appreciate all that was important to knowing the value of art, its influence on him, and, consequently, his influence on the world of art.

The Making Of An Artist

Elmyr's tutelage was serious and relentless, but without the corporal punishment that flourished in my public school upbringing or that friends of mine experienced in private Catholic schools at the hands of those tyrants in habits. Nonetheless, he knew he was giving me an opportunity, an education I could not receive anywhere else. Therefore I never wanted to suggest by word or deed that I didn't appreciate what he was doing for me. All I had to do was pay attention, do my homework, provide him the company he desired, and let him fashion me into the kind of person that might have earned his parent's approval—though learning what I did from his stories probably would have made that goal unattainable.

Despite signs of his precocious talent beyond the normal creative expressions of children, his conventional-minded parents may not have been ready to endorse his bohemian leanings. In view of their dispassionate connection to him, his interest in art blossomed on its own without encouragement or discouragement from his mother and father. Yet their divorce when he was sixteen perhaps made the decision to admit him to art school easier. They eventually accepted the notion of him pursuing formal training as an artist. His family's means and social position suggested no sense of urgency for him to decide on a future career. His father, showing his concern on the matter, had this to say: "I don't care what you do with your life. I just don't want you to do anything where you depend on tips from others—like a barber." As remote a prospect as this was, it reveals not only his parent's depth of thought on the subject but a shocking lack of expectations for their son.

Elmyr about 16 years old

While this emotional aloofness is hard for many of us to grasp, one must view it in the context of his era and upbringing. He had a succession of foreign governesses, French, German, and British. Their butler was British. Servants surrounded him. Private tutors guided his education. As in a corporate organizational chart, the parents were the CEOs and remained distant from the day-to-day operation of the household, while others raised their children. This may explain much, but it does not exonerate his parents' emotional vacuity, a trait that he fortunately never inherited. It would be easy to imagine how the apparently disengaged relationship with his seemingly uncaring parents might make their offspring crazy with resentment. However, he accepted this fact of life with composure, I thought, and never expressed a word of disrespect toward them in all the time I knew him.

In 1924 life was about to change dramatically for him. There would be no more luxurious family vacations at Europe's fashionable resorts, Karlsbad, Ostende, Biarritz, or Paris. What negligible attention he had received from his mother and father before would now seem lavish. After two years of study in Hungary at the famous art colony of Nagybánya, and feeling he had absorbed all he could learn there, he persuaded his parents to let him go to Munich. At the age of eighteen, Elmyr registered for art classes at the Akademie Heimann. "I received a strict education, heavily emphasizing classical art. I never knew that degree of discipline before, but I later appreciated it," he said. His teacher, Moritz Heiman, would have him do a study of a hand or a nude repeatedly for five or six hours each day for two weeks until he deemed his student's work satisfactory. "He was a rigid taskmaster," Elmyr added.

The Bavarian air suited him, highly oxygenated with freedom. For the first time in his life, he lived out of reach of his parents. He sensed his life was his own if only he were not still wholly dependant on his family for financial support. He was a well-bred young man of means and easily attracted new friends who were quick to take advantage of his largesse and cavalier attitude toward money. When he neared the end of his funds for enjoying life in Munich and the company of his less well-off companions, he simply sent a telegram home. His parents then immediately wired money to a local bank. The ease with which they replenished his account without a word of caution is surprising, given his family's ties to the prudent world of banking. He later lamented this lack of restraint or forethought, which "forever influenced my carefree view of money."

By the early 1920s, Europe had begun to rebound from the aftermath of the ruinous war. People sought relief from its trauma in the hedonistic pleasures of Munich's nightlife. Elmyr joined the revelry with abandon, and it was here that his youthful awakening assumed another dimension. He began to suspect the reason his parents never showed him the love he craved. Possibly, they knew before he did that he was homosexual. The cabarets, nightclubs, and *bier kellars* of the city offered him opportunities to meet attractive, sensually vibrant companions and receive long-desired attention. While he felt emancipated from any unwelcome disapproval from his family, an ingrained sense of social decorum and reserve inhibited an open expression of his sexuality outside his nighttime haunts. Even then, the importance of image, marshaled into his thinking, never lost its preeminence.

Munich was long an important center of artistic foment and rebellion. The Blue Rider (*Die Blaue Reiter*) group held important exhibitions there. Artists such as Franz Marc, Kandinsky, Paul Klee, and August Macke moved from a symbolic and emotional use of color of the expressionists toward pure abstraction. While Elmyr did not seem drawn to the conceptual philosophy of abstraction, the unconventional and bold use of color incited his imagination. Picasso, along with George Braque, already transformed early twentieth-century art, turning their interest in "Negro art" into cubism.

Picasso's flirtation with abstraction later reverted to the clean figurative lines of his classical period. Upon viewing one of Picasso's drawings from this period at the Galerie Tannheuser, Elmyr was "flabbergasted." At that time, he admitted, "I did not understand his cubist work at all." Given Elmyr's more traditional art education, he saw the same command of line and expression of old masters' drawings in Picasso's art. "The world," he later observed, "has never known an artist like Picasso. When, at an early age, he had already established his reputation as an artist—referring to Picasso's blue period—he had the courage to change, to completely reinvent himself, to experiment and explore new ideas." He added that, "If he had simply wanted to assure himself of a bourgeois life and guaranteed comfort, he could have continued to churn out work in that style for the rest of his life." This was precisely what Marc Chagall did, in his view, and, for his lack of courage to change, Elmyr had little respect for the artist. He expressed it like this: "For the last fifty years, he's been copying himself."

Again, feeling the restlessness of his age, in 1926 Elmyr lobbied hard, trying to persuade his family to allow him to continue his education in Paris, and of course to underwrite his move. They voiced no resistance or objections, displaying the same laissez-faire detachment toward him he long ago came to expect. "Paris was the center of the artistic universe," he explained, "and I savored the idea of living in that creative milieu." After visiting the city on several occasions with his parents and older brother on vacations, "I tingled with excitement," he said, "at the prospect of being on my own in Paris."

Elmyr thought he would easily leave Munich behind. The thrill of moving to France was all he could think about now. "I didn't feel good about leaving my friends. There was one boy I was infatuated with. He was blond, good-looking, tender-hearted, and the sole reason I would have stayed, but the allure of Paris was irresistible. There are few cities as beautiful and sophisticated as München, and it was a gateway to my adulthood. The Akademie Heimann also helped me a great deal, developing my artistic skills. It was more like a boot camp. The training was arduous but thorough. I also learned a lot about myself there, but it was time to move on after my two years there. I was twenty years old and eager to live in Paris."

The going-away party for him migrated from nightspot to nightspot until the revelers conveyed him to the train station, where an unusually inebriated Elmyr boarded a train that evening. Shouts of "good luck!" rose up from the group as the conductor signaled, "All aboard!" Elmyr leaned through the compartment's opened window and wished them all the best of futures, restraining his emotions until the train departed. The ker-chunk of the closing doors announced the train's departure and pulling his life in a new direction. Again he traveled first class as the train threaded its way through the night, crossing the Bavarian countryside, through pine forests, mountain tunnels, orderly farm land and neat villages, up to the Rhine, then through Alsace, the Voge Mountains, Lorraine, and ultimately to Paris. The overhead light in his compartment illuminated his reflection as he leaned his head against the window. He already mourned losing the companionship of his friends and first serious love interest. Their faces and personalities, the silent hours of extra drawing assignments in Munich's Alte Pinakothek Museum, capturing the sinewy musculature of the Greek and Roman statues, the cafés of Maximilianstrasse, he knew would momentarily join other memories of his past. As he sat alone with his thoughts, recapitulating the images of his last two years and feeling no fear of reprisal, the sadness of leaving hurt him now desperately. His tears mirrored the rain-streaked glass outside, the rocking click-clack of the train his remorseful lullaby.

Excitement and anticipation supplanted his waning sorrow as his train neared the French capital. Intermittent showers punctuated the gray, overcast sky when he arrived. Stepping down from the glistening train car, he wore the elegant raincoat he purchased from an exclusive men's clothing store in Munich. In his right hand, he carried his tan leather valise containing enough clothes for a week. Before leaving Germany, he arranged to have the rest of his possessions sent to him once he found permanent lodging. Looking up as he walked down the platform, he could see the glass-covered ceiling of Gare Saint Lazare. How appropriate it was to enter Paris here, he thought. Monet immortalized this famous landmark in at least a half dozen paintings, capturing it in all its subtle nuances of light and color. Swirling smoke and billowing steam from the locomotives depicted in oil paint fifty years earlier recalled the influence of Turner's ethereal and luminescent treatment of atmosphere that so inspired Monet and his fellow impressionists.

He enrolled at the Académie de la Grande Chaumière, a respected art  school headed by Fernand Leger. Elmyr found a modest but comfortable pension in Montparnasse, the new bohemian quarter that replaced Montmartre as the popular haunt of artists at the end of the nineteenth-century. Speaking French was second nature to him and had been since childhood, so his transition from Germany to France was a seamless one. He was now twenty years old, but unaware on the day of his arrival that Paris would, for the most part, be his home for the next twelve years.

Elmyr in his twenties

Throughout this time, Elmyr met or became acquainted with many of the cultural luminaries of the period. Since Leger was his teacher, he developed a close relationship with him and his wife. This friendship allowed him to meet Kees van Dongen, Albert Marquet, Andre Derain, Maurice Vlaminck, and others. Gertrude Stein, Alice Toklas, Fugita, Man Ray, Peggy

Elmyr in his thirties

Guggenheim, Hemingway, and Matisse frequented the popular cafés, Le Dome or La Rotunde, where he became a habitué. He enjoyed reading and became a regular visitor to Sylvia Beach's small bookstore on the rue de l'Odeon, where James Joyce would often give public readings of his books. Although Elmyr understood almost nothing of what Joyce was talking about, he still listened attentively. His sentiment "was probably not an isolated opinion, even among Joyce's English-speaking audience," he told me.

During the day he studied his craft, but by night he was a handsome playboy aristocrat. His title of baron also opened doors of French society, enabling him at once to associate with the upper crust and live *la vie bohème*. Easy access to his parent's wealth allowed him to make spontaneous trips to Deauville or Cap d'Antibes with his new friends or lovers, which was by now a lifestyle he considered normal. Through a widening network of personal connections, people introduced him to others like himself, rich socialites. With his increasingly proficient skill as an artist, Elmyr succeeded in procuring his first significant commissions.

After coming to Paris, he did a portrait of Prince Yussopov, who not only came from the richest family in Russia before the 1918 revolution, but also orchestrated the assassination of the charismatic monk Rasputin. His prestigious clients also included Mrs. Potter Palmer of Chicago and the Duke of Kent. It was an important turning point in his career; his future looked promising indeed. At the urging of his teacher and mentor, Elmyr submitted a painting he did in the south of France while on one of his impromptu getaways. The judges accepted his landscape of the coast at Cagnes-sur-Mer for the annual exhibition of the Salon d'Automne. In that same year, he participated in a group exhibition at the Redfern Gallery in London. While success seemed to come easily to him early, his career demanded discipline, which he favored less than his social life. When he recounted this period of his life to me, he offered this story as a parable to stress that he did not want me to have the same regrets. He was gifted, a skilled artist who, by his own admission, wasted opportunities by his lack of tenacity, guidance, and savoir faire to make a living by working for it. The mistakes of his youth haunted him for the rest of his life. At that time he could not see how radically different and difficult his life would soon become. In fact, he would not regain this worry-free self-sufficiency for almost forty years.

For the time being, though, life was both good and easy. Within a year of his moving to Paris, the French, in 1927, once again demonstrating their irrepressible joie de vivre, threw a nationwide party for an unexpected guest. A young, handsome American aviator named Charles Lindbergh excited the admiration of the world by flying solo for the first time from the United States to Paris. The sounds of champagne corks popping throughout the capital announced the celebration. Unfortunately, the gaiety would not last.

The three-year period following Elmyr's arrival in 1926 may have been his window of opportunity to establish himself as an artist, a goal within his grasp due to his auspicious beginning and burgeoning talent. However, other events beyond his control were about to change the course of his life.

Two years before he stepped from the train at the Gare Saint-Lazare, an obscure writer succeeded in becoming a published author. In Germany, his book initially received little attention, though Adolf Hitler's *Mein Kampf* was ultimately a best seller. In fact, it offered a remarkably frightening formula for reenacting a global war for slightly different reasons but with improved means. On the other side of the Atlantic, America's economic bubble burst with the stock market crash on Wall Street in 1929 that brought with it the Great Depression. Europe quickly felt its shock waves causing widespread unemployment. Barely ten years had passed since the Treaty of Versailles officially ended the First World War. Ironically, the tendency of people to search for strong leaders in times of crisis laid the groundwork for Hitler's rise to power.

Elmyr made one last trip to Germany before Hitler consolidated his unchallengeable supremacy as dictator of that country in 1933. "Nazi flags were displayed everywhere in Berlin," Elmyr said. "Uniformed soldiers seemed to almost outnumber civilians in the streets. It was not difficult to see where all this was leading. I stopped to watch a military parade near my hotel one day. They carried banners resembling a sinister Praetorian guard, wearing those high black polished boots, goose-stepping over those cobblestones. I'll never forget that image. When they passed, it sent shivers down my arms. I stupidly didn't raise my arm to show my support, and the people around me became so angry I thought they were going to beat me up. I explained that I was a foreigner, but that didn't seem to satisfy them at all. I knew then I had better leave the city for my own good." It would not be his last exposure to the Nazis.

After returning to Paris, the opportunities to sell his work diminished amid the depressed economy after 1929, even among his friends of the more-well-to-do nobility. The prospect of making a living from painting seemed more remote than ever. The uninterrupted subsidies from his family still allowed him live the life of a bon vivant. In reality, the views from his favorite sidewalk cafés were becoming increasingly grim.

In Spain, Germany, Italy, and Japan, the forces of totalitarianism under the guise of nationalist fervor or imperial designs cast an ominous specter over Europe and the Far East. "That decade of the thirties," Elmyr later observed, "was difficult for us all. Germany was rebuilding its military machine, and we all were powerless to stop it. Those that thought another war wasn't imminent were deluding themselves. You could only have been an ostrich with your head in a hole in the ground to not see it coming."

Hoping for a rapprochement with his family, from time to time he returned to Budapest. Letters to his family elicited replies in a sort of emotional shorthand, perfunctorily polite but glaringly unsentimental. He ultimately resigned himself to accept their detachment as an unbridgeable gulf between them. This unpleasant reality also made him think that no matter what he did, whatever accomplishment or accolade he might earn would somehow be unsatisfactory in their eyes. By this time, Elmyr had long ago become accustomed to seeking the love he needed from others.

By 1938, Germany annexed Austria with the Anschluss. The prospect of war looked imminent. In Hungary, the rising tide of fascism threatened the second-oldest tradition of representational democracy (after England). Germany had already reclaimed the Rhineland and the Saar regions. When Hitler's desire for lebensraum spread to Czechoslovakia, England's prime minister, Neville Chamberlain, spoke for the dwindling ostrich contingent that still believed war was avoidable when the western powers acceded to Nazi expansion. His famous exclamation of "peace with honor," referring to their dubious agreement and supposed appeasement of Hitler, showed the extent to which some were in profound denial of the coming war. "Perhaps the British and French would not have given away Czechoslovakia with the same alacrity if they had been conceding their own territory," Elmyr observed.

Elmyr again boarded a train for Budapest to be with his family. "We started putting some of our possessions in storage, the Louis XV and Louis XVI furniture, the Meissen china, the family portraits, tapestries…oriental rugs went to a large warehouse in Pest on the other side of the Danube. During the war it was hit by the German Stukas, the dive bombers, and everything was completely destroyed." He sadly recounted the unimaginable devastation and deprivation in the battle for Budapest "which was the second-longest siege, after Stalingrad, during the war."

Despite his urgings, he could not convince his family to leave Budapest, so he stayed on to help in whatever way he could. Within months of Germany's invasion of Poland and the Allied powers declaration of war, the Nazi *wermacht* overran Hungary and installed the pro-fascist Horty regime. They arrested Elmyr and his father. Although his father was Catholic, his status as a diplomat made him especially dangerous in the eyes of the Nazis and their puppet regime. They deported him to the infamous death camp at Auschwitz, where they focused on exterminating the Jews; but his fate, for the time being, remained uncertain.

Whatever remained of value in his family's estate, the Nazis confiscated. They also sent Elmyr to the scenic Carpathian Mountains, to a detention camp. "It was a particularly severe winter in Dracula's land, Transylvania," he told me while we appreciated the fire in the fireplace at his home one night. "The Carpathians are some of the most rugged mountains in Europe, and why they put the camp there I have no idea. There was probably two meters of snow covering everything, and the temperature was frequently below zero Fahrenheit. Somehow, the commandant learned that I was an artist so he had me do a portrait of him. He had a wood-burning stove in his quarters so I worked as slowly as possible so I could stay warm. I devoted minute detail to all his medals." It was unlikely that he ever thought of his artistic talent as a survival skill; however, it was a concept he more easily embraced later.

Perhaps the commandant intervened on Elmyr's behalf, but he was uncertain why they released him. Returning to Budapest, he found his mother reduced to poverty but still alive, while his father's fate was unknown. Servants that had long worked for them now helped them survive on meager food supplies they had hidden. The entire foundation of his life crumbled. Every vestige of wealth and privilege seemed like ancient history, and they all now huddled together in a democratic misery.

During his recollections of the bombings of the Hungarian capital, he remarked, "I thought it ironic how Paris jubilantly welcomed Charles Lindbergh after what I learned about him later." Lindberg, understandably an aviation enthusiast, had a warm spot in his heart for Herman Goering, Hitler's head of his Luftwaffe, and didn't think he was such a bad guy. Goering, apart from his passion for airplanes, and indulging his flair for theatrical designs of uniforms draped with ribbons and medals had more than a passing interest in art. His main preoccupation throughout the Second World War seemed to be methodically organizing the wholesale ransacking of Europe's public and private art treasures for the greater glory of himself—and the Third Reich. Then, Goering may have learned a thing or two about looting from Napoleon.

Within a year of his release, the Gestapo rearrested Elmyr once again, and this time they sent him to a prison camp on the outskirts of Berlin. There, under interrogation and methodical torture, they broke one of his legs. "Then, they sent me to a hospital where a very good German doctor reset the bones and put a cast on my leg." However, one day Elmyr noticed a rare lapse of attention to detail: the absence of a guard at the front door, although the soldier's coat draped over the back of a nearby chair. Thinking it was a perfect spring day for a walk; Elmyr threw the coat over his shoulders and hobbled out on his crutches. "A nurse then stopped me. She said, 'Where are you going, soldier?' I told her the doctor said I needed some exercise. I simply neglected to return. I had friends in Berlin that would help me, but it's a large city and I wasn't sure where to go. The Allies were bombing regularly, and you could see the destruction everywhere. If I were religious, I would say that a guardian angel was watching over me. I was probably a few blocks from the hospital when a car passed and came to a stop about twenty meters ahead of me. I thought, well, this is the end for me now. When I approached the car, I tried to hide my face in the collar of the coat. My heart stopped when the passenger door opened. Then I heard a woman's voice: 'El-myr, is it *you*?' I looked over and saw the sister of a friend I knew from when my father was in Berlin. I had no idea how she recognized me. I opened the back door and told her I just escaped from a hospital and would tell her the rest but first she should just start driving. We drove to her home that belonged to her parents. She and her brother inherited it after they both died. It was near a park and still intact despite the daily bombardment. She told me Erich, her brother, worked at the Reich Chancellery, and even if the Gestapo were looking for me, they would not come to their home. They hid me for a month and even procured false identity papers. They also arranged my travel documents so I could return to Budapest. They tried to talk me out of returning to Hungary. The Russians were already advancing in the east. They knew Germany was not going to win the war. They were among many of the Reich's reluctant supporters. No, they were not diehard Nazis by any means, just forced to conform like everyone else. I don't know what would have happened if they hadn't rescued me."

Within two months, he was back in Budapest. "Miraculously, we survived until the Russians took the city. We all nearly starved to death, and the winter of '45 was the coldest in a hundred years, I think. The Danube froze almost to the bottom, and tanks had no problem crossing the ice on the river. I know I was stupid to go back to Budapest, but I needed to help my family. Sometimes you do things that have nothing to do with logic or good sense. It was an impulse in my gut or my heart, but I know it wasn't the smart thing to do. We were living in the cellar of the house. I remember the constant sound of artillery. The husband of our cook watched from the cellar window, and machine gun fire killed him instantly. He died, and we could not even bury him. The next day Russian soldiers came. They found us hiding. One of the men shouted in Russian to my mother to give up her fur coat. She resisted and he shot her. I couldn't save her. They killed her for her…coat. That memory still haunts me. They took me with them but left the others, as they were all old and no threat to them.

"At that time, they didn't know the difference between a Nazi and Hungarian or a Frenchman. Many of those soldiers had probably never seen a toilet or indoor plumbing. There were only Bolsheviks, and everyone else was an enemy. I ended up in another prison camp with Germans, Poles, British, Serbs, Croats, and Americans. We were all heading on that long march through Besserabia and ultimately a Siberian gulag, if you survived that long. It turned out that my aunt found out that the soldiers had taken me. She was friendly with a Russian general from before the war and asked him for his help locating me. One day I heard my name announced repeatedly. By that time, you are so petrified from fear that if you move one inch to the left or right, you think you are going to die. Finally, I stood up. They took me to a captain, and he gave me papers guaranteeing safe conduct back to Budapest. I was one of the lucky ones, definitely."

Before her death, his mother confided in him. She had buried some of her jewelry in their green house. Careful to evade detection, he retrieved the buried treasure. One of their servants that survived sewed some of the loose stones from necklaces and earrings his mother wore what now seemed a thousand years past, into the lining of his coat. He also gave some of the valuable gems to her so she could help her family survive. Using his family's social connections, he was able to obtain Swedish-issued travel papers that he described as "useless." The diamonds, though, proved to an effective tool when it came to crossing borders.

Paris At War's End

Paris escaped the destruction that Hitler had ordered of his retreating armies. By September of 1945, Elmyr was back in the city that was home for most of his adult life. Friends from his past had also managed through the Nazi occupation. His former teacher and friend Fernand Leger, who'd spent the war years in New York, was there, as were Leon Zadkin, Philipe de Rothschild, and others. His cache of gems was nearly exhausted. What remained procured a small room on the rue Jacob, where he lived and used as a studio. Elmyr revealed that the city seemed filled with people like him trying to sell off valuables and family heirlooms for which there were few buyers. "I really wasn't sure how I would survive. Everything was in short supply after the war, and Paris was far better off than anywhere else."

Elmyr in Monte Carlo – 1946

Some friends helped him during this time. Countess Palfy, Tommy Esterhazy, Baron de Thierry, and Philipe de Rothschild bought his paintings or commissioned portraits for prices averaging a hundred dollars. Life was no longer worry-free, as he had known before. One day, while contemplating how to avoid his land-

Elmyr in his Paris studio – 1945

lord as his rent was past due, a friend visited him at his meager room on the rue Jacob. It was Lady Malcolm Campbell, who "appeared rather surprised when she saw where I was living." He proceeded to show her some oil paintings when a small ink drawing pinned to the wall caught her attention. Sounding surprised, she asked, "Where did you get that Picasso drawing?" He hesitantly asked her why she thought it was a Picasso. "Well, I know a Picasso when I see one," she responded. It was a simple line drawing, a nude figure that resembled something from his Greek period. "It was my turn to be surprised when she asked if I was willing to sell it," he said. "She offered me fifty pounds sterling, I think, so I sold it to her. I didn't feel good about it because she was a friend, but it was the day my rent was due and it assured my living for the next two months."

Three months later, she ran into Elmyr again and confessed she sold the Picasso to a London art dealer, made a nice little profit, and suggested he join her for lunch at the Ritz. While he was still feeling some twinges of guilt over the incident, he quickly recovered. When I knew Elmyr, he stated matter-of-factly that his teacher, Leger, admitted to faking Corots to make ends meet when he was desperate. He also repeated the well-known joke that "Corot painted six hundred paintings in his life, twelve hundred of which are in the United States." Vlaminck reputedly did Cézannes. Kisling did Modiglianis. He saw nothing new in what he had done, and it just enabled him to survive so he could continue to paint, pay his rent, and eat.

What intrigued him was the challenge of producing something that was as good as a drawing done by the greatest living artist of the century. He then went to a bookstore to find some catalogs of Picasso's early work. Returning to his studio, he proceeded to make a half-dozen pen and ink drawings, again in Picasso's Greek style. Of these, he chose the three he considered the best. The following day, dressed in his best (although aging) clothes, he went to a gallery on the Left Bank, the rue de Seine. Removing them from a cardboard portfolio, he explained to the dealer that Picasso, whom he knew from his time in Paris, gave them to him as a gift. In moments of nervousness, the palms of his hands always perspired. He wiped

portrait of Mme. George Auric – 1945

the perspiration on his pressed trousers as he looked through the gallery, waiting for a decision on the proposed sale. The dealer thought they were good and they agreed on a price, the equivalent of $400.

As unthinkable as this act may have been before the war, the world had radically changed. Life, no longer lined in satin, had acquired a harder, sharper edge. The ever-present safety net of his family's money had disappeared in 1946. He needed to survive by

portrait of Elmyr's mother by Elmyr

his own wits and talent, by mundane skills he never learned, and this was now more obvious than ever. The concept of a "budget" was foreign to him.

Elmyr quickly exhausted the money he made from his Picasso drawings. It was August, and he again faced the irritating nuisance of paying his rent. While having a coffee with a young friend one day, Elmyr confided his secret and his pressing need for cash. His friend, a dashing twenty-two-year-old, Jacques Chamberlin, saw an enterprising opportunity. Jacques had no money either, but he was extremely knowledgeable about art. His father, an industrialist from Bordeaux and passionate collector of the impressionists, lost everything to the Nazis, who were equally passionate about looting. The Gestapo moved the entire collection to the capital of the doomed thousand-year Reich. The Allied forces later destroyed it during their relentless bombing.

Jacques pressed Elmyr to let him sell his artwork. He couldn't fail, he insisted. They would form a partnership, split the money, travel through Europe, and enjoy themselves once again. The lure of recapturing the ease of living he knew before the war was precisely the sort of persuasion Elmyr was powerless to resist.

Elmyr faced another problem. His Swedish diplomatic papers were outdated, and Jacques, with the right connections, helped obtain a French passport for him. This sealed the deal. They prepared an itinerary and a plan. Since Elmyr had had success with his Picasso drawings, why stop, they thought. They were, after all, small and insignificant enough to not have been recorded by Picasso's longtime secretary, Sabartes. They were the artistic equivalent of an ATM card today, an easy source of cash.

Happily, Elmyr could once again savor the finer things in life, only now the former requisites were well-appreciated niceties. He desperately needed a new wardrobe and could no longer tolerate shoes with worn heals. Before leaving Paris, he returned to the Left Bank, scouring art supply shops for pre-war paper with the proper watermarks. After languishing for years in the recesses of these stores, the paper had already assumed the aged, yellowing edges that lent a visible sign of authenticity. Within a week of their departure, Elmyr made a dozen Picasso drawings. With the seriousness of a connoisseur, Jacques examined the new contributions to Picasso's body of work. For a moment, Elmyr thought they might not be good enough. Then, while Jacques looked squarely at his Hungarian friend, a broad smile overwhelming his face dispelled that doubt; Jacques assured him they were wonderful.

Jacques, along with his girlfriend and Elmyr, departed for Brussels first. There, they celebrated a quick sale with dinner at a first-class restaurant on the Grand Place. Crêpes with Grand Marnier followed the Belgians' world-famous mussels and a fine white wine. From there, they traveled to Amsterdam, London, Geneva, Lausanne, Zurich, and then back to the Côte d'Azur in the south of France. Everywhere they offered the drawings, art dealers eagerly bought them. Their uninterrupted success prompted spontaneous moments of creativity in Elmyr's hotel rooms that almost exhausted the entire supply of paper he had brought with him.

In early 1947, they returned to London. Elmyr visited the Redfern Gallery for the first time since he participated in the group exhibition there almost twenty years before. Jacques, however, had sold them one of Elmyr's Picassos the summer before. It was on display in their front room. It looked quite impressive in the ornate French frame with its monocle-popping price. Even with an exorbitant markup, he suspected that Jacques had given him something less than his share. He sensed an inequitable distribution of the proceeds before. With his waning trust in his young companion, Elmyr thought their business partnership should end. Broaching this subject was difficult, as he customarily fled from any unpleasantness. Predictably, arguments and recriminations followed.

When they parted company in February, Elmyr flew alone to Copenhagen. Encouraged by Jacques's flawless record of success, he thought he could now confidently repeat it. With about a thousand dollars in his pocket, he traveled from Denmark to Sweden, visiting some old friends from before the war. By the time he reached Stockholm, he steeled himself for the inevitable. Taking a room at the Grand Hotel, he used what remained of his supply of French paper. Five new Picassos emerged from an afternoon's efforts. Dapperly dressed, he assembled his collection of drawings and headed to a gallery.

He had no difficulty being partially truthful with the gallery director. He introduced himself as a Hungarian aristocrat-refugee, and forced to sell what remained of his family collection. "Would you be interested in acquiring these pen and ink drawings by Picasso?" he politely inquired.

When asked about their origin, this time Elmyr explained that his diplomat father bought them in Paris in 1937. He knew nothing more. The gallery director appeared interested but cautious. "Where are you staying?" he asked, and then proposed to meet with Elmyr later at his hotel.

Returning to his hotel, he once again had visions of the Gestapo interrogations when they broke his leg. His damp palms transferred their moisture to his trouser legs, though, he willed himself to a calm but manufactured composure as he sat on the edge of his bed awaiting his prospective client. When he responded to the knock at his door, he opened it to greet not one, but three grim-faced men. His English tweed suit coat barely disguised his pounding heart. The art dealer introduced his associates; one was a curator from the Stockholm Art Museum. They silently examined the drawings and then told Elmyr they wanted to confer on the works a bit more. While they went to the hotel bar Elmyr thought perhaps he should simply make a quick getaway, although the success of fleeing at that moment seemed unlikely. A half-hour later, they returned in a more cheerful mood and offered him the equivalent of $6,000. He graciously accepted.

His gratification was not instant; he waited three long days before receiving his windfall check. During that time he considered the array of options now in front of him. It was the most money he had possessed at one time. He had grown weary of Europe, still in the midst of postwar recovery. Entering a travel agency, a poster of Rio de Janeiro with its iconic Sugar Loaf and white sand beaches captured his attention. It was winter in Stockholm, and he wanted to escape its ice and snow. The cold weather reminded him of his wartime suffering, and he was ready for something different. "So I bought a one-way ticket to Rio," he recounted, with a smile so familiar to me.

Elmyr Discovers
The New World

"When I got off the plane, the heat and humidity struck me like opening the door of a sauna. I just left winter in northern Europe, and I was now in the middle of their tropical summer and could not get out of my long wool underwear fast enough," he recalled in amused delight. He went to the famous Copacabana Hotel that was highly recommended and the best in town. "I had just turned forty and hoped this change would be a new life, a new opportunity," is how he characterized this drastic move.

Five months after I first met Elmyr and began living with him, BBC television came to interview Elmyr. The British producer Richard Drewett collaborated with French filmmaker François Reichenbach and a French television channel. Their coproduction, entitled *Elmyr, The True Picture?* debuted in the fall of 1970. In one scene, Elmyr sits in front of the fireplace of his villa, La Falaise. A fire burns behind him. He fields questions from an off-scene interviewer. He briefly recounts some

Elmyr in Brazil – 1947

of his far-flung travels. Then, he responds to the question, "Why did you travel so much?" He said, "I don't know. What makes people travel? You think you want to see something different, meet someone better-looking in the next town...I don't know why." A seamless edit then shows Clifford Irving, Elmyr's first biographer and fellow Ibiza resident. Irving quickly adds, "Because the FBI and police in five states were hot on his trail, and when things got uncomfortable he had to leave town on a Greyhound bus..."

Elmyr would not have portrayed himself in the way Irving described. The disparity of their responses to the same question illustrates the difference in their views and spaciousness in interpretations of events. Elmyr saw his wanderlust in a romantic lilt. Irving saw him fleeing the law as a petty criminal. Well, there was truth in both those statements. At that time their relationship was already thorny. Irving, purportedly, was not paying Elmyr royalties from the book as their agreement stipulated. It is understandable that opposing perceptions had spread beyond this instance to the point that the artist and writer were no longer on speaking terms when I started working for Elmyr. They declared a temporary truce during the making of the documentary, but it was short-lived. Other factors contributed to the dissolution of their association, but mostly hinged on their dispute over the proceeds from sales of the book.

In any event, Elmyr's escape to the southern hemisphere reinvigorated his joie de vivre. Wearing the smile of someone first tasting chocolate, he reminisced in the BBC documentary, "If I didn't live in Ibiza, there are only two other places I would live...Rio de Janeiro or California." He further told me, "The Brazilians are physically beautiful people, with no hesitation to make love and enjoy life. They have an élan, a style I never experienced before. It was such a change from Europe coming out of the shadow of the war." The Brazilians' sensuality freed him from the ossified morality that relegated his sexual orientation to criminal status. The backlash of the 60s' counterculture that flourished in Ibiza likely emancipated him in much the same way.

Appreciating the gregarious, sophisticated, and fun-loving Brazilians, he made new friends easily. "They were very much lovers of life like their Latin ancestors," he insisted. Elmyr soon met an expatriate Frenchman and sublet his "small but lovely home in an area called Gloria Hill." Here, Elmyr set up a small studio and resumed painting, work that reflected a strong School of Paris influence but in a style that was his own. A photo of Elmyr from this period shows him happily at work, a thin, casually dressed artist standing before his easel. His smile suggests a blissful contentment and perhaps the sense of a promising future. With the remaining money from the $6,000 he earned from the sale of his Picasso drawings in Stockholm, he planned to revive his career as a painter of "Elmyrs" in South America. He succeeded in garnering some portrait commissions, but those were not enough to earn more than he spent. In fact, he never learned that kind of bourgeois bookkeeping or skill enabling him to do so.

"I loved life there," he told me, "but did not have the success I hoped for, so I decided I'd try out the United States. Fernand Leger talked about New York when I saw him in Paris after the war, and I thought it sounded like a city I should see." In August of 1947, growing restless once again, he left Rio for what he thought would be a brief visit to New York. "New York excited me, to see the Statue of Liberty, the Empire State Building, all those landmarks that, for us Europeans, symbolized the entire country. I later found out it was much bigger, more complex than Manhattan," he said. His old friend and teacher, Leger, along with Consuelo de St. Exupéry in Paris and some of his new friends from Rio, provided him introductions to people there. According to Elmyr, within three weeks of arriving he met Anita Loos, the author best known for *Gentlemen Prefer Blondes*; film star Lana Turner; Averell Harriman, the diplomat and one-time governor of New York; Dan Topping, who then owned the Yankees baseball team; and Hungarian compatriots Zsa Zsa Gabor and her mother, Magda. Elmyr later painted a portrait of Zsa Zsa nude, with a guitar "strategically placed in front of her." He later recalled, "She did pay me but very poorly, and complained that one of her tits was too much in the center." Lilienfeld Galleries exhibited it in January 1948 in a one-man show of Elmyr's work.

New York was vibrant, and the social life suited him. When his three-month tourist visa expired, he had only begun to savor the possibilities of living there. "Besides, it was a big country, and I did have a curiosity to see more of it. So, I decided I would stay longer," he admitted, with a nonchalant shrug of his shoulders. A small duplex apartment he rented on East Seventy-Eighth Street in Manhattan was a perfect pied-à-terre where he would hold court, receiving his illustrious guests and friends. One of these, René d' Harnoncourt, was, curiously, then director of the Museum of Modern Art. Elmyr unfortunately never provided me any anecdotes regarding their relationship, although it was common knowledge that Elmyr was an artist and had already done some portraits of d' Harnoncourt's society friends. All along, Elmyr intended to make a living from painting his own work, while he viewed his hidden talent as something to fall back on in emergencies. His secret, for the time being, was safe.

While in New York, he also became acquainted with some of the mythic figures of the famed Algonquin round table: Dorothy Parker and Robert Sherwood. His social life glittered, but it did not come cheaply. His fondness for fashionable tailored suits that were often $300 apiece, and his cocktail parties "where even the rich came hungry and thirsty" were expensive indulgences whose costs far exceeded the money he received from the occasional portrait commission. What he needed, he thought, was to have a successful exhibition. An offer came from a prestigious art dealer at Lilienfeld Galleries.

His financial reserves dwindled while he prepared for his show. He later pointed out that artists commonly pay for many of the expenses involved such as framing, catalogs, and sundries, along with a sizeable commission of the sale prices to the gallery. These details he blithely ignored, thinking that his little black book with its names of people from the A-list would guarantee success. Despite appearances, the country was still in a post-war recession. Nor did it dawn on him that January was historically the worst month of the year for retail sales. Combined with these overlooked realities, a severe snowstorm hit the city the day his show opened. Predictably, his planned moment of triumph dissolved into a crushing disappointment and personal disaster. Few people showed up. Elmyr said the show "was a critical success," which is showbiz-speak for death at the box office. According to one who described his work, it was "charming, capable, attractive, romantic in his approach" and "de Hory leans to an Expressionist palette in some of his best works." *Art News* wrote, "His lively realism, reckless paint and lush colors strike the well-known chord of the School of Paris as do his subjects—French ports, harlequins and facile portraits" (Irving 1969).

One small oil painting sold, but that did not cover even the cost of the exhibition's catalog. Elmyr's funds were almost exhausted, and he felt emotionally drained from this setback. Only one viable option remained to extricate him from this unpleasant predicament. There were no more sheets of vintage French paper at his disposal, and he didn't dare use anything with an American watermark. Instead, he searched through some of the used bookstores on Fourth Avenue and found two large volumes entitled, respectively, *Gothic Cathedrals* and *Views of Paris*. In each were blank pages, discolored from age and suitable for an important Picasso gouache. He used as his inspiration a bronze sculpture the Spanish master had done, *L'homme à L'Agneau*—the man with the lamb. On the vacant leaf from the smaller book, he executed another pen and ink, a Greek period line drawing that, by now, he could have done blindfolded.

On a Saturday morning, he brought the gouache to the gallery of Klaus Perls on Fifty-Eighth Street. After Elmyr's introducing himself and showing the dealer the Picassos, Perls asked if he could keep it over the weekend for closer examination. Not to appear overly anxious, Elmyr waited until Tuesday to return to the gallery, bringing with him the smaller drawing. "He seemed pleased that I brought something else to sell, and after haggling over the price, I think he offered me seven hundred and fifty dollars for the gouache and two hundred and fifty for the pen and ink. He was smiling because he knew he'd made a good deal," Elmyr recalled, with a smile of his own.

This may have reaffirmed faith in his own talent and helped temporarily mitigate his poverty, but his success and the rewards always seemed to fade faster than the pangs of conscience and the worry of retribution. He had already stayed well beyond his three-month visa, and since he could demonstrate no visible means of support, reapplying for an extension was out of the question. Buoyed by the recent sale, possessing a survivor's instinct and a desire to see the country, he thought

"God bless America!" He was heading west to California, but first he needed to find some old paper and buy some Chinese ink.

Whenever Elmyr talked about his past, his face immediately displayed his emotions before he articulated his thoughts. It was an incongruous trait for someone dependent on making a living by stealth and deception. This absence of a poker face of course delighted those trying to elbow their way to any card table where he sat. However, it remains difficult for me to imagine how he managed to manufacture the guile needed to deceive others. I just don't know how he did it. Repeatedly! Nor do I know at what point he developed the antipathy for art dealers, gallery directors, museum curators and "experts" that his facial features, words, and tone of voice would simultaneously convey. I do know this, though—the frequency with which he relied on his ability to do his fakes to make a living increased after he headed west.

Perhaps it was his seductive charm, polished manners, classy bearing, and intelligence that would ultimately make him one of the most effective and successful con men the world has ever known. More likely, it was his artistic skill upon which all his other attributes rested so securely—and made it all look so right. Sometimes, I wish I were a trained psychologist so I could offer plausible theories about the motive or intent or rationale behind what he did. On the other hand, from what I know and what I observed, his story doesn't require that degree of thoughtful analysis. It was all fairly simple. He was making a living using his only marketable skills.

By his own admission he considered himself "a weak person," yet this wasn't true. He proved to be a survivor through unthinkable ordeals. Yes, what he did was fraudulent, definitely against the law, but at the same time he was doubtlessly the kindest, gentlest, most humane being I ever had the pleasure of meeting. So, how can one reconcile criminal acts with morality, you may ask. This is how he saw it. He would have characterized his fakery in today's phraseology as "victimless crimes." He insisted that he never took advantage of a person who was outside the cognoscenti of the professional world. That made a huge difference to him.

"In Europe, a dealer could not prosecute you if he bought a piece of art as authentic and it was not, because he is supposed to know the difference. Cartier cannot sell you cut glass and call it a diamond. If you, however, offer to sell Cartier cut glass as a diamond and they buy it as such, then they should not be in that business; they should be selling hosiery or sausage in the market instead," is how he put it. In France today, antique dealers may legally sell you an antique as authentic if only 40 percent of the piece is authentic. They can cobble something together from other pieces. I believe Elmyr would have argued that 100 percent of his fakes at least looked authentic even to those who were the most knowledgeable and in a position to judge their merit. While it is impossible to determine exactly the extent that greed played in Elmyr's success, it would be fatuous to downplay its role.

It was 1948 when he finally set foot in Los Angeles, where image is everything. His suave manner and debonair appearance were his most credible credentials. Here, no acting was required, though. He just portrayed himself as himself, although increasingly under assumed aliases to confound the authorities' finding him. He was, after all, an illegal alien, though guilty only of some minor transgressions, he thought. A host of alter egos cropped up in L. E. Raynal, Elmyr Hoffman, Louis Cassou, Elmyr von Houry, Baron Herzog, and others.

Within hours of checking into the Ambassador Hotel, he found a bookstore, where he bought several volumes on drawings of Matisse and Renoir. He thought he would experiment with something new. Elmyr received the same classical education of these artists, which lent a familiarity of style in much the same way as students learn a certain cursive style of penmanship. After studying them for a day or two, he practiced making drawings in their individual styles. Female nudes were most popular, "and it was a subject I did countless times throughout my training, so these were rather easy to do" he told me. Of Matisse's draftsmanship, Elmyr declared in the BBC documentary, "Matisse's lines were never as sure as mine, never as flowing. He always added to, a little more and a little more. He was hesitant. I had to hesitate to make my drawings more Matisse-like."

Finding an art gallery in Beverly Hills was easy, and selling three newly created Matisse pen and ink drawings was equally easy. Elmyr found another dealer in Hollywood "who always bought everything I offered him," Elmyr confessed bemusedly. Each time he brought in something new from an oddly abundant supply, the dealer bubbled with the Christmas morning thrill of a child. The fresh fakes did not linger long in his gallery, as he quickly sold them to many of his show-business clientele at a "five hundred percent profit." One of this gallery's clients reputedly left his entire collection to a prestigious museum in Philadelphia, his hometown.

California had been good to him, and he discovered that not all artists had to starve. His experiences in detention camps brought him as near that slice of life as he cared to be. No, "my curiosity about that is satisfied!" is how he often finalized some thought he would rather not remember. If he did not dine at a good restaurant, he found that he had a knack for cooking and on occasion enjoyed whipping up some of his favorite Hungarian dishes. When not in the midst of his friends or with a special companion, he liked going to movies, and since he was spending much of his time in Hollywood, he thought what more appropriate place could there be other than Grauman's Chinese Theater. "It was a palace of kitsch, *tout à fait* Hollywood," he said.

One of his favorite genres of leisure reading was western novels,

Elmyr goes Texan

particularly those of Louis L'Amour. He liked to point out that "Hungary, too, had cowboys…a Central European variety, but still world-renowned equestrians." Whenever a new movie with Randolph Scott or some other six-gun-toting hero debuted, Elmyr would saunter off to the cinema for the matinee.

By 1949, rural parts of Texas started sprouting oil wells in backyards of a burgeoning new class of people—millionaires. Elmyr knew from childhood that those with wealth desired all the outward signs of their status. One of those cultural trappings was ART. "Who better to help them satisfy their cravings than *me*?" he wondered. Besides, he always wanted to see real cowboys in their ten-gallon hats and spurs on their boots. His urge to see something new had him packing his bags once again. He had one more Matisse to dispose of and thought of visiting his favorite dealer with the insatiable appetite for French art.

Between arranging for his departure, Elmyr stopped by the merchant's gallery. The joyous dealer warmly greeted Elmyr, who informed him that he was soon leaving for Texas. Perhaps sensing his source of quick and sure profits slipping away, he asked Elmyr if by chance he had anything from Picasso's cubist period he might consider selling. Elmyr carefully pondered the question as if trying to recall some obscure detail from his past. "My wife," he explained, "loves the cubists and has a small collection of her own. I would love to give her a gift." By an unforeseen twist of fate, Elmyr remembered that he actually *did* have a small cubist work by Picasso.

Returning to his hotel room, he spent a couple hours reviewing his books of Picasso's art. He then made a few preliminary sketches, borrowing a motif here and line there until a convincing pastiche evolved that had the "right feel" and something that satisfied his critical eye. Adding a few strokes of gouache for color, it now resembled a product of the Spaniard's early work from circa 1914. Removing the lampshade from the light on his night table next to his bed, Elmyr held the freshly painted paper close to the exposed bulb to dry it as fast as possible, but careful not to let its heat burn it.

Before leaving for the airport, he made one final stop at the gallery. Elmyr brought the requested cubist work of Picasso. Surprisingly, it evoked a tepid reaction from the dealer. His lack of enthusiasm surprised Elmyr. It was, after all, more his wife's interest than his. They agreed on $500 and, as usual, it was a bargain price. The check, however, was good, and it was traveling money to buy new adventures in the land of oil barons and cowboys.

Another of my favorite photos shows Elmyr dressed as cowboy on the back of a bucking bronco. One hand grips the saddle's horn. The other waves his hat over his head like a rodeo champion. Even though the horse was a fine example of western taxidermy, Elmyr's Texan-size grin was authentic. When I asked him about this wildly original souvenir, he explained, "I wanted to see the cowboys and savor the myths of those places I read about in my youth. When I went there, few Texans had much of a sense of geography outside the Lone Star State. They kept asking me about my accent, but I tired of the blank looks from people when I told them I was Hungarian. One day, when asked where I was from, I just said I was from Paris." The inquisitive Texan appeared flummoxed and said, "That's impossible. I know everyone in Paris." Bewildered by his assertion, Elmyr's rejoinder was "Well, Paris is a big place." It seems that Elmyr didn't know there was a Paris, Texas, and the Texan knew nothing of Paris, France. The snapshot only confirms what I witnessed about Elmyr's character. He dove headlong into whatever captured his interest and seemed as pleased with his cultural immersion as anthropologist Louis Leaky would be in a burlap sack full of old bones.

Los Angeles disappeared in a crimson sunset behind the silver wing of a TWA plane. Elmyr headed for Houston with a connecting flight in Dallas. All went according to plan but for a mix-up with his luggage that caused him to miss his plane to Houston. It left him, as Elmyr expressed in his own parlance, "stucked in Dallas." This temporary inconvenience turned out to be a good thing, he soon discovered.

He checked into the Adolphus Hotel and picked up a copy of the newspaper at the front desk. On its front page, one article caught his immediate notice. Fashion designer Jacques Fath, an old friend from Paris, was in town to promote a show of his work at the Nieman Marcus department store. Since the Adolphus was the best hotel in town, Elmyr called and asked what room Fath had. He guessed right. It was one o'clock in the morning, but he phoned his room anyway. Fath answered and was less shocked by the hour of the call than by hearing the voice of the caller. He was delighted to reconnect with his old friend. Elmyr mentioned that he was on his way to Houston. Fath urged him to stay a while and give Dallas a chance. Why not come with him to a party given by the Marcuses tomorrow night, he suggested.

Elmyr had no way of knowing that this would be the most exclusive conduit to Texan society anybody could wish for. Jacques introduced Elmyr to the Hunts, Halliburtons, and the Murchisons. They all entertained on a big Texan scale, lavishly and generously. Elmyr's personable nature and the fact that he wore a monocle made his old-world charm irresistible in this relaxed world of the southern drawl. His delayed flight stretched into a four-month sojourn. Through his new network of who's who of the Dallas elite, he was invited to do some portraits, but soon found out their ideas of art were different from his. "If they didn't look like colored photographs from a country fair, they didn't like them. I'm afraid I was a little too modern for their taste," he lamented. "I liked all these people immensely. They were delightful, open, and always invited me into their homes."

He went on to say, "I met a woman who inherited a lot of money when her husband died. She lived in Lubbock, in west Texas, and once sent her private plane to pick me up one day in Dallas to fly me to her ranch for lunch. She later invited me to join her on vacation in Colorado Springs at the Broadmoor Hotel. That's where I met Huntington Hartford, the A&P heir. When they told me he owned some grocery stores, I was used to thinking in terms of the greengrocer on the corner. I never had any idea they meant hundreds. Hunt was also very charming and invited me to stay with him at his place in Hollywood. At the time when I knew him, I don't think he knew the difference between an oil painting and a watercolor. I certainly would never have guessed that he would one day have an art museum named after him."

One discovery Elmyr was pleased to make in the Lone Star State was that the art dealers in Dallas had not only heard of Matisse, they were thrilled that Elmyr was willing to part with the few he had left from his family's collection. By autumn, he was seriously considering Hartford's invitation. September was a beautiful month in southern California, but what month wasn't, he thought.

Elmyr found out that Texas was a world unto itself, but it was a vast and varied state. Not everyone owned a horse, oil wells, or a ranch the size of Connecticut, although some of those he met did. During his return flight to Los Angeles, he reflected on his successful foray into an astounding circle of string-tie-wearing aristocracy, newly ordained by their sudden wealth. Money separated a supposedly classless society as much, if not more, than titles separated nobility from commoners in Europe. He recalled the anecdote one of the Marcus family told him of the farmer coming into their elegant department store looking for a winter coat for his wife. Elmyr smiled through its retelling. "He said he wanted a fur one. When he saw the expensive coats, he picked one out, a full-length chinchilla. When told the price—$25,000—he thought for a moment and said OK. The clerk then informed him that it was a fine, delicate fur and required careful handling. 'Well, if it's that fragile, you better give me two,'" he responded.

For years now, Elmyr had been honing his skills as an art forger. It was a craft requiring the same discipline, attention to detail, and dedicated practice that he learned during his years at the Akademie Heimann in Munich. He progressed from drawings to gouache and watercolors to oil paintings. With every step, he mastered techniques specific to the different media. Elmyr always made one important distinction to segregate himself from the common conception of a forger. "I'm not a copyist," he insisted. "I never copied anyone's work. I worked in the style of a certain artist. It could be in the style of Matisse, Picasso, or Modigliani. For example, they often found a subject they liked and did many variations of that subject. Mine might be another variation, but I never copied any of those works that already exit." His comfortable rationalization distanced him from that distasteful word—*forger*. "In the style of..." It sounded cleverer, less illegal. While this was not the career path he wanted, he was determined to show at least to himself, if not the world, that he was the equal of other artists who enjoyed a commercial success that had so far eluded him.

One day while visiting the former star of the Ziegfeld Follies, Fanny Brice, at her home in Hollywood, Elmyr noticed a large portrait done by Modigliani she had recently acquired. When he hesitantly inquired what she paid for the painting, she readily admitted it was $12,000. "She died not long after. I ran into her son later in New York, and he mentioned that someone offered him twenty-five-thousand dollars for the painting. Dealers and serious connoisseurs really prefer oil paintings, as they are the most desirable products of a painter's oeuvre. The rest they commonly refer to as 'paper,'" he commented.

Elmyr could only watch with mixed emotions as the prices of works by artists whom he sat with and drank coffee at Le Dome or La Rotonde steadily rose, and he was no nearer advancing his career than he had been then. It seemed to him that if one was not already established, prospective buyers, gallery owners, or collectors had neither the knowledge nor inclination to spend much money on unknown artists. There appeared to be one exception to this opinion, however.

A new movement called abstract expressionism was gaining currency in the art world. It was bold, colorful, exciting, and, coinciding with the mid-century modern era of design, resonated with notions of freshness. It was also championed by many dealers as a means to "invest" in art, which, for the first time, made the purchase of fine art a commodity like stocks and bonds, and more accessible to an increasingly affluent public. Elmyr viewed this thinking as fallacious and deceptive. It also left him despairing at the thought that any chance to establish himself and a career may have passed him by, making him and his art old-fashioned.

It were as though he had been given a fait accompli to which he had one recourse: do something there was a demand for, something he could supply, that would give him the means to make a living from his craft. Besides, he was unlikely to find a well-paying niche as a bon vivant.

Elmyr went back to New York in 1949, taking an apartment on East Sixty-Fourth Street. Here, he would attempt his first Modigliani painting. The money from just one sale would allow him to live worry-free for a long time. New York was like a huge warehouse full of antiques brought over from Europe by poor immigrants and wealthy collectors alike. He knew precisely what he needed, an old painting on a French stretcher. That was the foundation of a newly created artwork and essential to any hope of passing as authentic. He found one that was perfect for what he had in mind, measuring about twelve inches by twenty inches. The mundane pastoral theme vaguely reminiscent of Millais transformed into the portrait of a young girl with a rosy hue of freshly pinched cheeks. It exhibited the subliminal sexuality so familiar to Modigliani's style. Elmyr thought it a success and wanted to show it to a friend. The actor Montgomery Clift lived nearby. He and Elmyr were already well acquainted through mutual friends. Elmyr invited "Monty" over to his apartment and purposefully said nothing about the painting.

Elmyr reminisced about its private debut. "Monty knew something about art, too, so I was curious to know his reaction. When he came over, we had a drink, and he noticed immediately the Modigliani and thought it was beautiful. He was interested in it, but I wouldn't sell it to him because he was a friend." He went on, "There was a gallery called the Niveau Gallery, and I took it there after I baked it on a low heat in my kitchen oven for a few days to dry the oil paints. Depending on the impasto [thickness] oil paint can take years to dry completely. In those days, it was common to consult another expert, but they often made their decision on instinct. I spoke their language and had the right background, and my prices were always attractive. Invariably, they always said yes. The part I didn't like was the inevitable haggling over price. Anyway, we agreed on six thousand dollars for the Modigliani." It was, for him, "the start of something big," as the song lyric goes.

That same year, for the first time, he consigned work for sale at auction with the Kende Galleries on Fifty-Seventh Street and sold to M. Knoedler & Co., according to Elmyr. While he stayed in a suite at the Waldorf Astoria, he rented a room at Sloane House, a YMCA. Confiding in a longtime friend from Paris, Jean Louis, what he was doing, his incredulous friend visited him one day at the YMCA, where he found Elmyr in a paint-splattered smock working on a new Modigliani painting. Elmyr demurred, "Well, *mon cher*, I can't get paint on the carpet at the Waldorf, can I?"

By early 1951, Elmyr resumed his tour of America, visiting Florida for the first time; he enjoyed the Sunshine State and especially Miami. From there he traveled to New Orleans, with its reminders of its French heritage; its Creole cuisine was savory, and he loved its hot and spicy flavors. His passion for this kind of food was most evident when perspiration would trickle down from his temples, indicating that it was acceptably piquant. Once, wanting to amuse himself, he offered me a sliver of the smallest red pepper I had ever seen. It looked innocuous enough. Its five-alarm burning sensation literally had me hopping, tearfully running to the kitchen for water. He found the spectacle suitably entertaining. To assuage his guilt for the prank, he recounted an incident when he went to Colombo, Ceylon (Sri Lanka). Having just arrived, he went to a good restaurant, where he ordered a curried dish. "Do you want it hot or normal?" the waiter asked. "Hot," Elmyr replied. "When it came, I took one bite—it was so hot I fell off my chair!" he said. It was my turn to laugh.

New Orleans' *vieux quartier* was as close as he would get to Europe for some time. Its easygoing lifestyle and lively nightspots made him want to spend the winter there. "I found a pleasant apartment on the rue Royale," he recounted. This was a time before credit cards became so common. Cash was king, but his Matisses and Modiglianis turned out to be as good as legal tender. They, too, would find new homes among the culturally savvy clientele of some smooth-talking local art dealers. Perhaps for his own diversion, he began painting some of his own work.

He met playwright Tennessee Williams and writer/journalist Robert Ruark during his stay. Ruark had an apartment above the Old Absinthe House, and its owner possessed a historical museum. He asked Elmyr, "Would you be interested in two commissions? I'd like a painting of the blacksmith's shop and Café Lafitte on Bourbon Street. He then introduced me to the mayor of the city, Morrison deLesseps," Elmyr added, with noticeable name-dropping pride. His Magyar charm must have duly impressed the mayor, who then approached Elmyr with an unusual proposition. "Would you be interested in restoring several vintage historical paintings at city hall?" he asked. Elmyr accepted the challenge to do something close to what he was secretly doing already. Only now, it was under the aegis of special invitation of the mayor, himself! For the next few months, he labored to repair age-ravaged canvases commemorating the South's struggle in the Civil War, or War of Northern Aggression, as some southerners called it. In a gesture of civic appreciation on the completion of his task, the city paid him five thousand dollars and bestowed on him honorary citizenship and a key to the city. Unfortunately, he could not share the ironic humor of the situation with anyone. He suspected that it was unusual that illegal aliens receive these kinds of accolades.

Thinking this might be a propitious moment to renew his expired French passport, he filled out the appropriate forms at the French Consulate. They denied the application. His California driver's license would have to suffice for any form of identification. It was only good, of course, if the name on the license concurred with the alias he was then using.

His curiosity once more exhausted, he left New Orleans and headed north into the heartland, ending up in Kansas City for a few months, for reasons that he never made entirely clear. Like many American cities, it had an art museum—two, actually—and he was about to make their acquaintance. According to Elmyr, the William Rockhill Nelson Gallery of Art and the Atkins Museum of Fine Arts bought a Matisse and a Picasso, respectively. In St. Louis, his sanguine Renoir nudes "proved to be popular," he claimed. In Chicago, he established a good relation with a certain curator at the Chicago Art Institute.

Rather than traveling to these cities with the innocence of an eager explorer as he once felt, he realized his wanderings assumed the burdensome drudgery of an itinerant salesman. The dreary sameness of hotel rooms, the absence of someone special in his life, being reduced to making a living that at any moment could land him in jail all began to take a psychological and physical toll. Perhaps he had a little more time on his hands in the Midwest or noticed his increasingly graying hair in the bathroom mirrors of monotonously interchangeable hotel rooms. He felt adrift, as meandering as his itinerary, and was restless for a change. Was it too late to establish a career as a painter, doing his own work? This is what all his professional training was supposed to accomplish.

For the last six years, he told himself he would do the "fakes" (oh, how he hated that word) only as a last resort. If he had to tally up his output since '46, he wasn't sure he could do it. What was the point? It was just numbers, and by his own admission he was never very good at math. Besides, he didn't feel compelled to keep anything as incriminating as a ledger. He wasn't an accountant.

Deciding to go back to California seemed to make sense. Moving, after all, was easy. His entire worldly wealth was the cash in his pocket, elegantly tailored suits and shirts, some jewelry, and a few pairs of good shoes that he could pack in his leather luggage. Paint supplies, he could send Railway Express to whatever his destination was. He was a nomad, but a chic one. Even if he wanted to stop moving from place to place, he couldn't risk languishing in one spot long enough for the authorities and his past to catch up to him.

Elmyr had spent enough time in Los Angeles not to confuse Pershing Square with Bel Air, yet that is where he elected to live until he could make enough money from the sales of his own paintings. There, for eleven dollars a week, he found a room with a kitchenette. It was not a suite at the Waldorf with expensive carpeting to ruin from some errant dabs of oil paint. For the first time in his life, he imposed restrictions on his spending, abandoning ingrained habits that by force of his nature were difficult to break. He vowed to avoid buying his $300 Knize suits,

Brooks Brother's shoes, or dining out. This was as close to a meager working-class life that the fugitive aristocrat dared to venture. He bought canvas boards for his paintings instead of high quality canvas on stretchers.

The art galleries he approached were not interested in offering him an exhibition. A couple deigned to take a painting or two on consignment, but would not guarantee they would prominently display them or even hang them at all. Every honest effort to go straight was an ego-shattering disappointment. Showing an inordinate tenacity and honorable asceticism, he endured the wholesale disinterest and snubs to all his efforts at earning a gainful living from his work. It was galling, since he knew perfectly well that every rebuff would have been entirely different if those canvases bore another, better-known signature. He gave himself what he thought would be an adequate amount of time to get at least one big break—six months.

La Cienaga Boulevard was then, as it is today, thick with interior decorators' shops. Here, droopy-eyed boredom greeted his seascapes with furious waves dashing the shores or lushly rendered flowers or lyrical landscapes with fiery sunsets. They were not popular reproductions of Gainsborough's *Blue Boy*. "Now that is art that could go with *any* bedroom or living-room suite," one showroom savant told Elmyr. About this time, Elmyr felt the last residue of self-esteem draining out of him like the crush of a Mediterranean olive press. With just enough money in his pocket for bus fare home and a burger, he envisioned himself seated at the local diner, a modern-day Christ at the Last Supper. Rather than disciples, the marginalized society of Pershing Square surrounded him. It was all poetically depressing.

Even though he was again almost penniless, he persevered and ultimately found some decorators in Beverly Hills willing to buy his own art. Sensing the palpable desperation in his eagerness to sell *something*, the well-understood law of mercantile Darwinism allowed them to offer as little as possible for Elmyr's pictures. "Would you take ten dollars for this or twenty dollars for that?" they asked. He swallowed hard. Dignity often lodges in one's throat. "Is that in cash?" A slight haughtiness returned to his voice. On his way out, his new buyer remembered, "I have a customer who loves anything with pink poodles. Would you do some pink poodles for her?" asking as though it were the most common sort of request. Fully recovering his disdain by this time, Elmyr responded with an emphatic "No!" Circumstances soon revised that adamant reply, and Elmyr embarked on his "pink poodle period," as he characterized it.

The Aubusson rugs and gold-epauletted doorman of the Waldorf seemed a far-away memory. Instead, more than a few of his neighbors lived as human cockroaches in urine-soaked alleys, a film-noir existence, submerged in addiction, close to drowning in desperation, flailing to resurface one more day. It is unlikely the urbane sophisticate found anyone in his shabby neighborhood who would understand his self-imposed exile. The contrast, however, between a life of ease and refinement, and his current circumstances, reflects the depth of commitment to his own self-worth and faith in his talent that others so readily appreciated—under someone else's name.

Elmyr reluctantly resigned to living in his entertaining, if appreciably sleazy surroundings. Paris had its colorful equivalents, although one could not compare the gaiety of Toulouse Lautrec's Moulin Rouge to the bars around Pershing Square. They were not mixing bowls where the top and bottom layers of society mingled. It was a much more derelict world that Elmyr would normally choose to flee, but it was easy to meet people, and here no one cared what activities went on behind the doors of low-rent rooms. Elmyr soon met a former Marine and ex-boxing champion, Jimmy Damion. He was, as Elmyr described, "a sweet, undemanding, beautiful person."

I'm not sure if Elmyr expected to have the same out-of-the-blue stroke of luck, gaining instant success with his art as easily as Lana Turner's beauty earned her quick fame after someone discovered her at the counter of Schwab's Drugstore in Hollywood. One day, though, luck came his way when he desperately needed it. Among a disarray of forgotten papers in a suitcase, he found a receipt for a Derain watercolor left with a French art dealer in Chicago. He consigned it over two years before returning to California. Should he phone the dealer…why not, it couldn't make him any poorer, he thought.

Elmyr went to a corner phone booth and called the dealer—collect. With a little more luck, he reached him and accepted the charge for the long-distance call. Both were surprised to hear the other's voice. Elmyr excused his disappearance, claiming he had pneumonia *and* amnesia. (It must have sounded more convincing in French.) Elmyr was not dead, as the dealer had suspected, and was pleased to hear there was a buyer willing to pay $400 for the watercolor. Could he wire the money right away? Within two days, he once again had cash in his pocket, more than change for bus fare.

A week later, he and Jimmy found an apartment on Melrose Avenue between Hollywood and Griffith Park. Still, Elmyr tried to make an honest living, visiting decorators' shops with his portfolio of seascapes, still life flower arrangements, and bizarrely popular pink poodles. Jimmy had been urging Elmyr to buy a car with the money he received from Chicago. He was never good at resisting the overtures of anyone he had a relationship with. When a La Cienaga dealer offered an old '46 Chevy coupe in exchange for a number of Elmyr's paintings, he accepted, much to Jimmy's delight. More than a vehicle, though, he needed money to pay the rent, which he didn't have.

On a Friday afternoon, searching for ideas that might redeem him and Jimmy from the imminent prospect of getting kicked out of their apartment and taking up residence in the Chevrolet, Elmyr turned the pages of his art books and magazines. A photograph of Amedeo Modigliani caught his attention. The artist was strikingly handsome, his engaging stare self-assured. It was all Elmyr needed for inspiration. Thirty minutes later, Elmyr dressed in one of his expensive dark blue suits, monogrammed shirt, and Brooks Brothers shoes. On his Formica kitchen table lay a pencil drawing, a self-portrait of Modigliani. Elmyr captured the brevity of the young artist's life in the economy and surety of its lines.

Before leaving the apartment, Elmyr looked in his bathroom mirror and remarkably, the man gazing back was L. E. Raynal, the respected collector. His Windsor knot was perfect. Yes, he was quite distinguished. Jimmy drove him to the Ambassador Hotel, where the Dalzell Hatfield Galleries was located. Hatfield examined the drawing after hearing Elmyr's patented story of old-world aristocratic background and current hardship. This tact was to the art of negotiation what opening a major artery while swimming in a shark tank would be to the art of surgery. Yet Elmyr always seemed surprised that others so readily took advantage of him. He, on the other hand, consistently volunteered more than others asked of him. The fundamental nature of capitalism was a slippery notion indeed.

Hatfield said, "Sorry, I don't buy drawings, only paintings and important pieces, although my wife collects this sort of thing, small self-portraits. She might be interested. I'll call and see if she is." He returned and asked how much Elmyr wanted for the drawing. He needed the money, so he stated $250, with his voice rising to a question mark at the end of dollars. The dealer, sensing the vulnerability of wounded prey, replied, "I'll give you two hundred cash." Elmyr accepted with all the grace a desperate man can muster. Nor would it be the last time he would hear about an acquisitive wife of a seemingly disinterested dealer.

The paper used for the Modigliani drawing came from a book purchased at a junk shop for a dollar. Some months later Elmyr ran across an article about the recently discovered and previously unknown self-portrait. Apparently, Hatfield sold it to a buyer with one of the largest private collections of Modigliani's works. Ignited by curiosity, Elmyr phoned a New York dealer and asked if he knew how much the buyer paid for it. The dealer wasn't sure but suspected it sold for around $4,000. This news made Elmyr feel slightly nauseous. He furthermore had a momentary lapse of rare but clear business sense. He would have to sell four hundred paintings of pink poodles in order to make that kind of money.

In this instance—and there would be many more where he felt foolish or exploited—he felt outright cheated and angry for having let himself be used like this. If, in these moments of pique, anyone asserted that he was the one taking advantage of others, he would have been impenetrable to this suggestion. It was much easier for him to rationalize his actions based on his survivor's instinct. He was just trying to get by while habitually being a victim of the insatiable greed of dealers.

Modigliani self-portrait by Elmyr

The more he embraced this viewpoint, the easier it was to divorce himself from feelings of guilt associated with acts of fraud. He was a gentleman; ergo, gentlemen do not commit fraud. By whatever brain circuitry he needed to explain away his fakery, it was a pathway to a clearer conscience.

After learning that he made one-twentieth the money Hatfield made from the Modigliani, his ill humor was further aggravated when he found their Chevrolet was now falling apart. About this time Elmyr met another gallery owner in Pasadena who actually showed interest in his own paintings. He also proposed to barter for his artwork. This time the offer was a 1947 Lincoln Continental, a status symbol more in keeping with the image Elmyr had of himself and the lifestyle he aspired to. For a number of saleable canvases it could be his.

Like the mythic phoenix, he was about to resurrect himself from his near-the-bone existence. It took no special powers of persuasion when he suggested to Jimmy they take the offer of the Continental and head east. With an unfaltering conviction that all the money made from his skill should not just benefit others, Elmyr decided to satisfy the demand for the art he could supply.

He and Jimmy enjoyed the luxurious ride in the Continental and thought it the perfect conveyance for the cross-country trip. A week after leaving Los Angeles, Elmyr felt oriented once again, with New York City's familiar landmarks in view; Central Park, the Empire State Building, and the Statue of Liberty, perhaps the most famous symbol of hope in the world. Elmyr had already savored the promise of a better life on this side of the Atlantic. It was not El Dorado, the elusive, legendary city of gold pursued by the Spanish conquistadors. Lady Liberty's welcoming torch was intended more as a beacon for the "tempest-tost" refugees, which he was, but he would disabuse anyone's suggestion that *he* was one of the "huddled masses." No, those people were peasants or working-class laborers found by the thousands in third-class or steerage compartments aboard the passenger ships carrying newly arrived immigrants. Nor did he eagerly subscribe to the popular political principal of democracy so widely eulogized here. Egalitarianism may be well and good, but his idea of proper governance was probably closer to the Federalist thinking—the party of landowning, wealthy, and well-educated select few—than Jefferson's grassroots, populist notions. Even in

America, he never lost sight of his privileged background. It made him who he was, and he never felt compelled to assume a false modesty in this new, supposedly classless society.

What Elmyr found in the States was a stratified society whose uppermost members differed from European aristocracy perhaps only in the absence of titles. Wealth softened that distinction but was still a common denominator to both Europe's and America's elite. Since Elmyr already had a title and the bearing it conveyed, he just needed to make enough money to reestablish the lifestyle into which he had been born. He was about to make a little forward movement toward this goal.

Elmyr found a room at the Ansonia Hotel on West Seventy-Third Street. Within minutes of their arrival, Elmyr began phoning friends and acquaintances to see what prospects he could pursue. The few hundred dollars in his possession would dwindle fast if he did not make some money soon. He did not want to be standing on the street waiting for a bus with just the exact change in his pocket again, as he did once too often in California. An hour or so later, he was invited to a cocktail party that evening that sounded promising. By six o'clock, he showed up at his friend's apartment overlooking Central Park. His host quickly introduced him to a French art dealer who mistakenly thought Elmyr, like himself, was a fellow dealer. What the Hungarian refugee heard next was better than an engraved invitation to a front-row seat at a royal coronation. "Do you know anyone who has any drawings by Matisse and might be willing to sell?" the Frenchman asked, to Elmyr's surprised delight. Attempting to appear challenged by the question, he rejoined, "I do know *one* collector. I'm not sure if he would sell. I could ask him."

"Please *do* call me if he's interested. I'm staying at the Plaza," the dealer insisted. When Elmyr showed up at his hotel room with not one, but three Matisse drawings the following day, the dealer thought he was a miracle worker. *Conjurer* would have been more apt. He could have them for only five hundred apiece with a small sales commission for Elmyr included. Again, the prices were cheap and works the dealer could easily sell at twice the price. A check for $1500 separated the lining of Elmyr's inside suit pocket when he exited the Plaza's lobby doors. The dealer's words still rang in his ears: *superb, beautiful.*

At the Ansonia, a party atmosphere filled the room when Elmyr opened the crisply folded check to Jimmy. They discussed what they should do next. Elmyr's congenial companion had long lobbied for a trip to Florida. Whenever Elmyr had money, he predictably indulged himself and his friends. He could once again be generous without second thoughts. Jimmy enjoyed being Elmyr's chauffeur and on more than one occasion suggested he get a cap and gray gloves to look the part, which in turn might make Elmyr feel a little richer than he was. A week after selling the Matisse drawings, they loaded their luggage into the commodious trunk of their luxury vehicle. Jimmy talked about how he would eat oranges and grapefruit every day and wanted to discover the contents of those drinks that sloshed around inside coconuts and were sipped through straws. He couldn't remember sipping anything through a straw in his days as a Marine.

A gray overcast sky shrouded the city skyline the morning of their departure. They decided it was a good omen, confirming their wisdom to leave New York, seeking instead the warm air and sunshine of Florida's gold coast. Maybe it would be their real El Dorado. Their southward trek assumed the unhurried pace of life on an antebellum veranda. When their drive down the long Florida peninsula ended in Miami, they rented an apartment with an ocean view.

Elmyr never told me where he got the idea to start selling his art through an aggressive letter-writing campaign, but that new strategy proved to be an extremely efficient and effective tool for him over the next two years of his life in Miami. He first wrote to the City Art Museum of St. Louis. Stating briefly that he was in possession of a pen and ink drawing by Matisse from between 1920–25, representing a seated woman with a bouquet of flowers; he wanted to sell it. If they were interested, he would gladly send a photograph. His inquiry paid off. After sending the photo, an exchange of correspondence followed, addressing its price, which was of course contingent on examination of the drawing.

While he had a 100 percent success rate at selling his fakes, he prudently avoided compounding his crimes by not using the United States Postal Service when sending his works long distance. This cautionary measure would not draw the attention of the US Treasury Department or, worse yet, the FBI. He figured he did not need to know what arcane statutes he might violate, but sufficed grasping the concept of interstate commission of a crime. Years later, when I knew Elmyr and it was a period of relative tranquility and prosperity, with his illegal activities behind him, few things inspired fear in him as readily as the sight of someone in a police uniform. It was an unconscious but automatic reaction he was unable to overcome.

The museum in St. Louis requested and received the Matisse pen and ink drawing, carefully rolled in a tube and safely arriving by Railway Express. (In 2010, the Hillstrom Museum of Art borrowed an Elmyr fake from the St. Louis Art Museum, originally from

Renoir-style nude – pencil

Matisse drawing by Elmyr – purchased by the Main Street Gallery

the Main Street Gallery, for the exhibition: *Elmyr de Hory, Artist and Faker*, a Matisse pen and ink drawing of a woman. It was the first example of his fakes with a forged signature I had ever seen.)

A private collector with some connection to the institution purchased it after apparently getting their benediction on its authenticity. Elmyr found this method of selling less stressful than the sweat-inducing, tense face-to-face encounters with his prospective clients that invariably made him feel like a peddler. It was assuming that subclass status of merchant that he found more disquieting than slipping into one of his many gentrified personas that were simply a variation of his own background. After all, his deception at art was greater than his art of deception. Spending a little time with Elmyr, I learned not to confuse his animated nature and theatrical personality with a gift for theatrics. Even he realized that because of his transparency and inability to hide his thoughts or emotions, he would have been unconvincing outside his own limited range of experience.

From the refuge of his Miami apartment, he expanded his repertoire to doing more drawings, gouaches, watercolors, and oil paintings in the styles of Vlaminck, Derain, Bonnard, Braque, Matisse, Laurencin, Picasso, Degas, and Modigliani. Under his various assumed names, letters went out to galleries and museums in Chicago, St. Louis, Washington, Detroit, Dallas, Seattle, Cleveland, Baltimore, Philadelphia, and San Francisco. Without providing an expertise, or provenance of the works he offered for sale, he remained deliberately vague about their origins. "How did *you* acquire these artworks?" they asked. "They came from my family's collection," he told them. When or where they purchased them he didn't know, or they may have been a gift to him from the artist before the war, or acquired from a former mistress or someone with a personal connection who was now conveniently deceased.

Elmyr would soon meet the man who was singularly responsible for widening the scope and accelerating the pace of sales, along with perfecting the attendant documentation for his art, thereby creating a truly international market for his works. For the time being, however, the strength of his talent, along with the acquisitiveness of dealers and collectors, proved to be an alchemist's dream—turning base materials into gold—come true. Perhaps Elmyr was in a certain way a conquistador, although I know he would have bristled at this comparison. His perception of his profitable accomplishments was more self-effacing. In the 1970 BBC documentary made on Elmyr, he asserted that he never got rich off his efforts, that he "always sold everything very miserably and the really big money was made by the dealers and the people who resold them."

While still working from his Florida base, he offered and sold a Matisse pen and ink drawing, *A Lady with Flowers and Pomegranates*, to the Fogg Art Museum at Harvard University. It was, by Elmyr's description, "the foremost institution in America for the study of art," and he considered their purchase of a "Matisse by Elmyr" an accolade of the highest order. Following his initial success was an invitation to exhibit a number of other works in his private collection, which he quickly sent for their perusal. These included a number of Modiglianis and a Renoir drawing. The museum's assistant director, Agnes Mongan, examined the drawings, two of which aroused her suspicions, the Renoir and a Modigliani.

It may be a perfectly natural impulse to revisit any tried and proven formula for success. In this instance, his alacrity to offer too much too soon risked turning a good thing into something bad. One fundamental factor governing the price of art or any commodity is "scarcity value." In other words, the rarer an item is, the more likely it will have a higher price attached to it. Paintings by, say, Giorgione, Vermeer, or Leonardo, whose recognized oeuvres are relatively small, command staggeringly vast sums because the supply is minuscule compared to the demand. The sudden availability of Elmyr's drawings offered to the Fogg, and without sound pedigrees, could only have raised a huge red flag, not just there but most anywhere. The exception to this would be where the eagerness of others to acquire desirable works trumps all other considerations—and this occurred with other equally august institutions.

Ms. Mongan, referring to the two drawings she found questionable, allegedly stated, "They were not of any significance." Clifford Irving interpreted that quote to mean, "They were out-and-out fakes." Her doubts, in any event, started an investigation that continued for years. According to Irving, they contacted "hundreds of collectors and dealers about the situation." The museum began compiling photographs of Matisse's drawings from both public and private collections. It would not be surprising to find Elmyr's work á la Matisse on the "questionable" list when compared to those with an established history. The Fogg's Elmyr/Matisse decidedly came down on the questionable side. For a long time, they were uncertain if L. E. Raynal was deliberately attempting to sell them dubious artworks or if he was an unwitting recipient of them himself. The museum was not yet prepared to make any potentially libelous claims against him until they were certain, so they politely declined to buy anything else from his collection. By the time the assistant director's mounting evidence corroborated her doubts about their authenticity, they had long since returned the drawings. A few people now took on the challenge of untying this Gordian knot and finding the source of these spurious works of art. Fortunately for him, his multiple identities helped confound their search.

It was still unlikely that he knew the posse had unleashed the bloodhounds on his trail. Besides, they weren't sure *who* they were looking for. In the meantime, he moved to Miami Beach with Jimmy Damion. There, Elmyr met George Alberts, the owner of a P. T. Barnum emporium of sorts and a dealer that preyed on the tourist trade, selling everything that looked like what it was not: ersatz antiques, electroplated Georgian silver candelabras, fake Persian rugs etc. He found the merchant likable and entertaining, but probably saw no connection between himself and Alberts in any professional sense. Alberts deliberately took advantage of people's innocence and gullibility. Elmyr, on the other hand would never *dream* of doing that. The dealer liked Jimmy, too, with his honest face and genuine charm. He offered him a job, helping reel in the suckers, or rather, customers. Elmyr was pleased for his friend and had little inkling that it would signal an end to their relationship.

For the first time in the last ten years since he began generously contributing his works to the oeuvres of many of the great impressionist and postimpressionist artists, he was not constantly migrating from city to city, state to state. This unusual stability allowed him to focus on his craft, perfecting his techniques with the consummate dedication of a professional.

When I lived with Elmyr and became familiar with his temperament and idiosyncrasies, I often thought of the duality of his career. There was probably never a moment that he was unaware that every bit of skill devoted to creating art in other's styles went into creating his own art as well. If it caused me heartache to see how his sensibilities bruised so easily, I cannot begin to fathom the depth of frustration and pain he must have felt when almost unfailingly his efforts to establish himself as an artist in his own right failed. His family never provided the emotional support he desired, and now only his fakes earned critical and commercial acclaim.

By the time he moved to Florida, Elmyr had accrued significant tricks of the trade of professional restorers. His stint in New Orleans furthered his familiarity with practices he would employ throughout his stay in the US and later on in Europe. He knew, for example, how the Chinese cooked ivory in tea to give it an artificially aged appearance. By lightly rubbing cotton dipped in his day-old breakfast tea onto sheets of paper, they immediately assumed the brownish yellow tint mimicking the look they acquire over time from their acid content. Oil paintings still were his greatest challenge. They required authentic period French canvases. When he could not find them, he had to improvise. At one point, he brought an old European painting to a perplexed but accommodating Miami carpenter to make a few dozen copies of the proper style stretcher with its corner wedges to keep it taut and square. He then gave the new wood an old look by applying a mixture of turpentine, dirty linseed oil, and brown paint. To affect a splattered or speckled appearance he used a Flit gun or a more diluted mixture of his concoction in an atomizer. He repeated the process to the new French canvas he special ordered.

Elmyr's mail-order business was still thriving even as his bubble of peace and prosperity developed into an aneurism from the mishap with the Fogg Museum in Boston. He had more money now than he ever had before—about $40,000, by his estimate. In this blush of solvency, he decided to get rid of the old Lincoln and buy a new '56 Cadillac. Soon, he would need a reliable source of transportation.

On one of his meandering journeys through the Midwest two years earlier, he encountered respected art dealer Joseph W. Faulkner, owner of Main Street Galleries on North Michigan Avenue. Elmyr recalled, "They sold small Picassos and Braques, and some other postimpressionists. He bought a Picasso from me. I think it was a gouache. I later wrote him from Miami Beach, telling him I was willing to sell a Matisse drawing from my collection and asked if he was interested." Then, reenacting the dealer's excitement at his inquiry, Elmyr's eyes sparkled. He grinned broadly and exclaimed with joy, "Yes! Of course, I'm interested!" Anyway, this was how he interpreted Faulkner's response from his correspondence. He went on, suggesting that he was then under a lot of pressure from the dealer to part with other works as well. Elmyr feigned reluctance but predictably acceded to Faulkner's insistence, sending not only the proposed Matisse, but also some Modigliani drawings. Since he did not immediately need money to eat or pay his rent, he could afford the luxury of patience, giving his client several days to make up his mind. When he called the Chicago gallery, he discovered the dealer wanted *all* the drawings. Haggling over their prices was predictable, and even after years of practice he still wasn't any good at this hateful custom. They settled on $7,000 for the lot. It was $3,000 less than he wanted, but shortly afterward he received a cashier's check that made his concession less painful.

When Elmyr received word that Faulkner was coming to Miami for a vacation and wanted to meet with him personally to view his collection and discuss other possible acquisitions, he "spent a small fortune getting a number of paintings and drawings expertly framed." He went on to say, "A friend of mine, a dealer in Paris, once told me that you should never show art unframed. Proper presentation is everything. That's why I never felt good when I just pulled them out of some cheap portfolio."

Faulkner took a suite at the Fountainbleau Hotel. Later that day he and a friend paid Elmyr a visit at his apartment. One of the freshly framed Matisse oils captured the dealer's interest. It was a favorite theme of the French master, a woman seated next to a table with a predominantly red background. He had a specific client in mind but instead of buying it on the spot, he asked if Elmyr would allow him to take it back to Chicago to show him. Along with the Matisse, he carried away three more drawings. A little more time elapsed before they consummated the transaction. Elmyr settled for the original price he wanted for the painting alone—$10,000. The drawings were included.

It was interesting to observe years later a reprise of this scenario when eager customers flocked to Elmyr's home on Ibiza. People still attempted to bargain over price, although rather than reducing it, Elmyr would simply say, "No, that's still a fair price, but I tell you what...I'll include that drawing if you pay that price." It was a ploy that most often worked. His client felt he was getting a deal, and Elmyr didn't have to make a concession he didn't want to make. Besides, "the drawing may have taken me twenty minutes to do."

Clifford Irving reputedly interviewed Faulkner in 1968. The art dealer's account of his business transactions differed somewhat from that of Elmyr's. Faulkner claims Elmyr would not have duped him if he had not already received the imprimatur of Mr. Karl Schneidwind, curator of drawings at the Chicago Institute of Art. Schneidwind had bought two Matisse drawings from Elmyr and told Faulkner his reputation was good. Some of the works purchased by the Chicago dealer allegedly ended up in other museums.

In the early '70s, I accompanied Elmyr to a high-class cocktail party given by a Palm Beach society painter at the Ritz Hotel in London. Channing Hare was his name, but he preferred the cheerily Disney-esque moniker Uncle Bunny. At his suite, white-gloved, silver-tray-bearing staff offered hors d'oeuvres and fine French wine. Channing immediately led us to an enormous man sipping champagne. It looked like the man snatched his glass from a child's playroom; its thin stem pinched between his wurst-size thumb and forefinger. His family name was Block, which suited his physique. He was smartly dressed in everything that one could weave from silk—his suit, shirt, and tie. Channing introduced us, and we shook hands. My right hand disappeared in his clasp. He then folded his arms across his chest, standing like a well-attired sentinel. In case we had not caught it the first time, he repeated in an orotund voice and apparent enchantment with the sound of his own name, "I am Mr. Block from Chicago." Elmyr quickly pointed out, "I'm sure that even in Chicago there is more than *one* Mr. Block." Again, he stated matter-of-factly, "I am with the Chicago Institute of Art and I'm sure *we* never bought anything by you." Elmyr demurred, "Well, Mr. Block, you're doing the talking." Looking increasingly imperious, Block inquired, "Did you know anyone on the staff?" "Yes," Elmyr responded, "I knew Mr. Schneidwind." "He was a good man," was Block's final remark on the subject. He then looked past the tops of our heads, hoping perhaps for the arrival of the Four Horsemen of the Apocalypse, who might improve his mood and party spirit. We slowly parted company like separating polar ice sheets. Elmyr turned toward me, indicating with both hands, something thick, like the Chicago phone directory. Then, in a stage whisper, he admitted that Schneidwind bought a pile of his artwork that would fit nicely between his hands. Mr. Block had difficulty overcoming his professional esprit de corps, preferring not to acknowledge any fallibility or imperfection. This entrenched denial appeared to reflect a tacit don't-ask-don't-tell policy among many in the art community.

Schneidwind's expertise as the Institute's curator of drawings understandably lent a weighty seal of approval of Elmyr's work and convinced Faulkner he had no reason to worry. When the picture dealer later sent some of the drawings and a Matisse painting for exhibition at the Delius Gallery in New York, two Renoir drawings were supposedly not by Renoir—or even by Elmyr. According to Irving, they were Renoir facsimiles from a portfolio, reproductions from the Paul von Majowsky collection. The originals were in the Budapest Museum. It is a common practice of museums to periodically reissue or restrike editions of engravings or reproductions from their permanent collections. They usually bear some marking to distinguish them from originals. The embossed printer's stamp was absent from the Renoirs. Why Elmyr did this and risked exposing himself, I can't answer, because I never challenged him on the subject, nor did he ever satisfactorily explain himself to Irving on the matter. What we do know is that an angry Faulkner had sufficient reason to believe all the works from Elmyr may have been fraudulent and that he had been conned—totally. Elmyr recalled that when he last spoke to Faulkner, the dealer wanted him to furnish an expertise and provenance for each of his purchases. He euphemistically characterized the upset in his voice as "vaguely unpleasant." Elmyr told him he definitely had no papers of authentication but would send on any other documentation he could find. The next day, attempting to quell the rising unrest, he sent Faulkner a telegram. Somewhat defensively, he stated that he never pressed Faulkner for a decision on any purchases and allowed all the time the dealer needed to make up his mind. If necessary, he would come to Chicago but had to spend some time with a friend who had just arrived from Europe. Elmyr must have sensed disaster looming when he walked out of the Western Union office, got into his fully packed car, and left. He aligned the long hood of the Cadillac with the highway heading north. The setting sun warmed the car's interior. Palm trees' shadows like those of giant fence pickets lapped over his disconsolate face, marking his flight from Miami and the threat of trouble.

Things cascaded downhill rapidly after that. Delius sent a photo of the Matisse oil painting from the defunct exhibition to Matisse's former secretary in the south of France. Its authenticity now was no longer in doubt. The former secretary pronounced it a fake. Faulkner informed his clients that he would refund their monies for the works that came from Raynal, despite the fact that some art experts testified before FBI investigators that the paintings and drawings sold to him were authentic.

seated nude in the style of Matisse – oil

Matisse-style odalisque – oil

By the time Elmyr reached Atlanta, he called Jimmy Damion, who had stayed behind, electing to keep his job at the curio shop. "Two FBI agents came around," Jimmy told him. "They were looking for you and wanted to know when you'd be back. I said I have no idea." Elmyr was glad to be in another state and knew he made his escape just in time. He thanked Jimmy again for his kindness and told him he would miss him but thought it best to omit his next destination from their last conversation.

Since Elmyr never liked driving fast, he never worried about speeding tickets—or maybe it was a sensible way to avoid the police. For whatever reason, he took his time crossing the country. In Little Rock, Arkansas, the Cadillac broke down. While it was in a garage for repair, he stayed at a hotel. In some strange karmic twist of events, he made the acquaintance of the hotel's owner, who just happened to also own an art gallery. "It turned out to be perhaps the city's most serious gallery," is how Elmyr phrased it. Before the hydraulic lift lowered his car, Elmyr sold him two Matisse drawings for $1,800. "The art business wouldn't seem so difficult if all sales were this easy," he quipped.

One week later, he drove his Cadillac down Hollywood Boulevard. Happily, he still had his rumple-edged black address book whose familiar names sent a rush of nostalgia through his body when he opened it. He couldn't wait to once more visit his friends and not hide from them as he had when living in his dingy little apartment on Pershing Square. For a short time, he rented a fashionable apartment in the Hollywood Hills, then decided on Bel Air, the upscale neighborhood of doctors, lawyers, and those in the entertainment industry. He met a young actor and shared his house with him. It was here that he met the British actor Peter Lawford, who became better known as President Kennedy's brother-in-law and a member of Frank Sinatra's rat pack. Elmyr had learned as a young man that even if people were wealthy, that did not imply that they were also connoisseurs of art. Many of his Hollywood friends "weren't the least bit interested in art," he acknowledged. One exception was actor Vincent Price.

I had the pleasure of meeting Mr. Price one morning in Chelsea as Elmyr and I walked down the King's Road. He passed by, and I turned to Elmyr and asked if he recognized who just went by. He said no. When I told him, he abruptly turned around and shouted, "PRICE!" The actor returned. Each seemed pleased to see the other; Elmyr asked if he could join us for lunch. Unfortunately, he was leaving London later that day. I saw him once again in 1983, when he came to Minneapolis for a retrospective of his films at the Walker Art Center. We chatted briefly, and he later wrote me, mentioning that "Elmyr painted a lovely portrait of my wife." Curiously, I don't recall Elmyr ever telling me this, although I'd grown comfortable with Elmyr's A-list friends threading through his life and his being on a first-name basis with them. In any case, his friendship with Vincent Price conformed to the aura of glamour I took for granted.

Back in the land of movie stars and sunshine, the ripple effect from the Fogg Museum's investigation and misadventure with Faulkner began alerting the art community. The New York dealer Klaus Perls, who had purchased a number of Elmyr's works, had a brother, Frank, also a gallery owner in Beverly Hills. Irving claimed that Elmyr showed some of his Matisse, Modigliani, and Renoir drawings to Frank Perls in the late '40s. After careful examination, the drawings allegedly prompted the dealer's doubts. He then accused Elmyr of selling fakes, threw him out of his gallery, and chased him down the street. Elmyr told me that it never happened and that the story was an invention of Irving's. It is entirely plausible, however, that word of possible fakes circulating within the art establishment was gaining currency, given the propensity of dealers to buy and sell among themselves, and deleterious news of this kind would spread like brushfire.

It is likely that Elmyr was unable to gauge the jeopardy in which he placed himself. America was, after all, a big country, and he probably deluded himself into thinking his troubles were localized even after his near-encounter with the FBI in Miami. Despite having enough money to live comfortably and quietly for a while, his disregard of being caught allowed him to continue his business-as-usual approach to creating and selling his fakes. He resumed his clandestine manufacture of the finest examples of art from the School of Paris and was seriously thinking of paying another visit to Hatfield at his gallery in the Ambassador Hotel, where he had sold the Modigliani self-portrait. Before mustering the incautious bravura bred by success but imprudent in the face of recent events, he paused to reflect on his strategy. He thought it best to enlist the help of a friend, a young Canadian, to approach the dealer. He still may have wanted to exact revenge on him for making so much money from the drawing that earned him so little. "I'm just not on very good terms with him," he told his friend. Not since his partnership with Jacques Chamberlin did Elmyr let someone else attempt to sell his work.

Because Elmyr never divulged the extent of his confidences with his friend, it is impossible to know the degree of innocence or complicity the Canadian enjoyed as he walked into Hatfield's gallery with two watercolors, one a somewhat cubist-style by Derain and the other a would-be Vlaminck landscape. He left them with the dealer for the customary grace period for examination. Several days later, he received a check for the purchase of both—$2,000.

Just as General Custer had no inkling of any real danger, until, of course, it was too late, everything appeared copasetic to Elmyr. His inability to grasp the consequences of the risks he continued to take harbored in the self-deluding notion that his sins were insignificant. In his mind, he was just a struggling refugee just trying to make a living. After some months in Los Angeles, he thought a change of scenery might just be the salubrious change he needed. He was curious about Mexico and wanted to see it. The problem was that he had no valid passport. Then, remembering George Alberts, master procurer of all things not quite legitimate, he phoned his genial acquaintance in Miami. He explained that he needed some documentation to travel to Mexico, like a birth certificate. Could he help? Alberts assured him he could. That same week Elmyr sold his Cadillac and flew back to Miami. His resourceful friend came through for him. George gave him a forged birth certificate under the name Louis E. Raynal. Elmyr, George, and Jimmy enjoyed their reunion at a good restaurant the evening of his return. Jimmy assuaged Elmyr's worries for the moment when he mentioned the FBI had not been back to look for him. In any case, Elmyr was already booked on a return flight the following day to LA.

Elmyr stored some of his personal effects with friends in Los Angeles and flew to Mexico City. He found a nicely furnished five-room apartment to rent near the Hilton Hotel. The advantage of being an expert art forger was the luxury of an instant collection of fine art. He may have left his valuable reference books in California, but sheets of paper and canvas were easier to transport. His inventory of precious art came with him. Soon they would all be magnificently framed at a fraction of the price in the States. He reveled in the open markets with Technicolor produce and flowers. With his knowledge of French, Italian, and Portuguese, he found he could at least understand the gist of the language, with some room for error, of course.

By the time his pictures graced the walls of his home, he was ready to make his foray into Mexico City's high society. He frequented some of the elegant nightspots, and soon became acquainted with the community of artists, gallery owners, and wealthy patrons. Elmyr fit in wherever he went; he was charming, cosmopolitan, entertaining, and now a gracious host to his newly acquired friends. They flocked to his lavish cocktail parties. One gallery owner, Antonio Souza y Souza, was both young and rich. He quickly became a conduit for Elmyr to meet the kind of people most likely to buy his artwork. Antonio then asked Elmyr to show his entire collection at his gallery. He had just concluded a successful exhibition by the renowned Mexican painter Ruffino Tamayo, who also appealed to Elmyr's sense of civic duty. The public would be so grateful, he suggested.

"Someone I met from the museum in Mexico City asked if I would loan the collection for exhibition, but they wanted me to wait a while because they recently had a big show of the impressionists," he told me with an obvious air of pride. Elmyr thrived on the ego stroking and, giving in to their flattering overtures, said yes to Antonio. Opening night was a glorious cultural event. The way he described it to me made me think of one of those turkey farms with a cacophony of clucking birds, the poor creatures cramped so close together that if you threw a coin into the flock it wouldn't hit the ground. (Come to think of it, on many occasions I *was* one of those turkeys.) As much as Elmyr loved being the center of attention amid a flurry of social activity, the exhibition was a financial disaster. He explained that, "The prices of the artworks were much higher compared to what they were normally used to. If you asked more than two or three thousand dollars, they expected to see Rembrandt's signature on it." The show, however, garnered considerable press coverage that portrayed him as a "rich collector."

He would soon find himself in the spotlight again. The show closed. Elmyr had not sold one picture. Feeling the crush of disappointment and a need for cash, he approached Senora Montes de Oca Quijada, who owned Galeria Proteo, inquiring if she wished to purchase part of his collection outright. When he was willing to sell many of the Modigliani drawings averaging $350 apiece, she knew they were way below their market value. Politely telling Elmyr she would consider his offer, she then wrote to some American dealers with questions concerning Sr. Raynal, the collector. News circulating through the grapevine was not good. Elmyr knew his proposition probably seemed overly eager, especially for someone perceived as "rich." "Two or three weeks passed before I phoned her," he recalled as he relayed the incident to me. "Her voice was icy cold. There were no pleasantries. She just said, 'No! I'm not interested.'"

His Mexican adventure was beginning to look nothing like a rest at the spa in Baden Baden. Two months had passed since his arrival. Entertaining his would-be clients had not earned him one peso. It vividly reminded him of a Hungarian saying: "If you dine with the rich, you end up paying the bill." An unexpected turn of events was about to make him forget the failed show and dearth of success at selling anything. Responding to a few light knocks at his front door one morning, Elmyr opened it to find three uniformed police officers. His terror was instant. Mexican jails were rumored to be something out of Dante's *Inferno*. Would he accompany them to police headquarters, they asked. Any pretense of composure was out of the question. "I was in trouble and I knew it," he told me. His friend, Jean Louis, who was visiting him at the time, went with him.

At the stationhouse, they led him to an interrogation room, where he waited for an English-speaking translator. Again, the nightmarish memories of his treatment by the Gestapo brought him to the verge of tears, although he resisted this impulse so he would not appear to be an already-condemned man. Besides, they had not yet accused him of a crime. When the questioning began, "Remarkably, they said nothing about art, nothing at all," he continued. Nor was it about identity papers. While this might have relieved his tension, it did not. They in fact wanted to find out his connection to a murder. A sixty-year old homosexual Englishman was found strangled in his home. The police arrested a young man named Carlos and jailed him as a suspect in the case. They found Elmyr's phone number and address in his possession. He protested his total innocence in the matter. "Then why did he have your name and address, Sr. Raynal?" they wanted to know. A moment of intense concentration dredged up a faint recollection of a brief encounter with him at a cocktail party. It was a standard practice to offer one's *carte de visite* at these affaires, followed by the casual invitation of, "Call me sometime." The unthinking gesture now linked him to a capital offense.

While the police had only circumstantial evidence leading them to Elmyr, his questioning was routine procedure. Nor did they actually think he had any role in the crime. They did, however, suspect that he was guilty of being a homosexual. They also knew he was a rich foreigner. A little more than three hours passed in a bleak, hot room in the company of the rightfully feared Mexican police. It seemed a great deal longer. The topic ultimately returned to money. They suggested a mere thousand pesos (about ninety dollars) would cover their expenses and secure his release. Jean Louis then bargained them down to half that amount. An appreciably paler and weak-kneed Elmyr left the station with the support of his friend. His interrogating detectives then good-naturedly gave them a ride home.

Seven days later, they again picked him up for questioning. This time, though, they got directly to the point, wanting another five hundred pesos. He paid them without arguing, as Jean Louis, his flea-market negotiator par excellence, had returned to Paris. Elmyr at this point was probably beginning to feel somewhat like a New England maple tree, permanently tapped irrespective of the season. He protested the institutionalized extortion to the British ambassador, Sir Andrew Noble, who in turn recommended William O'Dwyer, former New York City mayor and ex-ambassador to Mexico. Now in private law practice in the capital city, he reassured Elmyr that this sort of harassment was not uncommon, and he would see that it stopped. True to his word, the authorities no longer bothered Elmyr. His lawyer's bill, though, sounded like another form of extortion at $1,000. O'Dwyer went on to explain that $500 of that went to the chief of police.

Despite rumors about fake artworks showing up in the United States, there was no definite proof linking Elmyr to those events. In Mexico City, his social life remained vibrant. One of the people who came to his exhibition was a fellow Central European, an Austrian named Oscar Herner. Elmyr shared this recollection: "He had a gallery, not filled with as much kitsch as George Alberts's in Miami, but close. His victims were also unsuspecting tourists. He also fled Vienna when the communists took over. Although a gallery owner, he wasn't that knowledgeable about art. My butcher in Ibiza knows more about art than he did; he was just a clever merchant. Oscar first proposed that we go into business together, opening a first-class gallery. He went so far as to have his lawyer draw up an agreement. When I showed it to another attorney, he assured me that I would be doing all the work and Oscar would make all the profit. That should have taught me something, but it didn't."

Elmyr lived as though money was still sent unquestioningly by his family whenever he needed. In fact, his funds were rapidly dwindling, and he was increasingly uneasy about his lack of sales. Nor were there any immediate prospects to assuage his concerns. Oscar still pressured Elmyr to do business with him. Elmyr later relayed that Herner made a few subtle remarks implying doubts about the authenticity of the collection, stressing again that these concerns were not due to his scholarship about art. It had more to do with the fact that he and Elmyr were both refugees, and Herner probably questioned Elmyr's ability to escape Hungary, in the aftermath of destruction, with a sizable art collection intact. His constant cajoling finally worked. Elmyr thought it was time to leave Mexico, but decided to consign half a dozen paintings to Oscar, who enthusiastically assured him he could find buyers for the works. One painting was a Matisse oil, a girl seated at a table with a vase of mimosa. "Matisse made innumerable versions of this favorite subject," he said. Elmyr created it in Miami Beach and thought it would have sold long before coming to Mexico. He told Oscar he wanted $10,000 for it, a remarkable deal. Herner gushed that he could find a buyer and offered Elmyr a $2,000 down payment. They agreed that anything above the ten grand would go to the Austrian.

When faced with any unpleasant realization as to when circumstances suggested imminent danger, Elmyr would borrow the Brits' knack for understatement. If, for example, a pitchfork- and-torch-carrying mob of villagers were coming after him, he would say of his visit to their town, "Maybe, I stayed a little too long," making his departure sound as genteel as possible. Without a doubt, his sojourn in the Mexican capital had run its course and his south-of-the-border experience was far less enriching than he had hoped. He was now worried about getting back to the States with his forged birth certificate. Elmyr thought it best to reenter through the back door, so he flew to Montreal. In Canada, Elmyr found a great number of his compatriots who had escaped after the Russians suppressed the Hungarian revolution in '56. Many of them were waiting for visas to get into the United States.

"I met a charming couple," he recalled. "They were Hungarian. How could they not be charming? Anyway, they owned a small jewelry store. When I told them about my art collection, they mentioned a cousin of theirs who was an avid collector." Elmyr brought a portfolio of drawings to show him and, "he had an immediate interest in them," he said, "but wanted me to leave them so he could have some experts examine them." All the experts concurred that they were genuine. A few days after Elmyr's depositing the drawings with him, the compatriot invited Elmyr to an elegant lunch at his home, where, over a plate of oysters, he managed to get a 25 percent reduction in the price. Still, Elmyr was extremely pleased to have the check for $12,000, and, for the first time in a while, he did not pay for the meal.

He also met a Frenchwoman who owned a gallery in Montreal, where, one day, Elmyr, looking distinguished in a dark suit and cashmere overcoat, presented himself as a collector. Rather than buying from her, he instead talked about a small Modigliani painting he was thinking of selling. She desperately wanted to see it. "Well…I suppose I could bring it by," he coyly suggested. She claimed she knew a big Canadian distiller who *must* see it. He was apparently interested but insisted on showing it to someone in New York, so he took it there. "A couple of weeks went by, and I hadn't heard anything from her. When I called, she told me that he became ill on the trip and was in a hospital. It was March, and I was tiring of the cold weather, so I wanted to get back to California. I then stupidly told her I was leaving, but I reluctantly gave her a forwarding address. Given my problems in Miami and Mexico, I was a little leery of doing this, but I did it anyway. Needless to say, I never saw a cent or the painting again," he reminisced, unable to hide the residual upset years later.

Others recommended going to Windsor, Ontario, and crossing into the US at Detroit. With the considerable traffic at this location, and minimal interference from immigration officials, it offered the easiest entry into the country. The long line of vehicles moved slowly but steadily past the checkpoint, except for his taxi. The grim-faced, uniformed officials waved the taxi driver aside. They asked Elmyr for his identification document. He then spent ten heart-thumping minutes as they leafed through large books; his pallor grew whiter by the minute. He prayed his name appeared nowhere on any of those pages. He was just a French Canadian sightseer, albeit a sickly one. When someone leaned into the cab and asked, "What do you want to see in Detroit?" he hesitantly said, "The art museum?" He then heard, "Have a good day." Besides the sweaty palms, an automatic response to stress was a strong gag reflex that I witnessed often. I know his panic precipitated a stomach-churning nausea that was difficult to suppress. His cab gathered speed, passing the Welcome to the United States sign; he opened the car window, admitting cold, damp spring air. Elmyr thought he was going to be sick, though, the fresh air and exhilaration of eluding the law and safely returning to the States thwarted that dreaded queasiness.

Oblivious of his complicity in smuggling in a felon and fugitive, his driver routinely deposited his passenger at the Detroit Museum of Art. By Elmyr's own description, he "walked through the galleries like a zombie until I came to their collection of modern French art. I couldn't believe it when I stood in front of a Matisse painting—by *me*. It was a gift from some foundation."

I don't recall him providing any other pertinent details about the picture. It should be remembered, however, that his works exchanged hands often in a robust market and, as I write this memoir, a large number, I imagine, have long since acquired a provenance of ownership distinguished by a lineage of prestigious public and private collections. Those works that have surfaced as acknowledged fakes by Elmyr among the hundreds (or thousands) he created represent, in my estimation, a small percentage of his output. Given that Elmyr kept no records of his production, let alone an accurate accounting by which to compare numbers or percentages, I can attribute that opinion to Elmyr's own assessment and the exposures for which there is a clear public record.

One day, months later, Elmyr was back in his old neighborhood in Los Angeles. He picked up a copy of *Art News Annual* from a magazine and newspaper kiosk at the corner of Hollywood and Vine Street. In it, much to his annoyance and surprise, he saw a full-page advertisement in color. Staring back was Matisse's young girl with the vase of mimosa, the painting he left with Herner in Mexico City. Elmyr was saucer-eyed in disbelief. Page twenty-two of the 1958 issue, devoted to *his* Matisse. Knoedler Galleries of New York was selling *Figure with Flowers*. Hurriedly returning to his hotel, he phoned the gallery, posing as an interested collector. Could they tell him the price, he politely inquired. "I'm sorry, but it's been sold," the gallery director told him. "We may be getting another smaller Matisse, not quite as important, but priced only around $60,000." With consternation audible in his voice, now an octave higher, he asked, "You mean the *Figure with Flowers* sold for more than *that*?" "Well," the gallery's representative calmly responded, "Matisse paintings of that quality are rare."

Elmyr then angrily fingered through the pages of his address book, looking for "that snake's, Herner's, telephone number of his tacky Bazaar." His indignation was unmistakable when retelling this anecdote.

Elmyr reached him at his "bazaar" in Mexico City. Oscar claimed total innocence but for the missing halo. He told Elmyr he consigned it to an agent in Geneva months earlier and had heard nothing since. The news of its sale in New York was also news to him, he protested. Attempting to defuse the volatile Hungarian, Oscar assured him he would unravel the mystery and fly to LA the following day to meet with him.

Thirty-six hours later, Herner showed up at Elmyr's Hollywood hotel; he claimed he was unable to reach the agent in Switzerland. While still standing in the doorway of the hotel room, almost chest-to-chest with the just-arrived dealer, Elmyr added, "And what happened to the other drawings I gave you?" Herner's head recoiled as if being breathed on by a tormented bull. The Modiglianis went to Geneva with the agent and the Renoirs were still at his gallery in Mexico. Then, in a scene eerily prescient of the dealings he would have countless times with Fernand Legros, Oscar consoled Elmyr with Hollywood melodrama, appearing convincingly contrite to the beleaguered painter, promising answers and restitution. His gloomy mood lightened when he offered to give Elmyr $3,000 on the spot. The rest of his money would be forthcoming when Oscar tracked down his wayward agent.

Regaining Elmyr's confidence somewhat after handing over the check, he suggested that they meet in two weeks in New York, as Herner expected to have this affair entirely resolved by that time. If not, he would fly to Switzerland to get the money each of them had coming. Before the slick Austrian left California, though, he managed to sufficiently weasel his way back into Elmyr's confidence and once more plumb the depths of his bottomless gullibility. When Elmyr walked up to the front desk of the Waldorf Astoria to check in for his appointed rendezvous with Oscar in New York City, he handed his leather valise to the bellhop. It contained a number of drawings, including two large Renoir pastels, a larger Modigliani painting, and a smaller oil of Matisse. The Matisse was another of his well-traveled canvases from Miami. Herner arranged to crate the art for shipment. While discussing the works and division of future sales profits, he pointed out to Elmyr the absence of one rather significant detail. The *e* was missing from Matisse's signature on the painting, and he thought it ought to be included. Elmyr then added the *e* while Herner looked on. As Elmyr explained the incriminating omission to me, he said, "I knew that he knew, and he knew that I knew that he knew. I felt that little mistake put me at a great disadvantage that did not bode well for me."

Herner headed for "the land of cheese and cuckoo clocks," Elmyr said, trying to make light of his egregious slipup. Elmyr returned to California, although this time his expectations were not as great as before. He sensed disaster from the moment he left New York. Two months later, he called the now firmly distrusted Austrian. From the unchallengeable safety of his Mexican stronghold, Herner spoke to his pursuer with marked annoyance. He had sold nothing, he coldly reported to Elmyr. When Elmyr pressed him for an accounting or return of his artwork, he curtly told Elmyr to come there if he wanted them. He then hung up on the righteously distraught artist. Elmyr called back. This time Herner made it clear that their partnership was over by informing his caller that it would be inadvisable for illegal aliens to come to Mexico, and pistoleros were cheap to hire.

Whatever comfort it may have been to Elmyr, there were consequences for Herner. The original Matisse exchanged hands, but not to the mysterious Swiss agent, as the wily Austrian had claimed. He actually sold it to an American collector, G. David Thompson, in Mexico. Its sale was contingent on experts' approval. Its examiners offered their opinion; they called it a fake. When Oscar Herner showed up in Philadelphia for the balance of payment on the painting, Mr. Thompson had a deputy sheriff there to arrest the mendacious dealer, who then generously volunteered a full refund and meekly departed with the Matisse under his arm. It circuitously was sold and resold, afterward ending up in the possession of E. Coe Kerr Jr., of Knoedler, Paris, according to Irving's account. Thompson then contacted Kerr, informing him that he purchased it earlier in Mexico and later discovered it was "wrong." Demonstrating that a good fake has more lives than a cat, it found a couple of more homes before becoming the focus of a trans-Atlantic dispute three years later involving Mme. Duthuit, Matisse's daughter. Since there was no record of the painting, she condemned it as she had with one of the works Elmyr sold to Faulkner in Chicago. The dust settled eventually. Elmyr alleged he heard it traveled around aboard the yacht of a Greek shipping magnate in the early sixties and was valued at that time at around $165,000.

Since the post-war economic shivers subsided, a healthy business climate had brought an uninterrupted prosperity to the United States, Europe, and now Japan. It also fueled a booming international trade in art. The value of works Elmyr once sold for a couple of hundred dollars were selling for thousands or tens of thousands of dollars, yet he was far from becoming rich from his efforts. At the same time, there seemed to be little unanimity among the scholars and experts called upon to decide his works' authenticity. Even those works discredited by Matisse's daughter appeared doubtful only because she could not corroborate their existence against recorded inventories. The quality of his work was never at the heart of these disputes. In fact, it was precisely *because* his fakes were so good that many were reluctant to condemn them, for the fakes slid so easily into the body of work of these renowned artists.

It was 1958. Elmyr was accustomed to life on the run. He heard from friends like Zsa Zsa Gabor that the FBI had asked her questions about him and seemed to have an active interest still in his whereabouts. The teeming streets of New York City always allowed him to hide in the crowds. One day, Elmyr browsed the shelves of the Fifth Avenue bookstore Brentano's. A new edition of drawings by Modigliani caught his attention there. Edited by the respected scholar Arthur Pfannstiel, it included, Elmyr claimed, three of his drawings that he was sure of and possibly two more he thought might have been his. By this time he had done so many, he could no longer be certain of his own authorship. Included in the volume was the self-portrait he sold to Hatfield. Scholarly eulogies accompanied the illustrations in terms reserved for those admitted to the pantheon of art history. The attendant reverence of these assessments all too often sprang from the clarity of hindsight. It could only make one wonder why, if these artists' works were so great in the first place, did it take decades after they died paupers' deaths for the obvious to be recognized.

As the market value of both authentic and inauthentic art climbed dramatically, the irony of Modigliani's wretched life was probably never far from Elmyr's mind. His story merits a garland of black roses. Two days after he died penniless in 1920 of tubercular meningitis, his inconsolable lover Jeanne Hébuterne killed herself. She was nine months pregnant. Elmyr was about to confront his own disconsolate feelings of desperation soon enough.

The specter of his past seemed to follow him everywhere. Other volumes of French masters began including Elmyr's artwork. They appeared repeatedly in auction catalogs. As he sat in the barber chair at the Hotel Pierre, he read an article about a Venezuelan oil millionaire. In the *place d'honeur* above his fireplace was a Modigliani portrait of Elmyr's. It was another he had "sold very miserably." Where these revelations once amused him, they now depressed him. An increasingly embittered man no longer felt the lament of regret he previously attached to selling his convincing creations. The respect he once harbored for many dealers, curators, and experts vanished. Unvarnished resentment replaced those sentiments. Experience, his illicit success, and not-forgotten failure to establish a legitimate career of his own now made him think of his judges as incompetent, pretentious fools.

His network of friends and acquaintances were the palliative he needed in order not to dwell on his personal setbacks. If he wasn't alone, he wouldn't be lonely, he thought. It may have been specious reasoning, but it was understandable in view of his incessant quest for love and reaffirmation. In his swank Murray Hill apartment, his social life continued unabated. Marilyn Monroe sipped cocktails there. "The front of my building resembled the lot of a Rolls Royce dealership, when my friends arrived," he told me. He never lost his flair for being a charming and entertaining host.

A frequent guest was a young Moroccan doctor, Josue Corcos. At one of these lavish parties, Corcos brought an uninvited friend. Elmyr's reaction was less than favorable. Fernand Legros was his name. His black thin hair, unshaven face, and long narrow nose gave him a Mephistophelean appearance. When Corcos presented him to his host, Elmyr's nose wrinkled with undisguised disdain. From the rancid odor emanating from Legros's rumpled suit, Elmyr also suspected he had not bathed in a few days and that the suit doubled as pajamas. Elmyr thought he looked like "a Bowery bum." Within moments, he pulled Corky aside, asking in a horrified voice, "Who *is* that? He stinks! Why did you bring him *here*? Please get him out of here!" Corcos sheepishly explained that the young man was half Greek, half French, and newly arrived in this country. "Someone asked me to help him out and, frankly, I didn't know how to get rid of him," the doctor admitted. The two men then left the apartment.

It is easy for me to visualize Elmyr's first encounter with Legros. Elmyr always sided with first impressions when meeting people, and anyone not passing this instant assessment may have just as well slid off the earth's edge. I witnessed these occasions. When introduced to a person who started these alarm bells clanging, he would extend his arm in full rigor and recoil his head as though pushing away with a stick something foul-smelling, trying to place as much distance between his nostrils and the object of his displeasure.

In contrast to Legros, this unsoigné party crasher, appearance was everything to Elmyr. Anyone failing his visual inspection *and* smell-test was someone he'd keep at a barge pole's length away from him. The one exception I can think of to this sensory aversion to anything malodorous was cheese, particularly French cheese. The more cadaverous its aroma, the better he liked it. Legros probably would have done better to roll in inside a giant wheel of stinky cheese, like a Trojan horse.

As long as Elmyr maintained an appearance of well-heeled respectability, it was easier to hide the underlying truth. He had been a fugitive for almost eleven years, committing fraud all the while, and was now the object of an FBI search. This, to his mind, was no reason to stop having drinks at the bar of the Plaza around five o'clock every day or enjoying the summer on Fire Island. In the midst of his cavalier incaution, though, he decided to scale back on his sales efforts. For the first time since he was a student in Munich, he would produce some lithographs—although these were not real lithographs. They too were fakes. You might call them fake fakes. They were actually original drawings done in lithographic crayon and sprayed with a fixative to inhibit smearing. He signed them as he would for a genuine limited edition, e.g., 22/50, meaning the twenty-second of fifty prints. They were quick, unobtrusive sales and easy money. Perhaps more importantly, they meant less risk to him. He sold them for two or three hundred dollars apiece.

Late that summer Elmyr traveled to Washington DC, after a friend invited him to stay at his apartment. He enjoyed the city, especially "the magnificent National Gallery. It ranks right up there with the Louvre or other great museums of Europe," he told me years later. There, he met an "independent art dealer," Charles Ouriel, who worked out of his apartment in Georgetown. Elmyr's finances were a choppy sea and now in a trough; he needed to sell something soon.

From his version of their encounter, Elmyr never made it entirely clear how or why he chose to confide in Ouriel about his unique talents or who initiated the proposed business arrangement by which they would mutually benefit. What is certain is that even at his perspicacious best, Elmyr was a poor judge of people, and his own sense of self-preservation was too often mystifyingly absent. Ouriel nevertheless possessed two paintings that would have been attributed to "the school of" Bonnard and Sisley. (Elmyr later described "the school of..." this way: "In most cases this designation is to an art connoisseur as vastly different from a first-rate work of art as *vin ordinaire* is compared to a *grand cru* for the wine lover." This epitaph accompanied his critique of the Ringling Museum in Sarasota, Florida, whose collection he largely dismissed as "not having *anything* to do with *the school of...*let alone *by* so-and-so," when he talked about their attributions to old masters.) In any event, Ouriel had Elmyr "enhance" them so they could pass for a genuine Bonnard and Sisley. He cautioned the dealer that the old and new paints would take a long time to meld and gain a uniform appearance. As Elmyr further related, he argued against showing the paintings too soon. Ouriel had, however, already arranged to take the Bonnard to one of Phillips Memorial Gallery's directors in the capital. Elmyr reluctantly went along, posing as the picture's owner. Upon examining the work, a woman in a home's interior, the director was allegedly convinced it was an original Bonnard.

Bolstered by the approval of the Bonnard, the Georgetown dealer sent both a black-and-white photograph and a color transparency of the Sisley to Lionel Venturi, an art scholar who authored *Painting and Painters: How to Look at a Picture*. (I have no idea if he resembled Ben Turpin, the famous cross-eyed actor.) Amazingly, he wrote back from Italy. Not only did he think the Sisley was original, but, more surprisingly, he offered his expertise on the back of the photograph.

After Elmyr transformed the Bonnard and Sisley canvases, Ouriel returned to New York with some more of his Matisse "lithographs" that he sold right away to a dealer. They, in turn, quickly ended up in the hands of Peter Deitsch, who specialized in drawings and prints and then made the unpleasant discovery the lithographs were "wrong." This shows how flourishing the in-trade market was. I had heard Elmyr refer to the art community as an "incestuous cabal." His disparaging characterization was tongue-in-cheek and always said with a sly grin. The subject of forgery, though, did not elicit a smile among any of the New York dealers.

A short time afterward, Ouriel walked into his gallery, seemingly unaware of the golden rule that in business (and comedy), timing is everything. He fell into a tiger trap. Charles Ouriel left the lithos with Deitsch for the customary grace period for examination. Deitsch recognized Elmyr's lithos as forgeries and similar to those he purchased from the other dealer. After making a few calls, Joseph Faulkner's name came up. The Chicago dealer was still sharpening his ax with Elmyr's name on it. Deitsch phoned him in the windy city and asked him about Elmyr. They concurred that all the lithos were probably the products of the Hungarian L. E. Raynal. The dealers from coast to coast were already watching for a man of Elmyr's description: short, well-spoken, cultured, and selling bogus art from his private collection. The irony here was that Elmyr and Ouriel looked a bit alike. At the end of their conversation, Deitsch was sure that Ouriel was the elusive collector/faker they and others were looking for.

This incident essentially ended Ouriel's career and made him persona non grata in New York. Showing then that his timing was as faulty as Ouriel's, Elmyr chose that magic moment—upon the dealer's return from his disastrous trip—to ask him for money for his work on the two paintings. Ouriel was furious and held Elmyr responsible for ruining him. Their brief affiliation ended on the spot. The shock of his anger and outburst crushed Elmyr's spirit, like some inferior species under the heel of a shoe. He was now desperate because he was broke, depressed by the prospect of being caught, feeling old, lonely, and, most of all, tired and disillusioned.

Elmyr returned to an empty apartment. His friend was away on business. The exhausted refugee wanted only to sleep. Elmyr went to the bathroom, emptied the contents of a bottle of prescription sleeping pills into his left hand, swallowed them, and drank a glass of water with his right hand—the one that created all the art.

When his friend returned the following day, he looked in the guest bedroom. The drapes remained closed. Elmyr was sound asleep, even though he was customarily up by that time of the morning. His friend left for work and would not be back until that evening. Passing Elmyr's room that night, he glanced in through the door he had left ajar that morning. Elmyr had not changed positions. Suddenly alarmed, he entered to find his guest barely breathing. A panicked call then brought an ambulance to rush him to a local hospital. Thirty-six hours after the attempted suicide, they pumped his stomach; he would spend the following four days in the hospital on the critical list. His improvement slowed when he developed pneumonia, requiring a three-week stay in the recovery ward.

His friends rallied round him, coming to DC to visit. Even his old friend George Alberts from Miami came to see him. George had moved back to New York, taking a penthouse apartment on Fifty-Fifth Street and Second Ave., and heard about Elmyr through a mutual acquaintance. Their kindness and concern were touching, and, as Elmyr told me this story on more than one occasion, it was a fond reminder that others *did* love him and his life *did* matter. George suggested that Elmyr take his apartment for a while to convalesce. He was leaving for Europe and it would be available. When Elmyr regained his strength, George said the weather in Florida would help him recuperate. George proposed to let him use his apartment in Miami Beach if he would drive his Cadillac down from New York. Elmyr weighed only 110 pounds and was barely capable of feeding himself.

Dr. Corcos drove down to the Washington hospital the day they discharged him, to bring him back to New York. Corky, in essence, became his nurse once they were back in Manhattan. A few days after their return, he stopped by to feed Elmyr and casually mentioned that Fernand Legros had just come back from Europe aboard a Greek freighter. Elmyr looked vacantly at his caregiver. He prompted him, "You remember— the young man I brought to your apartment in Murray Hill." His face then showing a sign of life, Elmyr exclaimed, "That horror?" His eyes were wide with shock as he recalled that walking social disaster, the smelly, unkempt, cheaply clothed person whose unpleasant image animated him enough to restore a tint of color temporarily to his pale face.

Corcos begged Elmyr to let him stay there and sleep on his sofa. "He will bathe regularly," the doctor promised. "He is intelligent—and could help you just until you are well again," he insisted. "He could then drive you to Florida or do anything you needed, anything at all. He just needs a break." Surely, Elmyr could understand that. Corcos knew that Elmyr was generous, kind, and too weak to resist the appeal to his humane instincts. He eventually gave in to his physician's pleading. When he asked Corcos where he was currently staying, the doctor went to the apartment door, opened it, and in walked his new roommate.

Elmyr felt uneasy about George Alberts's reaction to the uninvited second houseguest when he returned from Europe. On his arrival, it turned out there was little cause for concern. Elmyr introduced the two as graciously as he could, and Fernand was as charming as he could be. Elmyr discovered that Legros was actually born in Egypt, and Alberts was born in Syria. The two hit it off immediately, chatting away in Arabic like two hookah-smoking friends in a Kasbah café. The following day Legros capitalized on their instant bonhomie and promptly borrowed fifty dollars from George. He then packed Elmyr's suitcases, a small one of his own, and placed them in the spacious trunk of George's Cadillac. Before lunch they left the city, rolling south to Florida on the car's fat white-sidewall tires. Along the way, Elmyr slept, still exhausted and weak. Fernand stole frequent glimpses of himself in the rearview mirror, thinking himself every bit as stylish as George's Caddy. In Elmyr's words, "That turned out to be the beginning of everything."

From the time Fernand insinuated himself in Elmyr's life, their destinies were sealed. During their trip to Florida, Fernand was accommodating, helpful and deferential to his older and still-fragile traveling companion. The two were the unlikeliest pair conceivable, and their alliance by need would soon end. Despite Legros's attentiveness and Elmyr's forced civility, nothing in their manufactured cordialities predicted longevity of their relationship past their destination. They also shared their life stories along the way. Legros was born in Ismalia, Egypt, and his father worked for the Suez Canal Society. As he was half-Greek, perhaps, unsurprisingly, a relative had some connection in the shipping industry and gave him access to travel aboard freighters across the Mediterranean and later across the Atlantic to the United States. Elmyr probably thought his proposed journey to America evoked no protests from his family. Elmyr's distasteful first impression of the unwashed Legros was an image that still lingered in his mind, although he begrudgingly accorded him a little respect for his genial assistance during their trip.

Fernand left Cairo, where he had been living after the war, and went to France to serve his compulsory military service at age twenty. He told Elmyr, "I was almost immediately discharged," but was never clear about the reason for it. He was a lithe young man who then pursued a career as a dancer "in cheap cabarets," as Elmyr described it. Legros's own account of his life as a dancer is considerably more respectable, including stints with the Ballet of Monte Carlo, a member of the famed ballet of George de Cuevas, and even appearing on the *Ed Sullivan Show*. These claims all became part of a mytho-maniacal yarn, often recorded in the French press in later years, and a pipe-dream biography concocted by him and written by Roger Peyrefitte in the 1970s.

Given Elmyr's loquacious nature, it is not surprising that their conversations drifted into topics that were not only revealing, but also likely trespassed that line between candor and indiscretion. Admitting Fernand into that sanctum sanctorum of his secret life was not only thoughtless, it was dangerous. The fact that he was going back to Miami Beach, where the FBI came close to catching him before, should shed some light on the lack of forethought he displayed when most anyone else would have been more gun-shy. What possibly allowed Elmyr to share these keyhole insights into his illicit activities and daring past was Fernand's assertion that he had studied art at the L'Ecole du Louvre in Paris. This, according to Elmyr, seemed to be another invention of Fernand's imagination. When he told me this, he shrugged his shoulders dismissively and went on. "Even at the time when he was asking me to do everything he could get his hands on, he still didn't know the difference between a gouache and a watercolor or a Matisse and a Picasso. It's just that he had the cold-bloodedness and powers of persuasion of an oriental rug merchant that made him sound like he knew what he was talking about. He really was completely ignorant about art."

Before leaving New York, some of Elmyr's friends helped him with some of his bills, and George Alberts was kind enough to make him a small loan until he could later repay him. Two weeks after arriving in Miami Beach at George's apartment, Legros was still with him and Elmyr, naturally, was still paying the bills. He then suggested he was well enough that he no longer needed Fernand's help. His implication was clear that their temporary union of convenience was over. "Besides," Elmyr informed him, "it is not my intention to go on supporting you, and I have very little money left." Legros, blithely ignoring the first part of that declaration, exclaimed with alarm, "What are we going to do?" The elder statesman then volunteered an automatic response as if it were the most natural thing in the world to him. "You could go out and get a *job*." Fernand's soured expression immediately signaled how unsavory that idea was. Even though he was considerably younger than Elmyr, he learned early in life that by various means of manipulation it was preferable to use others to get what he wanted. He had precisely the kind of street smarts that Elmyr always lacked. Whether by temper tantrums, as Elmyr would discover soon enough; "emotional blackmail," as he called it; or a kind of seductive, evangelical oratory, others became his tools to do his bidding.

Elmyr told me much later how attentively Fernand listened by his bedside as he recovered from his attempted suicide. All the details of his personal history spilled from his lips into an eager vessel. His rapt attention could not have been greater than if Elmyr had given him the knowledge to spin straw into gold. This was essentially the alchemy of his thought processes. No sooner had the accent on the word "job" ended that Fernand rejoined Elmyr's proposal with one of his own, one much more palatable. "Why don't you just give me a couple drawings to sell?" he urged his keeper. "We could live for a month from selling just *one*." With the nonstop persistence of a street peddler, he shadowed Elmyr, relentlessly imploring his cooperation, trying hard to reverse his objections. Fernand correctly sensed that if he pestered him long enough, he would prevail. He was right. Elmyr caved in under the harangue of his endless, erosive rhetoric.

As strong as his doubts were, Elmyr had few options. He was nearly broke again, and a haunting recollection of J. Edgar Hoover's minions sniffing around for his scent required desperate measures for a desperate situation. Stepping back to look over Fernand from head to toe like an examining physician, he shuddered from the challenge before him. To pull off this charade, it would only take transforming the straw man from *The Wizard of Oz* into Cary Grant or some even more improbable metamorphosis. Elmyr felt weak and exhausted from Fernand's full frontal assault. With a sigh of resignation and extended right arm, he seized the taller Legros by his shirt collar and marched him in the direction of the bathroom. "You will never be a gentleman, but you can't smell like a bum. You *will* take a bath, shave, and put on clean socks," Elmyr insisted.

Elmyr retrieved blank sheets of paper from a suitcase. On the kitchen table, he drew three Matisse lithographs in the time Fernand took for his toilette. They then sat down together; Elmyr went over a plausible story for the gallery owner Fernand would visit. "Stick to the story I tell you," he admonished his would-be agent. Elmyr then looked through his wardrobe for something that Fernand could wear. He had him try on one of his tailored suits, a navy blue one. Until Elmyr regained all his lost weight, it looked better on the dark-eyed young man from Ismalia. Elmyr gave Fernand directions to a gallery whose owner was already acquainted with L. E. Raynal. "Remember, stick to the story and don't ad-lib," were his last words of caution as he exited George's apartment on a sunny Florida afternoon. Elmyr waited with the trepidation of a mother whose virgin daughter had a date with a sailor on shore leave. Returning two hours later, a grimacing Fernand entered the apartment with the portfolio under his arm. Before Elmyr could ask about the apparently failed sortie, he erupted in laughter and started doing pirouettes, holding a check for $750 in his raised hand. Elmyr may have felt like Pygmalion for the moment. Later he would feel more like Dr. Frankenstein.

Fernand bargained his percentage of the sale price up from 30 to 40 percent. Elmyr consistently said Legros's brashness and fearlessness never wavered throughout the years that he was associated with him. If anything, he became bolder and more confident with his success. That sense of youthful invincibility never left him. With utter conviction in his voice, Elmyr later described him to me as someone who "has a kind of diabolical charisma and can convince anyone of anything. If he spoke to your mother, he could convince her that the best thing she could do is kill you. She would do it!"

At that time, Fernand began to realize the potential wealth that *he* could gain if he handled Elmyr right. This thought became his "mission statement" and only business ethic. Any subservient role vis-à-vis Elmyr also ran contrary to his ego. He further knew a little flattery and attention thrown Elmyr's way would help get him what he wanted. Irving wrote of their burgeoning partnership: "Rising to the surface now in Fernand's character were two dominating traits—ambition and greed—with which Elmyr, for the better or for worse, had never been cursed." Before fully catching his breath after his celebratory dance performance around the apartment, Fernand urged Elmyr to do some watercolors or a few gouaches to sell. He was twenty-eight years old and saw no reason to put off getting rich.

A week after Fernand's successful venture as a seller of fine art, he exerted some more of his verbal Rolfing on Elmyr to try other markets. He had passed his test and apprenticeship nicely, he thought, and already hungered for bigger challenges. Elmyr agreed to fly with him to Chicago. Elmyr created a Braque watercolor, two Matisse drawings, and a Picasso lithograph. Fernand dispersed these among three galleries. Upon returning to Miami, Elmyr discovered that the FBI were again on his trail. The two men decided to leave Florida the next day. Nervously, Elmyr insisted on traveling alone to New Orleans. Legros was to join him only after a circuitous trip to Atlanta and then to Louisiana by bus. Fernand persuaded Elmyr to give him the portfolio containing a small trove of postimpressionist treasures. He played on his fears, telling Elmyr it would be safer for him if they were not in his possession. Elmyr conceded without objection.

While Elmyr, waiting to rejoin his new partner, dined on Cajun cuisine in the Latin Quarter or took in the nightlife in dimly lit bars or jazz clubs, a disgruntled Fernand traveled across four states by bus to their appointed rendezvous. He vowed it would be the last time he would take low-class public transportation. (I suspect it was.) Elmyr's snobbery seemed to have fertile ground in him, too. By the time they reunited, Fernand was given free reign to exercise his innate entrepreneurial spirit. Moving from New Orleans to Dallas to St. Louis and then to Denver, something akin to Henry Ford's assembly line was operating effectively, churning out convincing examples of impressionist and postimpressionist art for those better able to afford Cadillacs. When they were in Denver, Fernand booked a room at the elegant Brown Palace. Elmyr, for some peculiar reason, could afford only something less than his partner's five-star accommodations. He did his calculations again in Hungarian: two and two equals five. Yes, that's right. Something was not adding up. He suspected Fernand was paying him less than his 60 percent share. Despite that unpleasant revelation, he still did not want to upset their arrangement. He was, after all, making money again and not having to assume all the risk.

In Houston, their portfolio of fauve watercolors and drawings were popular with their clients. Fernand was pressuring Elmyr now for small oil paintings. "I explained the difficulties associated with paintings, but he didn't seem too concerned, or he was simply more concerned that they would bring in a greater amount of money," he recounted of Legros's insistence. Elmyr still enjoyed a wide network of friends and social connections he did not necessarily feel compelled to share with Fernand. Although Legros sought out exclusive men's clothing stores for tailored suits and shirts, Elmyr still thought he resembled a parvenu sponge diver.

One day Elmyr ran into an old friend in Houston, a French art dealer helping some well-healed Texans satisfy their desires for instant culture. The dealer asked if he knew of anyone who had a Modigliani portrait of Soutine for sale. Elmyr pondered thoughtfully for a moment, and said he knew a dealer in Chicago who had one and would probably sell it for the right price. Elmyr would find out. He then went to a bookstore, bought a book on the artist Chaim Soutine, returned to his hotel, and did his portrait à la Modigliani. He called the dealer and told him he could get the drawing in three days for $1,500. After the customary bickering over price, they settled on $1,250.

The dealer in this instance was François Reichenbach, who by 1970 had become a filmmaker and collaborator with the BBC on the documentary about Elmyr called *Elmyr, The True Picture?* Orson Welles later incorporated some of that footage in *F for Fake*. In that film, Reichenbach tells the story of this incident, leaving little doubt that he suspected Elmyr was manufacturing these artworks, but choosing to turn a blind eye. This just raises the question to what extent was there knowing complicity in the buying, selling, and reselling of Elmyr's work. I personally doubt this was an isolated instance.

Elmyr felt rather pleased with himself for his renewed initiative in selling his art, and without too much difficulty. When Elmyr mentioned it to Fernand, he let out the scream of a wounded howler monkey, awakening most, if not all the sleeping hotel guests on his and adjacent floors. Wild-eyed, profanity-laced protests made clear Fernand's upset at this news. He claimed Elmyr owed him 40 percent because they were partners and had a "gentlemen's agreement." Scenes of any sort were distasteful to Elmyr, and he avoided them whenever he could, but not only was he the target of Fernand's tirade, he could not escape as Fernand physically blocked the door. He continued his rant until he extracted a promise from Elmyr to pay him his share. Elmyr glimpsed Fernand's willingness to use his temper and public displays of anger to intimidate him and others around him. What he couldn't yet assess was the latent violence underlying Legros's outrage.

They continued their road show westward back to California, the place Elmyr most felt at home outside Budapest and Paris. Money was also flowing again, although thinking of life's demands beyond tomorrow was the kind of long-term planning better left to bankers, brokers, or fortune-tellers. His habitual insouciance about finances, cavalier spending, and generosity were simply part of his nature. Fernand was well aware of this behavior pattern by now. It soon became an important leveraging tool to manipulate Elmyr as long as their relationship lasted. Elmyr was also certain that Legros shortchanged him on sales, and this most likely prompted some solo sales calls when an opportunity arose. He just needed to avoid detection and triggering his partner's fury.

A young man Elmyr met and liked had some car problems, and the repair costs were more than he could afford. Taking the bus down to La Jolla and Laguna Beach, Elmyr paid a visit to a couple of art galleries and sold some of his lithographs. As predictable as his disregard for money was, his impulse to rescue others was even stronger. After giving his friend the cash to fix his car, the young man drove Elmyr back to his Hollywood apartment. There, in front of Fernand, he thanked Elmyr again for his help. Legros was by now the decided paymaster and quickly tallied a discrepancy in Elmyr's available funds and the cost of his friend's auto repair bill. Fernand instantly flew into a rage on the apartment's balcony where they stood. His audible tantrum began drawing curious spectators in the parking lot below in the way a fire would. A genuine Hollywood soap opera unfolded before their growing audience. Epithets rang out between strangulated refrains of, "You stole money from ME" or "You STOLE money from me," uncertain where to place the accent before his audition. Elmyr's friend stood back in shock. Elmyr, for a moment, huddled beside him, frozen in horror, then tried pushing Fernand back inside the apartment. Legros, who by then was more mindful of his audience that surely sympathized with his denouncement and discovery of this sinister betrayal, let out one last screech worthy of Sara Bernhardt, "YOU STOLE MONEY FROM *me!*" Oh, the treachery of betrayal —Fernand could honestly say he had the crowd on their feet.

Their 60/40 split now became 50/50. Fernand, however, was soon appreciably more subdued, not due to spiritual conversion, Zen meditation, or pharmaceutical drugs, but just a bout of infectious hepatitis. It seemed to be Elmyr's turn to help Fernand through bedridden days and nights for the next four weeks. Through Fernand's convalescence, Elmyr enjoyed the unexpected tranquility of his high-strung associate. He also took the time to tutor him in art history. If his teacher had not punctuated these stories of the great artists' lives with lurid accounts of their loves, intrigues, struggles, rise and fall from grace and so forth, he would have found them a huge soporific. What details Elmyr might have neglected to share about his own past, he now imparted to a sick, but listening Legros. These confidences were little more than chits to be used later for whatever advantage Fernand could gain from them. Still, this nurturing role came easily to Elmyr, being a caregiver by nature. During the years I knew Elmyr, I recognized this instinct and witnessed his abject incapacity to resist this "broken-wing syndrome," as I called it, as in rushing to aid a wounded bird. This impulse was also very much bound up in his notion of dependability, plainly helping anyone who needed help, and that others could count on him—even when the beneficiary was someone totally vacant of appreciating or reciprocating such gestures—like Fernand.

As soon as Fernand recovered from the hepatitis, his petulant temperament rebounded too. Elmyr was not used to living under the surveying eyes of anyone before now and was fed up with his petty jealousies and embarrassing public tantrums. He also thought that if he continued his illicit career, it was just a matter of time until his luck ran out. Since he narrowly escaped his suicide attempt, he had thought about much in its aftermath. For the last six months, he considered returning to Europe but wasn't sure how he would accomplish that. An unforeseen opportunity answered that question. Someone Fernand knew had the connections to procure a passport for him.

Elmyr and Fernand flew back to New York together to talk to an intermediary about the passport. They discussed going to Europe to do business. Fernand had visions of conquering Paris as a returning Bonaparte, a striking contrast to his impoverished youth in the French capital. They discussed arrangements for Elmyr to become Canada's newest citizen—for only a couple of thousand dollars. They just needed to work out the details and pay the money. They decided Fernand would travel to Ottawa to finalize the deal. In the meantime, they took separate rooms at the Winslow Hotel, on East Fifty-Fifth Street. Elmyr sequestered himself in his room and worked, producing drawings, Degas and Renoir pastels, and a Cezanne watercolor.

Again, details of this account are a bit fuzzy, but Elmyr thought there was a possible quick sale and easy money through an old friend from Europe. She was the Princess of Prussia, a granddaughter of Kaiser Wilhelm II. She was engaged to marry a rich Texan in San Antonio. Elmyr called her: "Yes, darling, do come down, I would love to see you...kiss, kiss," or something like that. Elmyr flew down that evening. After checking into a hotel with his luggage and portfolio, he phoned her again. Only now he discovered something unexpected came up and she had to leave for Europe. As long as he was there, he decided to visit the city's galleries. One gallery owner was particularly interested in seeing his collection and offered to do an exhibit on the spot. After a brief, feigned reluctance Elmyr said OK.

Elmyr arranged to have his collection of French impressionist art framed. The dealer then put together a private showing for some exclusive customers and sold a couple of the works immediately. One visitor was a rich cattleman. He and his wife asked if they could bring the Degas pastels and a Renoir to their ranch home. Their home was "palatial," in Elmyr's words. "They already had some fine original artwork, and they wanted to see how they would look on their walls. I must say, even I was impressed." Two days later the gleeful dealer presented him with a check for $30,000. It was singularly the most money he had ever made at once and almost had him belting out "God Bless America" or the Halleluiah chorus from Handle's *Messiah* on his way to the bank. There was nothing phony about the check. In order not to draw too much attention to himself, he told the bank officer he wanted to open a safe deposit box, which he did. The following day he returned with his portfolio, withdrew his box, and exchanged cut-up newspaper for the neatly banded bundles of cash, placing them in the portfolio. He then nervously exited the bank, perspiring and nauseous, feeling as though he had just committed a heist. A waiting taxi took him to the airport where he boarded a plane for Chicago. It was the last time he would see the land of the cowboys, oilmen, and unrestrained largesse of Texan hospitality.

Elmyr never told me why he went to Chicago from Texas. He did no business there other than indulge a whim to buy a car. He said he missed not having one, so he selected a blue Corvette convertible and thought he looked quite good in it, and of course paid cash for it. He then headed back to New York, crossing the Midwest and inaugurating his flashy new sports car. Once again lodging at the Winslow Hotel, this time he was alone. Fernand went ahead with arrangements to get Elmyr's passport. What he didn't know was that his new identity belonged to an actual living person. Fernand's accomplice found a copy of the man's birth certificate and used it in applying for the passport, an unoriginal if effective crime. He was a small-town clerk, a family man that they thought would never leave the country, named Joseph Boutin. Elmyr was about to assume his latest alias. It would not be without consequences.

In New York, Elmyr meticulously packed his suitcases. They, along with the Corvette, he would ship to Paris. He then demonstrated an uncharacteristic aberration in his normal behavior. He planned ahead—far ahead. One trunk containing several of his newest creations he placed in consignment at the hotel. If he ever needed to return for any reason, the artwork would be his insurance policy. "The Winslow Trunk" would later become the nexus of a battle royal between Elmyr and Fernand. When Fernand called his room, Elmyr picked up the phone. In oblique references any child's mother could see through, Fernand informed his partner that Elmyr needed to visit scenic Ottawa. Traveling to Niagara Falls, Elmyr crossed the border as a day-tourist carrying nothing with him—but $20,000 in cash and airline tickets to France. Fernand wanted to spend a week in Quebec before joining him in Paris. This was a fine idea, Elmyr thought.

Elmyr Returns To Europe

It was an overcast fall day in 1959 when he boarded a Pan Am jet bound for France. Elmyr had stretched his three-month tourist visa into a twelve-year stay in the United States. He evaded the hand of the law but not detection. Constantly looking over his shoulder for someone flashing a gold badge and uttering those dreaded words *you are under arrest* was an anguishing reality. No more, he thought. Europe would now be the fresh start Rio de Janeiro was in 1947. While he traveled first-class across the Atlantic, Elmyr felt emotionally spent, exhausted. Visions of his past overwhelmed him like a near-death experience; they would not let him sleep. For the last six months, he associated with a man he normally would never have invited to his dinner table. A saying he picked up in America expressed his true feelings about that unfortunate alliance with Fernand—"Good riddance to bad rubbish." The City of Light awaited him. It was his new beacon of hope, and there he intended to go it alone. Nothing felt strange about that. Elmyr, in all his various manifestations, was going home.

Elmyr wore a look of simultaneous disgust and surprise that by now had become instantly familiar when he relived any unpleasant remembrance of Fernand. While sharing this story, we sat comfortably in his living room, opposite one another in his matching leather easy chairs. His crossed legs rested atop the small table between us, parallel to mine. Some stories frequently lost me in a prologue sprinkled with unknown names and obscure facts. However, he kept them lively because they were meaningful to him and he told them with facial expressions a polished actor would envy. The accompanying pathos or humor in his voice compelled me to listen. I passed countless hours in this setting, absorbing his endless and captivating anecdotes. As a young man, I never thought my life would ever be interesting like his, although my association with him went a long way toward changing that assumption.

About Legros, he summed up again in his favorite understatement, "My curiosity was satisfied." This was Elmyr-speak—downplaying strong sentiments that many people would more easily express in expletives. His feelings, however, were no less adamant. In any event, he no longer had to endure his erstwhile insufferable partner. He wanted nothing more to do with Fernand or to ever see him again once he was back in Paris. Elmyr thought it best to just lead Fernand on, letting him think that when they reunited, their association would continue as before. His expression turned bitter, conveying unmistakable displeasure in relaying this detail, as though reliving a recurring nightmare. Elmyr booked a room at a hotel far from the one where Legros was to stay. It would be hard to judge who would be happier about his return to Europe, Elmyr or the consortium of museum directors and art dealers in America. The vagabond Hungarian, delighted by the prospect of renewing his Parisian friendships, thought he would start phoning people immediately.

Rather than updating his little black address book periodically, he customarily used them until they disintegrated into dust. Entries, telephone numbers, addresses, were crossed out and scribbled in elsewhere on the impossibly cryptic pages only he could understand. Nevertheless, as soon as the bellhop brought his luggage to his room, he removed the book that contained names and numbers of people on three continents whom he knew and who knew him (but under many different aliases). For the police it was a veritable Rosetta stone, unlocking secrets and incriminating links to his illegal activities for the past thirteen years. In order to find it, though, they first needed to find him, a quest he had so far successfully stymied.

Elmyr sat on his bedside and phoned number after number, setting the handset aglow, announcing to surprised listeners that it was *he*, Elmyr! He preferred sitting upright to lying down and talking. It just seemed easier to gesticulate that way with his free hand, and that enhanced communication—even by phone. Within an hour of initiating the calls, a friend invited Elmyr to join him in the south of France. Few spots were "as wonderful or as elegant as the Côte d'Azur," he emphasized when telling me this story. Within ten days of his return to Europe, he was once again on the move, driving slowly south in his light-blue American sports car.

In Cap d'Antibes, he felt at home, in his comfort zone. After Budapest, France was the place he was most at ease. It was sophisticated, exactly where people of his background came to enjoy that rarified lifestyle only wealth could provide. His current appreciation was perhaps greater now than before, as he could contrast it with a day-to-day existence and vivid recollections of his monastic accommodations on Pershing Square in Los Angeles. He hoped never to go through those kinds of deprivations and humiliations again.

Much like the weather of southern California he liked so much, the Riviera along the Mediterranean in the autumn was warm and sunny, and it was a beautiful drive along the coastal roads. An urge to go to Rome found little resistance in him. It was also one of the world's greatest cultural cities, he reasoned with himself as he crossed the French/Italian border with no worry. He had a fresh passport and spotless record as Joseph Boutin. By early October, he convinced himself that he should now call the Eternal City home. He found an apartment in a fashionable area of the city, off the Via Boncompagni near the American embassy. One room became his studio, where he resumed painting his own work, a luxury he was able to indulge because he still had money in his pockets from the sales in Texas. The illuminati of Roman society graced his parties, and Elmyr once more was a popular invitee of his old and new friends. He was a frequent guest of socialite Elsa Maxwell, perhaps the most celebrated party-giver of the twentieth century. Others included Crown Prince Constantine of Greece; the Borghesees; Count Esterhazy; Eva Bartók, wife of the Hungarian composer Béla Bartók; Ursula Andress; actor John Derek; and more. Between the cocktail parties, languorous luncheons, and dinners, Elmyr produced enough new work for an exhibition. He became acquainted with the owner of one of Italy's top galleries in Milan devoted to contemporary figurative art, the Galeria Monte Napoleone. When Elmyr showed him some of his paintings he was instantly offered a one-man show.

It was another dazzling success, socially, but something less than a financial success. While he felt vindicated that there were buyers interested enough to purchase art in the style of Elmyr, it brought in nowhere near the kind of money his fakes earned. He now had that reality to ponder. Friends from Paris came to the opening and reveled in the gaiety of the parties in Milan and Rome. His longtime friend Jean Louis was one of his staunchest allies and supporters. He arrived for the event, informing him, "Fernand Legros has been asking everyone where you are." Elmyr insisted that *no one* should tell Legros anything, let alone his whereabouts. "I would rather contract the black plague than see that man again," he said, politely characterizing how repulsive that would be.

Although his show did not garner the response he hoped for, it kept him in the flow of an exciting art scene and whirlwind of social activities that became even more frenetic as the 1960 Rome summer Olympics neared. Elmyr opted to get away to Paris and escape the summer heat of southern Italy in July. Upon his return to Paris, he visited the cafés of his youth in Montparnasse and Montmartre. Little had changed, and he was enchanted with the city's irresistible charm. "It truly is a jewel," he thought to himself as he sat at a sidewalk café one morning near the Gare Saint-Lazare. Unlike the impenetrable crowds in Rome, there was practically no one around that early Sunday morning. It was astonishingly peaceful. As he ate his breakfast croissant and drank his café au lait, a frightening spectacle turned his Roman tan ashen gray. Emerging from a nearby Metro stop, like Lazarus rising from the dead, a figure appeared. It did no good to ignore the specter of Fernand Legros walking directly toward him, as he had already noticed Elmyr. Now, however, he resembled his former self, before Elmyr's tutelage, unshaven and rather scruffy. Fernand held his arms open as if greeting his long-lost brother, which is about as elated as he felt when seeing his old business partner. The sight of him approaching immediately cast a pall over Elmyr's good mood. It was like the unwelcome news a woman might receive of an unwanted pregnancy or as referred to in religious terms—the Unexpected Visitation. Yes, that is probably close to describing the sickening realization that he was found by the one man he wanted most to avoid.

Fernand did his best to draw Elmyr in with his flypaper charm. Smiling broadly, he leaned into Elmyr to greet him in the traditional French manner, a kiss to both cheeks. Elmyr abruptly and stiffly extended his right arm forward to halt his attempt. Fernand still gushed, "*Mon cher Elmyr*, is it really you? Where are you living now?" Elmyr said, "Madrid." "Are you painting?" Fernand inquired. "Not at all," he replied. What he wanted most to know was if Elmyr had any money. With his arms folded across his chest, he said in a voice the hearing-impaired would not need repeating, "NO!" It resonated with all the believability of a child with a chocolate-smeared face and denying any knowledge of the missing cookies. "You're such a liar," Fernand calmly observed. Fernand went on to tell him he was disappointed that he disappeared without a word and that it was naughty of him to do that. His chiding did not move Elmyr. Fernand then tried a more persuasive appeal. Europe was not only a ripe art market, he claimed, but also people would be clamoring for Elmyr's brilliant work. "We could still make a fortune together," he insisted. The Hungarian remained uncharacteristically stoic and unimpressed with Fernand's cajoling. He told his suitor that he had done nothing and sold nothing since leaving the States. Legros then asked Elmyr to entrust him with just a few drawings or watercolors to sell to demonstrate that he could do it. Elmyr shook his head no. Fernand persisted like someone with an obsessive-compulsive disorder struggling to get a recalcitrant lid off a pickle jar. "What did you do with the rest of the work that remained from the trip to Texas? There was that very nice Cézanne watercolor. What happened to that?" He continued to pry like the Grand Inquisitor. This line of questioning was making Elmyr recall his unpleasant experience with the Mexican police. Hoping to terminate their conversation, he told Fernand that he did not have them. He left them in a trunk at the Winslow in New York.

Making a face of sad resignation, Fernand shrugged and then changed the topic of conversation. They chatted a bit longer about nothing special that Elmyr could remember. Fernand then excused himself and bid his old associate au revoir. Elmyr hoped it would be their last encounter. Fernand apparently rushed back to his hotel and placed a call to New York, the Winslow Hotel. He identified himself as Elmyr and asked if his trunk was still in consignment there. The desk clerk assured him that it was. "I will be having a friend come to collect it, Mr. Fernand Legros, and he will have a letter of introduction and proper identification," he informed him. He then promptly borrowed the airfare for a one-way ticket and $100 to fly to New York.

Fernand Legros – 1960's

Arriving at the Winslow, Fernand presented a letter of introduction and instructions to hand over his treasure chest to the swarthy guy with the eye patch. Well, that's what it amounted to. To the hotel director, I am sure the letter bore a reasonable facsimile of Elmyr's signature and looked convincingly proper. This easy conquest was an epiphany to the scheming Legros. It signaled the beginning of a career of fabricating forged documents accompanying Elmyr's fake art, thereby providing the missing ingredient in their chicanery. Fernand's inclination toward larceny, according to Elmyr, offered little resistance such as scruples.

The concierge had the trunk sent to his room. It was locked, naturally. Oh my, what should he do? Let's see, he just traveled three thousand miles to get something he wanted. He probably overlooked that small mechanical obstacle like a Yellowstone bear would, sniffing the scent of doughnuts in a camper's tent. No one knows for sure how Legros choreographed his celebratory dance after opening the trunk and finding a trove of highly marketable French impressionist and postimpressionist art. What I know from Elmyr's account is that Fernand sold the collection in North and South America and Europe, all very expensively. No information is available as to what Fernand sold in order to raise the money for the ticket home.

Elmyr said it was not until he made a trip to Hamburg in 1961, when visiting Arthur Pfannstiel, the expert on Modigliani who had already bought a number of Elmyr's Modigliani drawings, that he was reminded of the Winslow trunk. By that time, Elmyr had morphed into

Baron Herzog. The two men reputedly enjoyed the academic banter of intellectuals, exchanging thoughts on their particular focus of interest— i.e., Modigliani. With the childlike joy of showing a birthday present, Pfannstiel excused himself, returning with three drawings just sent him, done by Modigliani. A dealer wanted an expertise on them. You can imagine Elmyr's response when he recognized them from the famous Winslow collection. "What do you think?" his host asked eagerly. This instantly triggered Elmyr's sweat glands. He nervously offered a tepid note of approval, saying, "Well, they *do* look like his work…I think."

Elmyr tried to find out who had sent him the drawings, but Pfannstiel never told him. Elmyr later insisted that he saw them reproduced in a catalog from the Galeria de Arte Solarium of Sao Palo in Brazil. This anecdote also provides insight into the lengths Fernand went to to obtain legitimate certificates of authenticity to accompany his sales, but when they could not easily be secured, he would have them manufactured. These measures included fabricating phony pedigrees, indicating the art had passed through prestigious collections of people who were all now conveniently dead and could not contradict such claims. By the mid sixties, Fernand had genuine customs stamps copied that he needed for the international transport of works of art deemed national treasures. These were coincidentally the only commodity he trafficked. When I knew Elmyr, he still thought that Fernand's fortune and lavish lifestyle had to derive from something more than the monies made from his artwork. He believed that Fernand might have been involved with illegal drug trafficking. What ultimately surfaced was that he had worked his Svengali charm on an uncle who was allegedly an investment broker for retirees. Fernand swindled him out of two million dollars of their money, according to press reports.

Elmyr could still not believe his misfortunate encounter with Fernand near the Gare Saint-Lazare, the train station he arrived at when he was twenty and naive. One thing, though, had not changed in all those years: he remained naive. He still had his comfortable apartment in Rome, and with the closing ceremonies of the Olympic games now over, he felt he could return to resume life at a slower pace. Once back, however, he was uneasy, restless. His bank account was diminishing rapidly, and the inevitable consequences of that were depressing. Necessity, being the mother that it is, forced him back into a defensive mode. Rummaging through secondhand bookstores and art supply shops while he was in

Paris was a weathervane of the direction he was heading. He had the French canvas, stretchers, paper with French watermarks, paints, pastels, watercolors, and ink he needed in his apartment studio. Over the next month, he would produce a body of work that exhibited talent, knowledge, and verve that comes from a lifetime of familiarity with his profession. The temporary hiatus from his fakery had not softened his skill in the least. If anything, it appeared stronger and more confident.

Elmyr stood back, trying to examine objectively more than two dozen Renoir and Degas pastels, Matisse drawings, Derain watercolors, and Picasso pen and ink drawings. His history of success at selling his artwork in the styles of others suggested that what he had in front of him was the artistic equivalent of bearer bonds in the banking world. He later expressed his astonishment to me regarding the mythic stature and universal respect that made Picasso an unparalleled phenomenon of twentieth-century art. He said that no other artist throughout history could "transform a single line into gold" as he could. That was, providing it also bore his signature. Continuing in that vein, he suggested that this mercantile alchemy also debased the value of his work because it no longer had any rapport to its intrinsic artistic value. He opined that most of his work after *Guernica* (1937) was inferior, weak, and uninteresting when compared to his oeuvre before that creation.

Knowing there was a greater demand and that they fetched bigger prices, Elmyr preferred to mimic Picasso's earlier works. In the BBC documentary, Elmyr alleged that a dealer showed Picasso one of his paintings signed "Picasso." The artist then asked how much he paid for it. The dealer supposedly replied, $100,000, to which Picasso said, "Well, if you paid that much, it must be by me." By comparison, Elmyr boasted that he "never offered a painting or a drawing to a museum or a gallery that didn't buy it." This may be true, but unlike Picasso, buyers did not line up outside his door for his work. For Elmyr, the creating part was always far easier than the selling, and this sad fact eventually caused him to rejoin that unpleasant but profitable alliance with Legros. In any event, he was an effective, albeit unhinged and dishonest, agent for Elmyr's work, simply because he felt blissfully emancipated from any moral constraints whatsoever in pursuit of what he wanted. Legality? Morality? He would take careful aim in a Parisian pissoir at these things.

Everyone Elmyr knew in Rome who had any interest in art—or, rather, *his* art—had already bought an original Elmyr. It was not his style to pressure anyone to buy more if they did not specifically indicate further interest. That market had dried up, so to speak. It was time again to pack his well-traveled luggage. Before moving on, he invited his friends to a farewell party. Within days of deciding to leave, he packed economically around his precious portfolio in the meager trunk space of his Corvette and stored other items he could ship later on.

His internal compass wavered with no definite sense of direction or specific destination. Elmyr stopped in Switzerland, Germany, Holland, Belgium, and then London, making brief business calls along the way. No matter what his persona, his MO was the same: i.e., always appear smartly dressed, well spoken, plausible, and make them an offer they couldn't refuse. It was a formula that never failed him.

Meanwhile, Fernand was once again having new suits tailor-made in Paris to look the part of a successful art dealer. His enterprising spirit now soared, as did his ego. With the valuable art looted from the Winslow trunk in his possession, it was his bankroll in a high-stakes poker game where he viewed the competition as chumps.

On his meandering trip northward, Elmyr reflected on the European market. He preferred to obliterate souvenirs of his association with Legros, but the words of his unsavory supplicant rang in his ears during their brief encounter in Paris. People would be "clamoring" for his masterpieces. The ego-caressing compliment would have meant more coming from someone he respected—a titled person, for sure. Coming from any quarter, though, like a natural sponge he absorbed a kind word. He was a vacuum, in fact, for the slightest demonstration of kindness or affection, whether they were genuine or insincere. In Fernand's view, this made him the perfect sucker. It must have been an enormous source of amusement for him that he could con a fellow con so easily.

The art community had excellent communication channels, and, despite a voracious appetite for the kind of art Elmyr provided, he did not want to inundate the market with his work. It should filter in slowly, he thought, like an intravenous drip. He then made a strategic business plan for himself. Traveling from Ostende, Belgium, by ferry to England, he drove north to London. There, he sold a Derain watercolor to a Mayfair gallery. He booked a room at the Dorchester on Park Lane.

It was good to be back in the land of Earl Gray tea, elegant men's haberdasheries, and civilized manners. Then, strolling into a travel agency on Knightsbridge one day, he bought another one-way ticket to Rio de Janeiro. That very afternoon, he sold his Corvette to a London auto dealer who was happy to pay him $2,000 for it.

On the flight to Brazil, he once again relived those memories of arriving from Stockholm wearing long wool underwear and nearly fainting from the tropical heat. Now he knew what to expect. Maybe this time he would live in Buenos Aires. The Argentines were also beautiful people, he recalled. There was one major obstacle to Elmyr's long-range plans, though; he gauged them in months, never years. He was restless by nature. His relationships were fleeting. His profession was risky. A fortune-teller would read nothing in his tea leaves that foretold any permanent stability in his life.

Visions of residing in the southern hemisphere "faded like a mirage" as he described the rapidly changing plan for his future. "Things just did not work out as I hoped," he wistfully shared with me. In Sao Palo, he enjoyed some success, selling his works to a museum and later to art dealers in Buenos Aires. The pursuit of happiness he knew was far more elusive than pulling out some map and planning an itinerary. After two months, no one place appealed to him enough to call a permanent home. Nor was South America the booming market that was the United States or Europe. He had about $5,000 remaining for his efforts and time there, but still felt vacant, purposeless. He wanted to return to Europe.

An Iberia Airlines flight brought him back to Spain from Argentina. An exhausted, itinerant art forger arrived in Madrid and checked into the Ritz Hotel. Unlike before, he did not immediately reach for his address book, sit on the edge of his bed, and make call after call until his social agenda was filled. Looking back at him in the bathroom mirror was an appreciably older, though, no wiser man with graying hair. He was not just physically tired from the long trip; his joy of life seemed gone. The hotel with its refined accommodations would be a salubrious spot to rest a few days, he thought. Madrid was a city he liked. There were fine restaurants, sidewalk cafés, the great Prado Museum, and even within the firm grip of Franco's police state, there were gay bars, although many were literally underground.

A friend from Paris told him about the quaint island of Ibiza. It was one of the lesser-known Balearic chain and overshadowed by the larger, popular tourist destination, Mallorca. In the two years since he left America, there seemed to be something missing, besides a legal occupation. Remembering the easygoing companionship of his friend Jimmy Damion in Los Angeles and then Miami Beach, he longed for someone special in his life. No matter how much he enjoyed the company of his friends, there was an emotional void he needed to fill. He was now fifty-five years old and began to question if his life would ever assume any semblance of normalcy. His friend also told him Ibiza was a sanctuary for bohemians, writers, and artists, being cosmopolitan and intimate at the same time.

He boarded a plane for Barcelona with a connecting flight to Ibiza. As the plane circled, making its runway approach, he could see the island dotted with its ancient white farmhouses, and the walled fortress of the Old City of Ibiza town. The translucent blue-green of the Mediterranean Sea gave it an instant visual appeal, possessing the same quality of light he loved about the south of France. Elmyr arrived inconspicuously, like an alien species there to just observe but not interfere with the indigenous life forms.

Ibiza town – watercolor by Elmyr

painting of matadors in Elmyr's own style

He found the island "simpatico, as they say in Chinese," as he later quipped. A casual encounter at a sidewalk café led him to the owner of a small home overlooking the Bay of Figueretas near Ibiza town. So far, he liked what he saw and decided to rent the house, Villa Platero. It was inexpensive, as were the restaurants and bars. Could this be the place destined to be his home? Still, the notion of settling down in one place, after moving around like a nomad his entire life, was foreign.

Later that summer, he went to Greece, visiting the island of Hydra. At that time, the filmmaker Jules Dassin was filming *Phaedra* with the Greek actress Melina Mercouri. (She was a longtime political activist and became minister of culture in the socialist government that came to power in 1981. Retrieving the Parthenon's famed "Elgin Marbles" from Great Britain was her cause célèbre.) Elmyr befriended both Mercouri and Dassin, who offered him a walk-on part in their movie. He did not come away starry-eyed enough from the experience to make a career leap to acting. Besides, he already was an actor. Greece and its myriad islands might be a possibility for a discreet retirement home, he thought, although his assessment was pragmatic. "It did not have a major airport and I knew one useless language, Hungarian; I didn't see a need to learn another, Greek," he remarked to me later.

It was time to attend to business once again. Intending to return to Paris, he chose to stop in Vienna, where he sold two Matisse drawings. On his arrival in Paris, he checked into a hotel in Saint-Germain-des-Pres. That evening he went back to one of his old haunts, the Café Flore, where, in a city of millions of people, he ran into the starkly unavoidable Fernand Legros—again. This time he appeared better groomed but still oozing the affected charm of a gigolo. Parisian sophistication seemed to be rubbing off on him. Yet, Elmyr could not account for the confidence in his strut and absence of cloying deference he always used to get what he wanted. A whiff of something rotten in Denmark wafted under his nostrils in France. What Elmyr didn't know was that he had unwittingly helped Legros become an enterprising hustler with a patina of authenticity that derived from sales of work stolen from his trunk at the Winslow Hotel. Fernand moved swiftly with the deft agility of his former cabaret dancing to meet art and antique dealers and collectors. Making contacts by networking the gay community and employing Kasbah marketing techniques, he now had money in his pockets, which only reinforced his natural bravado. Elmyr, in fact, would have liked to have the money Fernand had. At that moment, he also could not imagine that this role reversal would endure for several years to come.

Fernand knew Elmyr was generous by nature, so he could be as well. The difference was in the character of the two men. Elmyr's gestures of kindness were the product of genuine altruism, while with Fernand they were like a loan on which he would exact a usurious interest and soul-snatching future payback. For the latter, the interest invariably exceeded the principle. That evening at their café table, they had a couple of aperitifs together in a cordial and relaxed setting. It was not the tense, unpleasant encounter of the year before near the Gare Saint-Lazare. Legros checkmated Elmyr's custom of reaching for the bill when the waiter brought it. The unexpected largesse disarmed him even further, to the extent that he actually told Fernand where he was staying.

Legros's lack of desperation lulled Elmyr into the scheming web he was weaving for the gullible Hungarian. Fernand found an apartment on the rue de la Pompe. Despite its good location, it was modest next to the one he moved to later on and had decorated to suit an Ottoman pasha. Elmyr still was clueless about the connection between himself and Fernand's current bourgeois comfort. He was astonished, though, to find three original watercolors by Raoul Dufy framed on Legros's apartment walls. He never dreamed his former partner could so quickly become a legitimate art dealer. Never mind that these outward signs of prosperity came directly from the booty stolen from Elmyr, which made Fernand a kind of bipedal magpie. I should not disparage magpies by this comparison, and I'm sure they feel guiltier for their thievery than did Fernand. This would not be his last visit to Legros's new residence, but the first of several over the next few weeks.

Elmyr was not idle at this time either. He produced two Modigliani drawings that he thought were "quite good." He was so confident in their quality that he went to see a representative of Madame Modigliani, the artist's daughter, who allegedly provided an expertise verifying their authenticity. An eager dealer on the Avenue Matignon promptly bought them from him.

During their conversation at the Café Flore, Elmyr told Fernand about his visit to Greece, and the sketches and watercolors he did there. The ingratiating Fernand asked to see them. When Elmyr brought his portfolio with the artwork from his Grecian holiday, the once-more fawning con man praised him. "How much are you asking for them?" he inquired after he had carefully examined each one. "Fifty dollars for this, a hundred dollars for that," Elmyr unassumingly stated. His voice rose to more of a question mark at the end. "They are absolutely wonderful. *I'll buy them all!*" Fernand bellowed to emphasize the moment of his proclamation, his cunning past unnoticed by the painter. Elmyr was now mellow with good humor and as they chatted more. Sharing a bottle of Chateau Margaux '47, he told Fernand of his fresh triumph with the gallery owner on the Avenue Matignon.

With a grave but caring look, he then leaned into Elmyr as if to share a secret and confided with the wisdom of an older brother, "Elmyr, *mon cher*, it is too dangerous for you to continue to take these risks! Look, you can see I'm doing well. We could help each other. I have some *real* Dufys here. We could hang some of your work alongside, and not only would they look more authentic, I could probably ask better prices for my pieces. Then we could discreetly sell a small Modigliani by you, or a Matisse. That way we both could profit, and you would no longer have to take any chances. You could live quietly and peacefully on that island you talked about, and we could split the profits like we did in the States." One could almost hear the snake charmer's flute in the background. There was no doubt about it. Fernand's powers of persuasion were impressive *and* effective. Elmyr had just succumbed to the aural equivalent of a date-rape drug, insidious and stupefying. He was about to partner with a man he had described as loathsome and odious, but Fernand's low-key euphonious evangelizing had just thoroughly seduced him, his once and future business associate.

By now Elmyr not only had replenished his coffers, he was certain that the island of Ibiza was where he was going to live. It was in the western end of the Mediterranean, where the rest of Western Europe was easily accessible, and it was nowhere near as expensive as city life. During his flight back to Spain, he mulled over the new strategy for the rest of his life. He would live an unhurried existence where work is incidental to siestas. The climate was like that of his beloved California. For less than $160 a month, he could pay his rent *and* have a house cleaner. Before leaving Paris, Fernand promised he would receive a stipend of $400 monthly from a Swiss bank and gave him a $500 advance with a 50 percent split of future sales. It was, in the words of George Bernard Shaw, "too true to be good."

Elmyr indeed thought that his worries were over and his career as an art forger would draw no more attention than if he were an honest corner greengrocer in Shepard's Bush. To his delight, he discovered that his $400 salary was roughly double what he needed to live comfortably in those days. True to form, he shared his good fortune with others, helping many struggling artists on the island by buying their work. He also met a young Canadian whom he mentored and helped develop into a talented artist with his assistance and encouragement. The long-lacking companionship in his life was no longer the emotional void his constant wandering had made a sad fact. To the local residents, he was *Señor* Elmyr. Everyone, in fact, knew others only by their first names, and it seemed everyone soon knew Elmyr.

One local gallery owner and resident since before anyone could remember was an expatriate Brit, Ivan Spence. A shock of magnificent straight white hair combed back from a broad, perpetually tanned forehead sat atop his thick six-foot-four-inch frame, making him seem like a mobile snow-capped mountain. Even more riveting was his sonorous BBC voice and articulate erudition that made it easy to think of him as Jehovah's schoolmaster. When standing next to Ivan, Elmyr would look up at him as though he were peering up at something way above the tree line. The disparity in their stature was nary noticed when they were lost in twinkle-eyed rapture, discussing art in its nebulae of minutia. Two sandbox playmates could not have been more oblivious to the concept of time than were these aged children locked in their private world of mutual interest.

Elmyr visited Ivan's gallery regularly and enjoyed the entertaining exhibition openings. This is where he acquired a reputation as a collector, buying pictures or sculptures from artists of varying talent, but who were invariably thankful. His patronage also conveniently presented him and everyone else a respectable image as someone of means. Living on a small island was akin to a small town where little or nothing goes unobserved, and even less escapes becoming the topic of gossip by others. Most assumed he had family money. Even the more inventively curious did not concoct any naughty rumors that might have an echo of truth about Elmyr's fantastic life and closely guarded secret. Any other kind of speculation really did not bother him.

For the first half-year, Fernand sent Elmyr his stipend and once even included a $1,200 bonus. On occasion, he would come down from Paris and hand-deliver his check and wish list of works he wanted from his employee. I do not recall ever asking Elmyr directly if he realized that Fernand had succeeded in pulling off a bloodless coup the moment he lured him into their renewed partnership. Nor can I say with certainty whether he actually believed Legros's unctuous overtures or simply deluded himself. What is certain is that the master/apprentice relationship that began on their trip from New York to Miami now flip-flopped. Fernand was in charge, and Elmyr was doing his bidding.

orchestral scene in the style of Raoul Dufy – watercolor

'fauve landscape in the style of Vlaminck

Fernand was prodding his employee to produce more works that would pass for the cheery freewheeling brushwork of the popular colorist Raoul Dufy. He insisted there was a huge demand for Dufy's watercolors, reflecting his serious-minded themes—regattas, orchestral scenes, and horseracing. Knowing Elmyr's studious habits and love of books, Fernand came to visit him and even brought gifts. Well, it was actually a fresh supply of old *arche* paper and a stack of new reference books Elmyr would need to produce the art he wanted. What Elmyr failed to notice was that his partner also seemed enchanted with his Mediterranean hideaway, or rather, home. This sparked an idea like all his others, one that would benefit Fernand. He urged Elmyr to build a house of his own. Villa Platero was pleasant but too small for the *two* of them. Elmyr rejected his suggestion instantly. To do business with him was one thing; to have him as a houseguest was another.

Modigliani-style portrait of a woman – oil

Before long, Elmyr received special cardboard tubes from Paris. Inside his packages, he discovered large color transparencies of works by artists meant to give him a more exact idea of color and brush techniques so he could better replicate their styles. More high-quality art books from the Swiss publisher Skira followed. Fernand, in fact, spared no expense in supplying Elmyr with the tools necessary for creating his expert fakes. He asked for more Van Dongen fauve-period paintings, Matisse oils, Degas, Renoir pastels, and Picasso cubist drawings, and still wanted to know why he had not yet received his Modigliani and Derain drawings. Elmyr made daily trips to the post office to collect his mail and was by now friendly with the old postal worker who regularly handed over the frequent packages too large for his letterbox. Under a barrage of special requests, Elmyr's repertoire expanded, and he accepted his new challenges as he had from his exacting teacher at the Akademie Heiman in Munich. His craft may have been illegal, but that was no reason not to do it as well as he could, and his years of success suggested he was good at what he did.

When Elmyr prepared old canvases on their stretchers, it was like an alchemist pursuing his forbidden craft. He first carefully soaked the canvases with an alkali solution to soften the old paint and then scrape them clean

Modigliani-style portrait of a woman – pencil

with a palette knife. The tricky part was separating the surface paint while leaving the underlying primer in tact. It was a time-consuming chore that he found tedious and demanding. Another restorer's device he used was applying a golden-hued varnish that simulated a *craquelure* or that "alligatoring" appearance of old cracked painted surfaces. These techniques were so effective and visually deceiving that they fooled many experts. In Elmyr's wake, the whole art establishment became extremely apprehensive about offering definitive opinions on a work's authenticity. Now, before millions of dollars exchange hands, they commonly undergo a rigorous scientific scrutiny. There still is no infallibility in this realm, which is why a vigorous debate continues over the authorship of many works of art—and fakery persists. Imitation and fraud these days have moved more easily to items that lend themselves to mass production—e.g., clothing, pharmaceuticals, software, and machine parts—where illicit profits are tens or hundreds of millions of dollars annually.

In emulating Dufy's painting technique, Elmyr recounted how attentive he had been to detail, noticing the Frenchman's habit of building an impasto on his canvases by adding layers of white paint. After some experimenting and comparison, Elmyr concluded that he had used a zinc white that seemed to match well against his enlarged transparencies. Leonardo wrote his notebooks in a reverse script that one could only read in a mirror; Elmyr made notations in the margins of his books in Hungarian that were about as indecipherable as the great Renaissance master's. If anyone found these encrypted messages, they would not risk incriminating him or revealing their purpose.

Cloistered away in his small Ibiza villa, Elmyr seemed to be the much more discreet of the collaborative duo. Elmyr let it slip out to a few people that he also liked to do a little art on the side after a friend found him down at the port early one morning with his sketchbook, making drawings of the fishermen repairing their nets. In order to allay any unwanted attention, Elmyr said that his efforts were strictly those of a dilettante Sunday painter. During one of Fernand's brief visits, he spotted Elmyr's portside sketches. Fernand's ever-fulminating personality erupted in anger. "How could you be so careless?" he chided his ruffled partner. Elmyr later suggested that Legros had only two behavioral modes: his oily, affected charm, and the maniacally enraged victim.

"When anything displeased him," Elmyr said, "he would say, 'How can you do this to *me*?' " He then apparently responded like a cuckolded lover, hurling epithets and dishes at the one that caused him some slight or perceived injustice. The mere threat of these volatile scenes and tirades were sufficiently intimidating that Elmyr realized he needed to weigh his words carefully in Legros's presence.

Fernand, for his part, profited nicely from the sales of his business associate's new work. He found a more upscale apartment on the Avenue de Suffren, where the upwardly mobile merchant created an aura of respectability that impressed his clients, those easily swayed by appearances. Like any common street corner shill, though, he thought of these people as dupes and only respected someone he couldn't con. However, they continued to entrust him with legitimate artworks. Fernand even sometimes bought these consignments or traded for Elmyr's work. Hanging next to Elmyr's art, his increasingly believable collection and expanding connections were making him a force to reckon with in Parisian art circles.

While Elmyr thought Fernand limited his sales to the French market, he actually sold his impressionist and postimpressionist masterpieces in Chicago, New York, and Switzerland. Elmyr told me that someone offered to buy one of his Matisse oils from Fernand for $75,000 at that time, but Mme. Duthuit, the artist's daughter, virtually controlled the traffic in her father's work where authenticity was concerned. Fernand reputedly told Elmyr that if he could poison her chocolate bonbons, he would gladly do it. Around this time, she died. Legros, he thought, probably celebrated her passing with bottles of Veuve Clicquot and a party at the George V Hotel. Any obstacle in his path he of course viewed as a malicious act uniquely designed to thwart *him*. There was a similarly shared sentiment between the two men. They both revered success, and each felt vindicated by it. For Elmyr it validated his talent. For Fernand it justified any means necessary to achieve it. With each sale, Legros became more focused, single-minded, and dedicated to his conquests like a self-appointed Napoleon, a shrewd self-aggrandizing tactician with Vegas showgirl flamboyance.

By the first anniversary of their reunited business venture, Elmyr had made new friends on the island, and found someone to remedy the dreaded loneliness that had previously forced him into late-night bars and terminal encounters. He wasn't rich, but he was now happy. Fernand was now rich, but he wasn't happy—but that had more to do with his not being rich enough for his liking. He would try mightily to remedy this over the next few years. Like a marauding, silver-tongued human variety of a Venus flytrap, he traveled thousands of kilometers, luring his prey to purchase his valuable, rare offerings. In 1963 alone, he carried his handmade black portfolio or shipped carefully packed crates of art from Paris to Rio de Janeiro, Buenos Aires, Cape town, Johannesburg, and then Tokyo. The benefits from these selling trips bought Fernand new cars, wardrobes, five-star hotel suites, an art gallery, and a retinue of young men to be his paid fawning courtiers.

Fernand took advantage of well-respected auction houses, making them accomplices in his schemes to defraud the "suckers" as he thought of his buyers. Parke Bernet in New York and Sotheby's in London were certain destinations when he was in those cities. Auction houses legally emancipate themselves from responsibility for a work's authenticity. It offers them a convenient and guilt-free loophole that shifts the burden of proof to the seller. They still possess staffs of extremely competent experts who will offer an opinion on the merit and possible auction value, but by their own admission, they are not in the business of "authenticating" what goes on the auction block.

While in New York, Legros met a husband and wife who were art dealers, Rose and Edwin Bachmann. They introduced the dealer of important French art to many of their friends and clients in Manhattan. Through some of these new contacts, he obtained a powerful marketing tool that was the equivalent of the Holy Grail for a devoted Christian. It was a privately printed tome containing the names, numbers, addresses, and special interests of collectors throughout the States. He could now appeal directly to an exclusive clientele with rare tastes, desires, and the means to indulge them. This decoder ring was going to be extremely useful to Fernand when he would begin to pursue some of his deep-pocketed American customers.

Legros was too familiar with the system of providing or seeking customary documentation indicating a work's legitimacy—along with Mme. Duthuit and Mme. Modigliani, only a few renowned experts who held the fate of an artwork in their hands shared their power and influence. The French term *aupres du tribunal* described those individuals officially recognized by the government as scholars, or those having a direct personal connection to an artist, who were authorized to provide a judgment on the authenticity of the artwork. For their opinions, they received a small fee. While Fernand may have thought this nuisance custom existed specifically to hamper his sales efforts, it long preceded his entry into the picture-dealing trade. With his usual pluck and tenacity to find a path to what he wanted, he decided to do whatever was necessary to obtain the expertises that legitimized Elmyr's fakes and make the money he deserved. Some experts unhesitatingly corroborated Fernand's attempts to procure these authentications. Elmyr's works were so good that they found their quality unimpeachable. This fact apparently overwhelmed whatever questions may have arisen about the artworks' lineage. Since these legal attestations from the experts made a painting or a drawing instantly marketable, and meant tens of thousands of dollars in potential sales to Fernand, in his own subtle way he helped the experts come to the right conclusions. If he detected any hesitancy on the part of the examining expert, he voluntarily increased their paid fee by dropping a thousand dollars on the table. If not picked up right away, he dropped another thousand down. "People like round numbers," he claimed.

Legros enlisted one respected authority, André Pacitti, who was so cooperative in giving him his imprimatur on his growing collection of Dufy watercolors that he seemingly became more doubtful of original Dufys later on. In a characteristically bold move, Fernand had contacted the elderly Dutch painter, Kees van Dongen, who lived in the south of France, near Monte Carlo, for the last forty-five years. As Elmyr proudly recounted this story, he said, "Van Dongen was shown a painting done by me. It was a portrait of a woman in his fauve-period style that Fernand called *Woman with a Pearl Necklace*. If he had painted it, it would have complimented a portrait he did in 1908, called *Woman with Hat*. Legros said he not only recognized it as one of his, but also told him all the sensual details about how he interrupted his work to make love to her. Needless to say, he got the expertise from the ninety-year-old van Dongen."

"Later," he further explained to me, "Legros found a Japanese engraver to copy the official stamp that authorities used [*Expert aupres des Douanes Francaises*], like Pacitti, André Schoeller, Malingue, or

Epstein." Fernand also acquainted himself with a number of Parisian collectors whom he "persuaded" to supply him letters verifying that various works by Elmyr had been in their private collections. These lubricated the process, allowing much of his production to slide into the ranks of bona fide works of art and, I believe, remain unchallenged to this day.

With all the attendant documentation in order, it was easier to submit these artworks for sale at the government-sponsored auction house in Paris, the Hôtel Druot. Elmyr estimated that between forty-five and fifty pieces by him went to public auctions in New York, London, and Paris from 1962–65 alone. "It may have been a higher number, but I'm not sure," he confided to me later. Fernand told him that if he thought a bid was not high enough, he would buy back the work and pay the ten percent seller's fee to the auction house. This, however, bought him a well-placed photograph of the work in the catalog of a prominent auction house and further enhanced both the artwork's legitimacy and value. To show that the depth of his ingenuity continued to amaze even Elmyr, Fernand demonstrated another stroke of his inexhaustible and adroitly clever mind.

Many high-quality volumes of art books or portfolios have color or black-and-white plates only slightly affixed on the page opposite the description of the artwork, called tip-ins. Fernand scoured secondhand bookstores for discontinued editions that featured, say, a fauve painting by Vlaminck. He then sent Elmyr the original from the book and asked him to do a similar painting of the same dimensions and subject. After exerting a little gentle persuasion and financial incentive, he found a Parisian printer to provide him his new "old" reproduction of the painting on the right paper and insert it in the art book. This enabled Fernand to show variations of the same theme to buyers in São Paulo, Chicago, Tokyo, or Zurich, and impress them every time.

Fernand's veneer as a dealer of important works of art, along with an armory of marketing strategies and an unrelenting hard-sell approach to business, made him unstoppable. No matter how successful he was as a new potentate of the Paris art world, his growing wealth fell farther behind his soaring ego. At the same time, he demanded of his male harem and sycophants the total fealty accorded a nervous, insecure despot. Clearly, he had Elmyr exactly where he wanted him, away from witnessing the lavish lifestyle Elmyr would have rightly assumed derived from sales whose profits were not going to him. Fernand was also familiar with Elmyr's habit of becoming unproductive when he prospered, and he was not about to do anything to staunch his revenue stream that seemed to be hemorrhaging from his own spendthrift habits.

It was on one of his globe-trotting sales calls to Tokyo in 1963 that Legros had his Japanese engraver fabricate a complete set of customs stamps to accompany the other phony documentation he needed in trafficking these treasures across international frontiers. This was not wholly the product of his prodigious schemes to swindle people. Those *Swiss*, those little watchmakers, he thought, were annoyingly fixated on details. A little more than ten months earlier, Fernand left Switzerland with a portfolio containing several different works according to Elmyr. They included Vlaminck gouaches, Matisse drawings, and a Dufy watercolor. The customs officials gave him a temporary exit permit for three months for the artwork. The significance of this was most likely forgotten the moment he passed the border. Fernand quickly disposed of the works among buyers forgotten with commensurate speed. When the Swiss authorities asked for the artworks' return, his attorney assured him he could not ignore their request that bore serious consequences— like prison. He made a hasty visit to Elmyr in Ibiza, entreating him to replace immediately the old fakes with new ones. Elmyr naturally asked if he had sold the others. "No...ah...they're all on consignment, but I did sell a small Matisse drawing. I forgot my checkbook in Paris. I'll send you a check as soon as I return," he assured Elmyr. He later told me that he discovered the reason for his trip from a lover of Fernand. "He stayed with me five long days until I completed everything he wanted. If I had known he had sold everything I would have asked for much more than the $750 he promised...that I never received, by the way," he admitted, shaking his head, but still grinning for his own incorrigible naivety.

The rich Swiss market was too lucrative to jeopardize by not conforming to their niggling legal requisites. Fernand's natural response would have been to spit in their faces, although he showed admirable restraint in not acting on this impulse. If they were patient enough, Fernand might one day feel magnanimous, and with a sweeping gesture from his royal scepter, deign to forgive the little cheese makers for inconveniencing him so. He now possessed not only French, but Swiss customs stamps as well. Those infernal functionaries could no longer pester him.

Throughout the years of their association, Elmyr explained away his ignorance of the extent of Fernand's success at selling his work with some partially believable rationalizations. Yes, he was inherently gullible. Yes, he had no head for numbers or business. (This may explain why his parents never groomed him for the family banking business.) Yes, others easily manipulated him. In the seven years that I knew him and lived with him, he vigorously downplayed his knowledge of what was really going on, but this simply does not tally with his output at that time. He knew the truth was far more incriminating than a lie. I call this the Lenny Bruce Defense. The comedian advised that if "your wife catches you in bed with another woman—deny it!" This prudent counsel, it seems, has been widely embraced by a good share of our elected officials.

During those years of 1963 and 1964, Fernand established some solid business connections in Japan with dealers and collectors, and even sold a number of works to the National Museum of Western Art in Tokyo. Elmyr later discovered, when the sale of his art to the museum was pending, that the cautious Japanese buyers solicited the advice of the visiting French minister of culture, André Malraux, the great art connoisseur and writer. He reputedly remarked that their prices seemed extremely reasonable. However, he was surprised how the paintings ever got out of France. The sales went through, and Fernand allegedly pocketed a cool quarter of a million dollars. Elmyr's share was substantially less. When Fernand next went to Ibiza, he carried on about what a wasted effort the trip had been. It cost him a lot of money, and claimed he just could not get them to commit to buy anything, but he generously brought his friend a small Japanese television as a gift anyway.

After Fernand thoroughly charmed his clients in Japan to open their checkbooks, he purchased a Paris apartment for $350,000 on Avenue Henri Martin, previously owned by King Hassan of Morocco. As Elmyr recounted this story, his tone turned increasingly peevish as it usually did with these testimonies of his gullibility and self-professed stupidity. "Fernand," he went on, "spent something like a $160,000 to remodel it. He wanted to surpass the opulence of its last owner, I think. I heard about the new apartment, but he always tried to keep me away—but I did see it in 1965 when I made an unannounced visit to Paris. When I saw it, it looked like a set design from Scheherazade. Red brocade covered the walls with gilt trim. There were three large bathrooms in marble; the sinks and bathtubs all had gold faucets. It was *trop voyant*—too showy. I told him it might impress the nouveau riche, but…he laughed and said his clients *were* nouveau riche.

"I also told him I thought the ambiance overwhelmed the artwork, and mentioned that most dealers show their pictures in a more subdued, even somber setting to focus on the artwork." Fernand then vigorously waved his arms like an orchestra conductor bringing a rehearsal to an abrupt halt upon hearing a sour note. "Mon cher," he explained to Elmyr, oozing his self-assured charm once more, "please, let *me* do the selling, and *you* do the artwork." The in-command confidence of his demeanor turned dark instantly, as though just informed of a plot to poison him, when Elmyr asked for some of his long-awaited bonus money most likely already spent on interior decoration. Fernand's bile ducts were probably backing up when he sat down to write Elmyr a check for $2,000. With that distasteful burden out of the way, his mood morphed quickly back to joy. Like Beelzebub expecting new contracts relinquishing fresh souls, he enthusiastically rubbed his hands together and asked Elmyr what art he had brought him.

Since business was wildly profitable for him that year, Fernand purchased a Renault limousine for himself, a mink coat and jewelry for his mother, two new Corvettes for his boyfriends to use, wardrobes for them, and even a new Mustang for Elmyr. For obvious reasons Fernand speedily tried to dispatch Elmyr once he had his current masterpiece-on-demand list fulfilled. He knew the flagrant spectacles of prosperity might cause his gold-egg-laying Hungarian goose sudden constipation. If his theatrics and bogus excuses for withholding his ill-gotten gains from Elmyr were less than convincing, his elder partner could be stubborn and uncooperative. Elmyr's temperament needed careful handling, but any miscue in that regard was still not like handing a vile of nitroglycerine to an agitated chimp, as Fernand's volatility always suggested.

Any slight, real or imagined, was enough to nudge Fernand into a rampage that terrorized those around him, and who were powerless to stop him because no one had an elephant gun loaded with a tranquilizing dart. Elmyr cited stories of Fernand's fits of jealous pique that would cause any reasoning person to flee. One famous incident Elmyr relayed involved a bitter quarrel that erupted between Fernand and his lover who just purchased a new cream-colored Alpha Romeo sports car. As they drove it from the dealership down the Champs Elysee in Paris, Fernand put out his cigarette on the carpet and started berating his driver. With a freshly lit cigarette, he began burning holes in the red-leather seats. Mutual accusations escalated to blows as the car careened through traffic. Then, pulling up to the nearest gendarme, the driver angrily told the police officer that the man next to him sexually propositioned him and he wanted him arrested. The cop took them both to the police station, where they stayed until Legros's bruised friend dropped the charges. Fernand promised a truce and full reparations for the damages after renewing pledges of love and fidelity.

Another time in New York, visions of his lover's betrayal seized his overactive imagination because his boyfriend neglected to tell him he was going to a movie. When he arrived two hours later than expected, Fernand, it seems, had already exacted punishment for his treachery by throwing all the traitor's clothes from their fifth-floor hotel room to amazed but open-armed, joyous spectators on the sidewalk below. Pierre Cardin suits, tailored shirts, and silk ties rained down like a sartorial wet dream. New, inventive ways to avenge *any* offense as he saw it, never failed to invigorate Legros. These challenges found him at his resourceful best.

For as slippery as Fernand's grasp was of his own mercurial behavior, he was still an astute observer, and consequently, manipulator of others. His manufactured altruism possessed as much stagecraft as his cabaret choreography. He enjoyed the showmanship of spontaneous generosity although it was rarely, if ever, unpremeditated. These gestures, in all probability, were regular steroid injections for his self-image—better still, reminders of his power and control over others. Gifts of cash, on the other hand, were more fleeting and promoted dangerous independent thinking. This simple fact made it necessary to dole out just enough money to Elmyr to not weaken his dependence on him, yet still give him enough incentive to continue producing his paintings, gouaches, watercolors, and drawings. This tactic did not pass unnoticed.

Even though Elmyr deduced what one could not easily ignore, that Fernand was lying to him about the profits from sales, he could prove nothing. Ibiza was by now not just a safe house removing him from harm's way. It was his home. For the first time in his life, that previously unknown impulse to live permanently in one place had become an idée fixe. Fernand's once-improbable suggestion of building a place of his own did not now seem so far-fetched. He also thought Fernand would happily contribute to its construction costs in exchange for the artwork he wanted. Yes, it was an epiphany for Elmyr, and it made perfect sense, a claim he rarely made about anything he did.

Elmyr Builds His Villa

Through a friend on the island, Elmyr found a small piece of land on a hillside between the old walled city of Ibiza town and the Bay of Figueretas with a commanding view of the countryside and the Mediterranean. The property's edge plummeted down a rocky precipice about forty meters to a beach. On this site Elmyr eventually had his villa, La Falaise, constructed. A resident German architect, Irwin Brauner, designed his home. Elmyr's intention to leverage his talent to get his house was clever in its conception, although Fernand's devious wiles ultimately conjured it away from him. He agreed to pay for the home's building costs by setting up a special account at a local bank. These funds were to be dedicated to building costs. When Fernand found that Elmyr was actually using a little of the money for his personal living expenses, he exploded in a late-night call from Paris. Not only did he accuse Elmyr of violating their compact of sacred trust, but he screamed that his ungrateful boyfriend and Elmyr were plotting against him. Elmyr found his paranoid rants always discomforting, but their shock value had dulled somewhat over the years of their association. It was just when there was an audience present that he found his outbursts an insufferable breach of social decorum.

Even though he had an ample stipend to cover his modest living expenses, *modest* was one of those words he liked to say was "open to interpretation." However one chose to define it, it was too imprecise to frequent his vocabulary, so he was less likely to see that it applied to him in any way. It is perhaps because Elmyr did not feel bound by the vagueness of their financial arrangement that he saw nothing wrong with augmenting his "modest" salary from the unaccountable Legros.

Fernand once suggested that Elmyr rent a small studio in the old city of Ibiza so as not to arouse his neighbors' suspicions around Villa Platero. Elmyr parried this idea, explaining that within days people would be peering through windows and keyholes to see what he was up to. Satisfying one's curiosity on Ibiza was at least as important as nutritional sustenance. He found one way to slip under the gossip radar was to escape the small island altogether. During the winter he often went to Kitzbuhle in Austria or Lisbon, Portugal, where in a creative flurry he produced all that Fernand requested—and more. His extracurricular activity always paid off; he would produce some Dufy watercolors, Vlaminck gouaches, or Matisse drawings that he sold for easy money in Munich, Vienna, or Milan. Since Legros was certainly withholding monies from him, he saw no reason to share the proceeds from his own entrepreneurial efforts. On one of his trips to the Austrian ski resort, however, Fernand sent along his boyfriend from Paris to make sure "mother"—or the "gypsy," as they derisively referred to Elmyr—might not cheat him.

Legros's penetrating ability to see demonic subterfuge among those entrusted to be faithful and demonstrate proper veneration to him, made the Grand Inquisitor, Torquemada's, suspicions look cheerily optimistic by comparison. In view of this inescapable reality, the inspiration behind Legros's right-angle logic is as freshly mystifying today as it was then. His confidante and lover, who was to keep an eye on Elmyr, was himself the most common object of Fernand's fits of jealousy and rage, a constantly ducking target in his personal shooting gallery. Elmyr never had difficulty making friends of his own, so he never coveted Fernand's bevy of boyfriends, even though Legros forever anguished over such thoughts.

The surprise in Elmyr's voice as he regaled me with this story is still unforgettable. Legros's spy drove his Corvette down from Paris to

Munich, where he was to meet Elmyr. As it had been snowing heavily that winter, they needed to get snow tires for the American car to safely negotiate the slippery Alpine roads to Kitzbuhle. They waited patiently at the luxury Hotel Bayerischerhof a couple of days for the tires to arrive. About one o'clock in the morning on the second night at the hotel, the phone rang in Elmyr's room. An irate Fernand demanded to know his companion's whereabouts and insisted on speaking to him. Elmyr curtly informed him that he was not his guardian and said, "Why don't you ask *him*?" and then hung up the phone, knowing how that would likely soothe Legros's troubled mind. Elmyr finished his nighttime reading and went to sleep. About an hour later, he awakened to an aggressive staccato of knocks at his door. In walked Fernand's friend, the blood drained from his face like someone about to go into shock. The phone rang once more. Again, it was Fernand. Elmyr held the phone away from his ear and with the audibility of a bullhorn, it announced for all to hear, between the strangulated cursing, "If I were there, I would kill you both!"

Elmyr didn't know Fernand's threat was not for him. However, Legros's cross-eyed indignation seemed to justify every former and future tirade against his friend, who weathered his verbal assaults with the practice of a battered spouse. Fernand once more phrased his denunciation in the *insane imperfect tense* of someone dressed in a canvas jacket with overly long sleeves clasped in the back. In anticipation of their arrival, Fernand had the forethought to bribe the hotel desk clerk to report their every movement. It was through him that Legros discovered his friend's return to his room, but his friend was not alone. He unwisely invited an acquaintance to come back with him. Elmyr, his face still signaling his disbelief, then said the accusatory call Legros made was from Orly airport in Paris. He knew every detail about the boy that returned to the room with his wretched companion.

The following day, the new snow tires arrived, so they could depart Munich for the ski resort and ascend the switchback roads through the Austrian Alps to Kitzbuhel. Amazingly, but not surprisingly, Fernand arrived two hours after they did by taking a cab from the Munich airport and traveling the hundred-mile distance. Dressed only in casual trousers and red sweater to match the color of his face, he had no coat, no luggage, and no money, but somehow managed to find their rented chalet.

Elmyr was flabbergasted to hear his familiar shrieks and see his violent arm-flapping, as though trying to disprove the notion that one cannot simultaneously become airborne and argue with a German-speaking cab driver. Fernand demanded that Elmyr pay the driver, and he did, to stave off Legros's one-man reenactment of the Second World War. At the sight of his unfaithful friend, Fernand uncorked his recriminations once more. Elmyr found himself in the middle of the combative couple and, like a prizefight referee, forced the two apart. At times like these, loneliness probably seemed an attractive alternative to him.

Over the next several weeks, Elmyr sequestered himself in the mountainside chalet, locked his door, and worked prodigiously. These moments of single-minded purpose were rare for him; the lack of distraction contributed greatly to his focus. Fernand appeared less convulsed by anxiety and suspicion now that he could personally observe everyone's activity. Well, according to Elmyr, the fights were fewer, at least. Fernand's strategy was to have Elmyr do enough Dufys to mount an exhibition in Paris by late November. He secured the Galerie Pont-Royale Hotel for a show entitled "Homage to Raoul Dufy." Of the thirty-three works they planned to display, twenty-six of the watercolors and oil paintings were by Elmyr. True to form, when Fernand and his companion returned to Paris with Elmyr's work, he stayed behind, probably to recover from the Sturm und Drang of the not-so-dear but thankfully departed others.

By the time the show opened in Paris, Elmyr had returned to Ibiza. A well-known critic, Gerald Messadie, wrote some suitably pontifical praise in the exhibition catalog. Curiously, a real Dufy graced its cover, *Les Courses, Deauville 1925*, an oil painting from the private collection of Fernand's attorney. The smattering of legitimate works among the fakes was apparently an effective trompe l'oeil to make the show a huge success. The news of this social, artistic, and financial triumph never quite reached Elmyr, tucked away on his Mediterranean isle. No surprise there.

Fernand was again feeling spontaneously generous on the heels of the profitable Dufy exhibition. He showered those benefits first on himself and then his growing entourage of young boys, who seemed to be getting younger all the time. Elmyr later told me in order to pacify the families of his underage harem, Fernand paid hush money for their silence as well. There may well have been little money left to give Elmyr. In any event, Legros knew how to handle him—or exploit him properly.

Elmyr not only knew nothing of the money Fernand made from the Dufy show, he was also unaware that a fauve-style Derain painting he did in Kitzbuhel reputedly sold through a gallery in New York for around $115,000. This was also part of the booty Fernand took to Paris after his winter ski vacation in Austria. This instance, like so many others, points to Elmyr's dismal negligence of even keeping any record of his output for which he could hold Fernand accountable. It seems that once he handed over the artwork to Legros he became lost in a fog of amnesia.

I consistently witnessed his inability to keep track of records, receipts, or documents that became irretrievably lost within piles of newspapers, magazines, or correspondence. While I tried to bring some order to the chaos, his lifelong pattern of disorder routinely thwarted my efforts. These mountains of paper he then often relegated to boxes or suitcases and left with friends when he moved between ever-changing addresses.

To further illustrate this point, I returned to the States in 1975 to visit my family. This included a trip to Los Angeles to see my brother. While I was there, I looked up someone I met in London, a wildly entertaining bantam fellow with the incongruous name Samson. In his small home tucked away in the shadows of one of the movie studios, he lived in a time capsule like a diminutive Miss Haversham. Everything was vintage 1900 art nouveau and a delight to behold. Knowing my connection to Elmyr, he led me to a back room where he brought out a suitcase of Elmyr's and let me browse through it. There was a wealth of letters from various museums regarding the purchase and selling of paintings; I found mementos and other personal effects that were intimate and revealing. I wish I had had the presence of mind to ask for the valise, but I did not. I believe that material would have been exceedingly insightful in writing this book. Alas, I still have more than can be confined to these pages.

Nineteen sixty-four was an eventful year for both Elmyr and Fernand. Elmyr continued living quietly on Ibiza, receiving his monthly allowance, and occasionally, a begrudgingly sent bonus check, but it was never enough to declare his independence from his partner. In April, construction began on La Falaise. At age fifty-eight, ownership of his first home ought to have been a turning point in his life, signifying stability and finally reversing years of impermanence. Fernand still exerted an irresistibly persuasive influence over Elmyr and convinced him that since he was a refugee with no legal citizenship, it was too risky to put the house in his name. "Don't you agree, mon cher," Legros said to him, "that it would be better not to have anything to do with the courts and banks that might bring attention to you, attention you don't want? I think it would be safer to put it in my name, since I'm an American citizen and they're not likely to make any trouble for me. We can have a contract stating that you have a right to use and live in the house as long as you live." This was simply more of Legros's oral conjuring he used so well in hypnotizing his victims. The promise of long-term happiness in his home was another mirage. Even though Elmyr knew every peseta paid for the villa's construction had some residue of oil paint, he again acceded to Fernand's spurious overtures. Elmyr later characterized this as the "worst decision of my life."

Not to let lifestyle or homosexuality stand in the way of what he wanted, Fernand put a clothespin on his nose and married a woman in the 1950s for the sole purpose of acquiring US citizenship. While this ploy is unoriginal, the union had the believability of his wedding Carmen Miranda and producing an offspring named Fruit Cocktail. (Well, given his background as a cabaret dancer, that may not be such a stretch.)

Crossing international borders was not the angst-ridden experience for Legros that it was for Elmyr. Elmyr may well have been envious of the cachet of Fernand's American passport, as it earned him easy entry to just about any country on earth. Legros was still attracted to the lucrative market in the States and Americans' tremendous appetite for art, which was only less voracious than his craving for wealth. While Elmyr successfully plumbed the acquisitiveness of this free-market culture during his twelve-year stay, Fernand was looking to strip-mine it. His slash-and-burn approach to business seemed to be very much in keeping with the still-lively impulse to divorce profit motive from morality. Fernand definitely fancied himself a shark and others his prey; ethics had little to do with survival.

One reason Elmyr may have been disposed to Legros's specious argument about putting the house in his name was that his own Canadian passport used to return to Europe was about to expire, and the grueling process of obtaining a new one might have been weighing heavily on him. Around this time, he decided to apply for a Nansen Pass. This document allowed stateless refugees the right to travel, conceived as a means to deal with the huge numbers of displaced persons after World War II. Some friends helped him through the multi-layered bureaucracy of the Spanish government. Here, again, he found that as long as he knew the right people and was able to pay them, almost anything is possible. It remains unclear to me today how he emerged from the onerous paper-shuffling in Madrid with an entirely new identity. He was now officially Elmyr Joseph Dory Boutin. Perhaps unsurprisingly, the name on his driver's license morphed from Elmyr to Elementer. Immigrants that arrived by the millions through Ellis Island in New York were certainly familiar with the quixotic spelling transformations of their names, which often had little to do with their original identities. Elmyr suggested, "Anything that didn't sound Spanish left them totally flummoxed."

As Elmyr thought increasingly of Ibiza as his home, he paid great attention to appear as normal and law-abiding as possible. His decision to pursue his new state-sanctioned identity papers, however, was probably born out of impure motives. Shortly before his Canadian passport reached its expiration date, Fernand asked a friend to take it to the Canadian Embassy in Rotterdam for renewal, where he made a surprising and unpleasant discovery. Elmyr explained the mess in a tone of unforgotten disgust: "The passport that I paid very expensively to get was actually someone's real identity. Legros said, 'Don't worry, he is some *petit functionaire*,' in some small town who would never apply for a passport. It turned out the Royal Canadian Mounted Police were looking for him for some crimes—including bigamy. When they presented my passport at the embassy, my or his name appeared in one of those big books with the names of undesirables. Fernand's friend fled the building when they started asking him questions."

regatta in the style of Raoul Dufy – oil

While Elmyr watched laborers laying the foundation for his new house, Fernand began a courtship of sorts with a Texan oil tycoon named Algur Meadows, an art-collecting philanthropist. His previous gestures of magnanimity included endowing Southern Methodist University with an art museum that housed a collection of over a million dollars' worth of art he purchased in Madrid. It included paintings by El Greco, Goya, and other Spanish masters. Since irony has no limits, he later discovered that these treasures were mostly worthless, yet this public embarrassment did nothing to thwart his zeal to collect. Legros was more than willing to accommodate his unsinkable optimism. Cliff Irving alleged that over a thirty-month period, he sold the oilman an estimated "fifteen Dufys, seven Modiglianis, five Vlamincks, eight Derains, three Matisses, two Bonnards, one Chagall, one Degas, one Marquet, one Laurencin, one Gauguin, and a Picasso." His purchases netted hundreds of thousands of dollars for the aggressively persistent art dealer. When the daring duo, Fernand and Elmyr, were ultimately exposed, the ensuing scandal had the entire art world blushing from embarrassment, and none felt more foolish than Algur Meadows. There are many ways one can earn fame. He may have cemented his reputation by owning the world's largest collection of fake paintings. Former Texas governor John Connelly later bought many of these—he thought, although the would-be modern masterpieces also turned out to be—*fake* Elmyrs. His place in history was quite different from Meadows's. He accompanied President John Kennedy on November 22, 1963, the day Lee Harvey Oswald assassinated him in Dallas. Governor Connelly, also shot, survived his wounds from the assassin's bullets but not his misadventures in the art business.

There is not a lot on public record concerning Meadows's thoughts on his disastrous foray into the dark waters of the art world. Those close to him may have been privy to his views on the topic. At the same time, it probably would have been prudent not to broach the subject at all if one wanted to remain on speaking terms with him. After his convincing singular reenactment of the Spanish Armada, his alacrity to repeat the debacle a second time, or numerous times, comes back to Voltaire's haunting observation that "history never repeats itself but people always do." Both he and Elmyr could have commiserated a long while on this, I suspect. Elmyr's skill at fooling others never surpassed his propensity to let others fool him. He recognized this weakness but like an Alzheimer sufferer started each new day afresh, willing to invest confidence in others, warranted or not.

Elmyr alleged that Meadows's dealings with Legros suggested the Texan millionaire was a tough negotiator and frequently succeeded in bargaining down the prices of the art he bought. His hard-edged business acumen, however, did little to make up for not understanding what he was buying. Then again, Elmyr consistently fooled experts, curators, and dealers who made it their business to know better.

A film made about a retired over-the-road truck driver who bought a painting in a junk shop stirred up controversy in the refined world of art. She had no idea that what she purchased may be an original work by the abstract expressionist artist Jackson Pollack. Excerpted from the documentary for the television newsmagazine program *60 Minutes* is a segment showing former Metropolitan Museum director Thomas

Hoving studying the painting. He looked at the tableau of paint drippings with head tilted back, using the end of his nose like a rifle sight. Then, he proclaimed it "DOA—dead on arrival." Never mind that a fingerprint found embedded in paint on the disputed canvas purportedly matched one on another recognized Pollack. All I know is that Elmyr spent twenty years of his life debunking the oracular self-importance of people like Hoving. In the BBC documentary on Elmyr, he expressed his opinion thus: Museum directors may be very good at raising money for their institutions, but their knowledge of art is absolutely *négligeable*. If her junk-shop find is ultimately determined to be an authentic Pollack, its current market value is estimated around 75 million dollars. Not a bad price for paint drippings. The experts can then pontificate on why this artist's paint dribblings are worth that. It should be no surprise that many see the art world as dysfunctional.

At this point in Elmyr's career, he succeeded in reducing his exposure to danger but was also reduced to creating whatever Fernand asked of him. He no longer had the artistic license to do as he wished and consequently became bored with some of the monotonous repetition of his commissions. Legros always prodded Elmyr for more oil paintings to maximize profits, explaining that it took just as much effort to sell a drawing as a painting and the latter was far more lucrative. He further insisted that Elmyr add more red color to the works. Fernand's predilection to red, Elmyr explained, was because "when he was growing up in Egypt, it was the color most closely associated with King Farouk." His color preference consequently mimicked royal tastes while his ego assumed regal grandiosity. Yet, with a practical eye toward sales, he insisted it was a good choice of color, well suited to American living rooms. It also happened to be a color Dufy lavished on his light and airy themes, one of which was a crowd scene entitled *Reception at Elysee Palace*. Fernand had Elmyr do numerous variations of this in the visual shorthand of the Frenchman. They were easy to sell, colorful, and possessed the psychic depth of a dinner plate, which is perhaps why they were so popular.

The uninspiring sameness of this particular subject prompted Elmyr to warn Fernand that he found his efforts unsatisfactory and made him promise that if he encountered a problem with any of his work that might be "weak," he was to return it to him immediately. He intended to destroy anything that could be viewed as doubtful and arouse suspicions. His dissatisfaction with the Dufys proved prescient. Predictably, one of his Dufys went to Fred Schoneman, of Schoneman Galleries in New York, for an appraisal. Like its creator, he also found it mediocre enough to think it was not genuine. Armed with his damning assessment, its buyer went back to Legros for return of his money. To placate his client, Fernand rushed out and bought a painting by Georges Rouault for $30,000, and offered it in exchange for the fake Dufy. He accepted. Rather than returning the suspicious Dufy to Elmyr, he later sold it to Algur Meadows.

News of the incident unfortunately followed Fernand back to Paris. If they could not find the source of the fake painting, he reasoned, he could successfully limbo under that stick the French police, given the slightest provocation, would freely wield against him. Worrying that the nosy authorities might discover some link between him and Elmyr, he flew from Paris to Zurich and then drove to Kitzbuhel, finding Elmyr was once again ensconced in his winter ski chalet, at work on a new order of masterpieces. No sooner had he arrived at the snowbound getaway, that he began making calls to Paris. For reasons no longer understood, he believed the French Duxieme Bureau, the government branch that deals with espionage cases, was looking for him.

Whatever that gland was in his body that secreted paranoia, Fernand possibly thought *his* was in perfect working order. He informed Elmyr that his recent brush with Schoneman in New York, of which he knew nothing until that moment, was causing, in Elmyr's words, "a little unpleasantness" in Paris. After picking up the gist of Legros's panicked phone conversation that his apartment on Avenue Henri Martin was about to be searched, Elmyr's inner alarm bells sounded as well. The pounding at his chalet door heralding Fernand's unannounced arrival at four o'clock in the morning had frightened any remaining impulse to sleep from his body. To make things worse, Fernand informed him that *he* might be in trouble too. It seems the art community in New York was once again invoking the name of L. E. Raynal. His past was coming back to haunt him as sure as a rising miasma over a low-lying graveyard.

It was February 1965. Construction of La Falaise was not yet finished. Fernand reminded him of this and in the same breath asked, "How would you like to go to Australia?" Elmyr replied, "Can I have breakfast first?" Fernand's face remained serious, and Elmyr then realized he was not joking. "Why would I want to go to Australia," he asked, "all they have there is kangaroos!" He objected further when Legros wanted to ship him off with only a one-way ticket. "OK," he responded, "I'll get you a two-way ticket. You can take the Mustang with you since you'll need to stay a while. You could open a gallery in Sidney. Anyway, you can't go back to Ibiza. The police might be watching the house."

Elmyr was again no match for his partner's insistence. He flew from Austria to Madrid and stayed at the Hotel Ritz. Fernand's friend arranged the car's shipment to Gibraltar, where Elmyr boarded the liner *Canberra* for Australia. What he discovered later upon his return home was that Fernand destroyed all his artwork and sketchbooks—not any Matisses or Modiglianis, just Elmyr's own work.

Even though Fernand manipulated him with less resistance than wet clay on a potter's wheel, it was surprising how quickly he agreed to go to Australia. His resentment once more percolated to the surface in conveying this story. Legros again placated his reluctance by stuffing $3,000 in his pocket while they concluded planning the trip in Madrid. Short of his ship sinking en route, his voyage to the southern hemisphere could hardly have been more disastrous.

Two unforeseen details set the tone for his visit. First, Elmyr's body hosted an unwelcome visitor. A food-borne microbe commonly transmitted in goat's milk or cheese called Malta fever, incubated in him during the tedious voyage. He most likely contracted it in Ibiza, so the nasty little bug had been using him as its personal amusement park for a number of weeks already. Its symptoms include sweating, muscle and body aches, weakness, fever, and depression. He told me that if it is untreated, paralysis occurs in its advanced stage. During the years I spent with him, he strongly believed in the ameliorative value of pharmaceutical drugs, so I do not know if that viewpoint preceded or followed his tendency toward hypochondria. His doctors never properly diagnosed his illness during his sojourn on the Australian continent, so I have no doubt he was dismayed that any pill offered did not cure him. His general listlessness and concurrent side effect of depression, along with his coerced departure from Europe for a destination that seemed to him at the end of the earth, dispirited him.

I have already established that Elmyr was no raving democrat. His idea of egalitarianism was, for instance, the generous notion that luxury hotels allow *anyone* to stay there if one can afford it. I'm sure he expected to hobnob with other open-minded patricians like himself among Canberra's first-class passengers. As he recounted this episode, the pucker factor appeared in his face, as though he just swallowed a dose of alum. "I wasn't disappointed with the accommodations," he claimed, "it was the other people I was stuck with. They were retired shopkeepers from Brighton or Manchester, and boring. The only one I found interesting to talk to was a Jesuit priest. We played chess every day." I suspect his physical malaise may have influenced this opinion, or there might just have been a dearth of titled aristocrats and tiara-wearing dowagers onboard. He knew they all had not vanished with the Titanic. For once his bohemian instincts prevailed over his natural snobbism when he recounted that he could not enter second- and third-class areas. This, he suspected, was where all the fun-loving people were hiding.

The other glitch in the hasty travel arrangements he did not discover until the ship docked in Sydney. No one told him in advance that Australian customs required a large cash deposit on his imported vehicle before he could bring it into the country. While this unpleasant surprise most likely prompted an angry rebuke even in his physically diminished condition, one can only imagine the kind of profanity-laced tantrum that would have had Fernand ricocheting off the walls if this had happened to him. Port officials seized his sporty Mustang convertible the instant it was off the ship. He was feeling weak *and* distraught. It was not a propitious beginning to his newest adventure.

Elmyr rented a house in Sydney, where he had only enough energy to paint and draw as his debilitating fatigue encroached on his withering stamina and psyche. Fernand came out to visit him in April, only to find a weaker, sicker, and more forlorn painter. The new supply of artwork produced by his lethargic and unhappy partner, however, considerably buoyed *his* spirits. As Legros crated the oils, watercolors, and gouaches for shipment to Paris; Elmyr's complaints and deteriorating health went unnoticed. Fernand insisted on attending to business and seemed annoyed by conversation that had nothing to do with him. He was astounded that Elmyr had not even acknowledged that *he* just made a long trip there and did not adequately appreciate the trouble he went to just to see *him*. Fernand probably thought the self-pitying Hungarian was the most self-absorbed person on earth.

During Elmyr's stay in Sydney, he managed to venture out to some of the city's art galleries. According to Elmyr, "They were *all* very happy to make my acquaintance." Without much difficulty, he sold some works from his private collection to "eager buyers." By June, he realized if he did not get back to Europe for the medical care he needed, the land Down Under would be six feet over his coffin. Although his condition nearly warranted his return on a stretcher, he boarded a flight to Spain, looking half-alive with the pallor of an anemic Kabuki actor. When he reached Madrid, he checked himself into a hospital. His doctors there were more familiar with his disease, as it is common in countries around the Mediterranean. This time he received the medications he needed and slowly regained his health.

That same month, workers completed La Falaise. He moved into his villa with renewed vitality and hope. To prove that his mood was still fragile and easily dashed like dishware hurled against a wall, Fernand promptly announced that he and his "guests" were arriving for a two-week stay in July. Given the fact that the house was in his name, Elmyr could not very well object. While his private contract guaranteed him lifetime use of the home, it actually meant that the two business associates would have to share the domicile. It was yet another instance of his lack of vision to see future consequences of present or past actions. All he had to do was threaten to withhold the artwork Fernand wanted until he signed over the ownership of the house to him. He did not, and the consequences played out dramatically when I was there to witness the turmoil. For the moment, no matter how unpalatable the prospect of Legros's visit was, he had no recourse to his fait accompli. He could, however, leave for that period, and that is what he elected to do. Elmyr also concluded that he found Legros increasingly unbearable and disliked being even in the same room with him.

Their relationship was, after all, strictly one of convenience, and that unique aspect had pretty much evaporated in well-founded distrust. Despite the trappings of wealth and genteelness, Fernand had not actually risen in Elmyr's esteem since the first day they met, though, he had more reasons to find him intolerable now. For once, his instincts did not fail him; placing some distance between him and Fernand was a good idea. Lapsing a moment longer into lucidity and giving the devil his due, Elmyr thought his selfish partner may have been good at business, but that talent was designed to serve himself, and he was just Fernand's tool to be used toward that end. For as obvious a fact as this might have been to any casual observer, Elmyr was consistently impenetrable to this marrow-sucking reality because his perceptions routinely passed through a filter of humane optimism; he always tried to live by the golden rule, and his true friends recognized this trait. This fleeting clarity about Fernand, though, did not assuage his worries about what scandal he might create during his vacation on the island.

The day Legros and company arrived, Elmyr left for the south of Spain. He knew that in the best of circumstances, any visible link between him and Legros could bring their house of cards crashing down. Unlike the incautious art dealer, Elmyr was always a strict observer of social convention. Even in pursuit of his private life, he was discreet and did as little as possible to ruffle local sensibilities. Conversely, Fernand thought nothing of behaving outrageously, and if others were offended, it was unimportant. Elmyr sensed his dreaded visit was a bad omen, and his suspicions would unfortunately prove correct. Legros was about to make a sort of Normandy Beach landing of the Follies Bergère.

Fernand took the hippy mantra of "if it feels good, do it," and embraced it with a bear hug. Ibiza was now under a siege of foreigners invading its quaint fishing villages, renting countryside farmhouses and introducing their counterculture values to the local population that was barely aware of living in the twentieth century. Ironically, those throngs looking for unspoiled bucolic simplicity were in a way their own worst enemies. This sudden influx of new residents and tourists catapulted the island's economy forward, and boosted land values like the California gold rush. It was rapidly becoming the new Riviera, where everyone enjoyed the sun and fun, none more so than an ex-cabaret dancer turned flamboyant entrepreneur.

At Fernand's urging, the spacious guest quarters of La Falaise boasted his favorite color, aptly christened, "the red room." It was mostly white, but had red wool curtains and matching cushions for the sitting area banquette. He took the guest suite, and the rest of his entourage moved into Elmyr's bedroom and the small, attached servant's quarters. Over the following two weeks, Elmyr's new home more accurately resembled a portside bar, with parties occurring almost nightly after Legros and his inebriated retinue returned, expressing their festive spirits and drinking all the liquor and wine on hand. When the supply of alcohol ran out, Fernand simply had more delivered from a nearby bodega and promptly signed Elmyr's name to the bill. Even though Fernand had a new boyfriend, he continued to cast his net each night at the bars and nightclubs to see what fresh fish he could catch. Life at the new villa was making Sodom and Gomorrah look like a convent of Benedictine monks. Neighbors started complaining about the late night music and noise; the local police began responding regularly to bacchanals at the cliff-top nightspot. Elmyr's visions of Fernand's shocking comportment lived up to his worst fears.

Legros most likely enjoyed being the grist of the café society's rumor mill. He was, in fact, the bipedal social disaster that Elmyr desperately wanted to avoid since the beginning of their association. In a matter of days, Fernand triumphantly ruined his cohort's image of respectable model citizen he had diligently worked to cultivate since he first came to Ibiza. Upon his return, he would not only have to confront the immediate ordeal of public relations damage control, but clean up the wreckage in the wake of the ransacking revelers.

Only weeks before Legros's marauding visit, he had recovered from his long and debilitating Malta fever and moved into his new home. His spirit was the most upbeat it had been in months or even years. As he opened the front door of the villa, the destruction Legros and his friends left behind was instantly apparent. Cigarette burns and stamped-out butts destroyed his cream-colored area rugs he had recently bought in Madrid. Shards of broken crystal glasses lay undisturbed on the tile floor. Patio furniture rested peacefully submerged at the bottom of his pool. Other objects vanished as likely souvenirs with the departed night-trippers. Elmyr sat down in his living room easy chair, disheartened by the thoughtless vandalism, rested his elbows on his knees, sunk his face into his opened hands, and cried. He cried for the senselessness of it all. He cried for every glimmer of hope in his life that always seemed quickly extinguished. Still, he survived. Slowly his sorrow turned to anger. He now detested Legros and knew a divorce was imminent. The question was how to sever his bond with him and not become a victim of his paranoid vindictiveness.

Elmyr had long thought there was much about Fernand's instability that justified a lengthy sojourn in a psychiatric ward. He cared less about the reasons for his dangerous irrationality than its damaging effects that could easily swallow those around him down the vortex of his own predictable self-destruction. He was just one of many seduced by Legros's wiles and now knew he somehow had to redeem his soul and extricate himself from his grasp.

At the same time, another continent away, an equally poignant drama of Hollywood dimensions was playing offstage. Fernand's favorite victim in the Lone Star State, Algur Meadows, was about to host many of the art world's cognoscenti gathering in Dallas for an important Picasso show. The Texan art collector thought it an auspicious occasion to invite some of them to coo over his private gallery of modern masters. The forty-six works gracing the walls of his home would make it not just significant, but über important. His list of invitees included some iconic figures. Among them were Dan Vogel, a respected Dallas dealer; the Perls brothers, Frank and Klaus, who were unfortunately familiar with Elmyr's work; and Mr. and Mrs. Daniel Saidenberg. Daniel Saidenberg replaced Paul Rosenberg as Picasso's American representative.

Upon entering Meadows's mansion, one of his illustrious guests asked if he preferred their opinions in writing or an immediate oral assessment. He opted for the latter, without the benefit of anesthesia. It is unclear who drew the first drop of blood, but the feeding frenzy was on. They collectively savaged his personal pantheon, condemning everything in sight. Expressed in erudite terms, their unambiguous displeasure ticked off every conceivable objection why this or that piece was not right. In the tumult, the scholarly piranhas gnawed every bit of flesh from the artworks' bones. Only the teeth marks remained on the frames. It was, of course, akin to calling in the grim reaper to write the coroner's report and cause of death.

One should also remember there is a collegial esprit de corps at work here, and if one chimes in his doubts, it can signal a chorus of criticism like an upset Vienna Boy's Choir. Conversely, one critic's positive review may be as contagiously influential. One reason Elmyr may have been as successful as he was for so long is that unanimity

147

of opinion among experts is almost unheard of, and that inconclusiveness frequently worked in his favor. In any event, familiar phraseology couched the professionals' autopsies. This artist would never have drawn a line like this or that. The shading and colors are all wrong, etc. In some instances, their objections may have been correct. Elmyr knew that some of his work might have been weaker than he liked, and he had expressed his reservations to Legros. It is still remarkable how few of his works have surfaced after all these years.

No matter the reasons for their bleak critiques, the bottom line was that Mr. Meadows would be viewed as the biggest rube the world of art has ever known—for the second time. The mood at his dinner table could have been merrier only if they had dined in a slaughterhouse. To add to the funereal atmosphere at Meadows's Mortuary of Modern Art, I imagine the neatly engraved menu for their meal might have read, "Dead Fish" on a platter, followed by "Cooked Goose." Well, you get the idea.

On Fernand's last sales trip to Texas, Meadows failed to connect the dots when one of his last views of Fernand was of him standing behind cell bars of the Dallas City Jail. His incarceration surprisingly had nothing to do with swindling his now slightly less rich client. It was the result of a criminal complaint filed by his former companion who had long benefited from Legros's nefarious activities and was the most frequent target of his jealous rage. The incident revolved around a stolen briefcase that not only contained damning evidence against Fernand, but, worse yet, reams of papers documenting his own business affairs, indicating a personal and financial independence from Legros. This not only confirmed Fernand's longstanding suspicions of betrayal; he could not support the idea of his former protégé and lover no longer subservient to him. Since Fernand and his friend were together when the briefcase disappeared from his hotel room, he did not suspect him of the theft. Not long afterward, however, Elmyr was again acting as Legros's long-distance therapist, listening to his sputtering rage and death threats against the weasel-eyed monster he used to let sleep with him. Fernand had no idea his friend was with Elmyr when he called and heard for himself his tirade fueled by information locked inside that attaché case. He then took the first available flight to Dallas and had Legros arrested for felony theft.

Oddly enough, when Fernand stood wailing and crying in his jail cell, it was Algur Meadows who came to bail him out. Had he then known the verdict on his art collection, he likely would have been less disposed to come to Fernand's aid. The negotiated terms of his release were that he had to return the stolen property and admit to the theft. In return, his former boyfriend would drop the charges against Fernand. Cliff Irving later reported that Meadows's misplaced sympathy deteriorated significantly when he allegedly stated, "The thing I most regret is that the day they let him out of the Dallas jail, there was no Jack Ruby waiting in the courtyard." His escapade with the police initiated Meadows's nervousness about the picture dealer's integrity. That prompted the convocation that was the death knell of his career as a collector of fine art.

I suspect few things gave Fernand the adrenalin rush of money in his hand or exacting punishment on his enemies. With the righteous indignation of a jihad, he declared a personal vendetta against his former lover for the shame he had to endure at the hands of the police in Dallas. It would be just the kind of cage match, fight-to-the-death, wholesale bloodletting he relished. A scorching letter he wrote to Elmyr offers a revealing glimpse of his gladiatorial feistiness. He starts somewhat tepidly, stating, "*...and a lifetime won't be long enough to punish him, his entire family, mother, father, and little brothers, to punish that son of a bitch. If necessary I would mind to kill the man myself in public, in front of everyone, and afterwards I don't mind to spend the rest of my life in jail...*" (Irving 1969). His intent and tone become even less kind as his declaration of war continues. This scary rant was not just hollow threats; he meant every word of it, and Elmyr knew it. He also knew that in an equally frightening way, he remained tethered to a lunatic.

Legros's campaign of vengeance now became his newest cause célèbre. His incentive for payback was, in fact, so great that like Martin Luther, he enumerated his grievances in a lengthy denunciation against his heretical former confidante. The document accused him of crimes that Legros had commissioned him to do and thereby incriminated *him* as well. Such details were mere inconveniences against the big picture of settling a score. Fernand strategically timed his reprisal for January 26. It was his thirty-fifth birthday. That morning he made a call to the Paris police station nearest the Hôtel Montalambert on the Left Bank, where his traitorous companion was living. He then proceeded to rattle off a litany of crimes his cohort committed and that *he*, as a good law-abiding citizen, felt compelled to report him to the authorities. If they checked his luggage in the hotel consignment, he suggested, they would find evidence of his illegal activities, and promptly hung up the phone. On the anonymous tip, the police investigated the claim. Upon opening the valise in question, they found a package that included four van Dongen paintings, one Marquet, and a Bonnard, all with their attendant phony expertises and fake customs stamps used to export the works from France.

When the police brought him in handcuffs to the station, Fernand, parked out front, sat on the hood of his red Ferrari, holding a long-stemmed glass in one hand and an uncorked bottle of Dom Perignon in the other. He drank his expensive champagne as they led his arrested enemy up the steps. Fernand then shrieked "Bravo! Bravo!" and rejoiced for putting that "turd" in a cage where he belonged. His premeditated little plot, however, left an open door leading directly to himself. Despite costing him a quarter of a million dollars in confiscated artwork, his brief moment of sweet revenge was apparently worth it.

Unlike Fernand's stay of a few hours in the Dallas City Jail, the victim of his newly celebrated retribution would spend the next four weeks becoming better acquainted with the Parisian gendarmes. The blood feud between the two would later play a significant role in the final unraveling of Legros's lucrative art business.

As usual, Elmyr knew more about who was sleeping with whom from the sidewalk café banter on Ibiza then he did of the uncivil war that broke out in Paris. He was habitually uneasy over his now insufficient stipend and infrequent bonus money from his shifty and unreliable dealer. His ever-precarious personal finances often left him without funds and his bank account overdrawn. Fortunately, his local safety net of friends helped. They knew he consistently repaid their short-term loans and never thought twice about assisting him until some check expected from somewhere abroad came through. It was just mystifying that at times he appeared so flush with cash and then struggled to make ends meet. Many of the foreigners were familiar with currency restrictions of numerous countries and Spain's almost Byzantine banking system, so these glitches with money transfers were normal.

Fernand may have had a hiccup of pragmatism after he realized what his cold-blooded Threepenny Opera at the Left Bank police station had actually cost him. Within days, Legros was back in Ibiza, trying to ingratiate himself once more with Elmyr. He made all the right noises to placate his partner. On his hands and knees, the remorseful supplicant begged Elmyr's forgiveness for trashing his home during his stay there. Other people damaged the house, he explained, not him. "I will pay for everything that is broken or missing," he swore with believable sincerity. Because of his current penury and Fernand waving a check for $2,000 in front of his face, Elmyr felt obliged to set aside his resentment and once again do business with the devil.

Fernand was a master of theatrics, but not timing. No sooner had he brought Elmyr back into the fold like a champion border collie than he chose that magic moment to tell him of the devastating Texas twister that ripped through Meadows's collection in the form of art experts. Elmyr was livid. When he told Elmyr that Meadows's lawyers were willing to accept financial restitution rather than proceed with a criminal complaint, Fernand laughed. The palms of Elmyr's hands perspired profusely as he digested the disturbing news and doomsday scenario. He nervously insisted that Legros do what was necessary to avoid impending disaster. Fernand's entreaties of moments before now turned to petulant defiance. He did not want to talk about that but rather discuss his latest scheme to make more money.

While Elmyr stood silent, becoming nauseous from worry, Legros's mood quickly changed again; he now displayed the triumphant smirk of a child whose untiring obstinacy overwhelms a relenting parent. Fernand was cheerily oblivious to the fallout from the mushroom cloud rapidly enveloping Dallas and the shock waves heading toward them both. He could focus only on the new commissions he wanted from Elmyr. They included a number of Dufy watercolors, his usual light-hearted fare; a fauve-period painting of Vlaminck; perhaps a Marquet painting, or one by Derain. "Just outside of Paris, in Pontoise, there is a government-sanctioned auction house," he explained to the distracted artist. "There is an important sale scheduled there in early April," he continued, attempting to pacify his disbelieving listener, assuring him that he would have someone else submit the artworks under *their* name. When Elmyr cautioned him that it would be too dangerous, Fernand abruptly disarmed his protests by hinting that Elmyr was in no position to refuse his request.

Elmyr recounted this with a sigh of resignation. "What was I supposed to do?" he asked. "I knew Legros was crazy, but I depended on the son of a bitch." Any whiff of scandal circulated like an out-of-control prairie fire in the art world, and Fernand simply had no idea of what he had ignited. Elmyr found himself caught between two options, neither of which was safe. He could again cave in to Legros's coercion and veiled threats, or not cooperate and risk violating the unholy compact he had with a violent, vindictive nut. Elmyr reluctantly decided to give him the artwork he wanted, although he subsequently labored over his creations with the gusto of a condemned man. Near the end of February, he rendezvoused with Fernand at Barcelona's airport. Elmyr had everything ready but for one Vlaminck oil painting. Legros took his package, then wrote out a check for $2,000 on his Swiss account and handed it to his visibly tired and subdued partner.

Their reunion in the airport bar was brief and businesslike. Fernand returned to Paris with little or no thought given to his recent troubles. Elmyr returned to Ibiza, and that was all he was able to ponder. A week later, a despondent Elmyr received unwelcome news from his local bank that Fernand's check had bounced. Anger displaced his melancholy when he realized he was again almost penniless. He called Legros in Paris. "Bonjour, mon cher," Fernand bubbled with the conscience-free gaiety of a sociopath whose basement floor covers the bodies of mysteriously missing people. "Don't *mon cher* me, you son of a bitch. You gave me another of your worthless checks. I'm sorry I ever met you, and I want nothing to do with you ever again!" Elmyr hung up the phone, but Fernand was not one to let someone else have the last word. Several more truncated dialogues ensued before Fernand regained control of the crisis. "I'll send you another check," Legros promised. "This time it will be a good one."

It is difficult to assess whether Legros's own finances oscillated as much as Elmyr's. He made a tremendous amount of money, but his expenditures were enormous. Elmyr told me that when Fernand was together with his longtime partner, they commonly signed checks for each other. The banks routinely returned the checks when the signatures did not match those of the given account. They later sent checks with their proper signatures. It was their personal game of juggling their money and delaying payment. Once, according to Elmyr, Fernand had his friend sign his check for a large bill for tailored suits in Madrid. Then, after one of their frequent quarrels, Fernand filed a criminal complaint against his friend for forging his name to the check, even though the tailor witnessed his asking him to do this.

That spring of 1967, the auction in Pontoise was approaching, and Fernand still had not received the Vlaminck landscape he had ordered from Elmyr, although he already officially listed it in the forthcoming sale. While he could have withdrawn or exchanged the Vlaminck for another, Fernand elected to check one of the three Parisian warehouses where he stashed his trove of art treasures. In one of the crates, he found a fauve period Vlaminck he thought was about two years old. The golden-hued Rembrandt varnish adorned the canvas, giving it its instantly aged appearance. He promptly submitted it to the auction house. About a week before the sale, the artwork went on display for prospective buyers' examination. Elmyr's eyes widened with amazement at this part of the story. He said, "One of the auction house employees thought the Vlaminck apparently looked a little dirty, so he attempted to clean it with a cloth." When he removed the rag from the picture's surface, he noticed that some of the paint from the 1906 canvas came off with the dust. This anomaly elicited an immediate call to the police, who promptly confiscated it and the rest of the pictures from Legros.

Fernand expected the sale to net him around $150,000. Now the gendarmes wanted to net him. As soon as he found out about the incident, he raced to Pontoise, hoping to collect the rest of the pictures. Upon his arrival, he discovered the police had seized the others too, and wanted to speak to their owner. What remained of Fernand's thinning black hair atop his high forehead, he nearly pulled out in a rare moment of panic. Then, rushing back to his opulent apartment on Avenue Henri Martin, he gathered all his personal files and burned them. His American friend whom he had persuaded to act as the seller of the Pontoise tableaux was now "a person of interest" in a criminal investigation. Together, the two men frantically grabbed items from drawers and closets and threw them into nine large suitcases. Their bulging contents erupted at the seams; sleeves of tailored silk shirts trailed on the ground as the two men carried the suitcases to their getaway car, Legros's luxury Buick. Tossing the leather luggage into the trunk, resembling thieves fleeing a clothing-store heist, they jumped in the vehicle and sped off, heading south.

The humor in Elmyr's voice and the smile on his face showed how much he enjoyed relaying Fernand's torment of that moment. In an instant, his mood turned serious. "They drove to Barcelona," he continued, "and took the ferry to Ibiza. I was in Madrid at the time, attending the premiere of Robin Maugham's play, and knew nothing of their arrival. They broke into the house in my absence and changed the locks on the doors. I later got the bill for that from the carpenter he hired to do it. You can imagine my surprise when I came back to find Legros and his friend living in my home and telling me they were staying a while. I was not at all happy about it."

Back in Paris, the police quickly established Legros's connection to the scandal of the Pontoise auction. His many buyers were probably slapping their foreheads in what must have sounded like thunderclaps announcing the coming storm and uttering in dread, *mon dieu*! Napoleon, a person whose ego looked circumspect next to Fernand's, said that Europe ended at the Pyrenees. Now that Legros was south of that mountain range, he felt safe because he never sold any artwork in Spain and mistakenly assumed the authorities would not extradite him for his troubles in France. From the security of the villa, his characteristic pluck and defiance returned, claiming his current setback was the result of his competitors, their rampant petty jealousies, and who had plotted it all just to undermine him.

Many of Fernand's young male "concubinage," as Elmyr described his paid admirers, were once more turning La Falaise into a Turkish brothel. "They were little more than knife-wielding hoodlums," he said of Legros's harem with unforgotten alarm, "and I didn't feel safe in my own home." Fernand, on the other hand, so enjoyed the freewheeling lifestyle of the island that he put a down payment on a portside building that he felt inspired to turn into a bar, and fittingly planned to call "Sharks."

The damage caused by Fernand's last visit was fresh in his mind. It was also an inherently repugnant notion to Legros that anyone else be happier than he was, so, if he were miserable, he would do his best to make those around him equally miserable. At that time, Elmyr probably would have signed over his soul to any other bloodsucking monster to get Legros and his hyenas off the island. It was now perfectly clear that the dynamic between the two men had irretrievably changed. Fernand's career as an art dealer essentially ended with the debacle of Pontoise. Both men, aware that the other could no longer be a source of income, saw no need for the phony cordialities that had previously allowed a civil but dysfunctional relationship. Fernand, on the other hand, was far more disposed to instantly dropping the kid-glove treatment of his now-former partner and showing the bare-knuckle brutality of his nature. Elmyr pleaded with him to leave, that his presence would certainly bring Interpol agents to his front door. Legros not only laughed at his nervous appeal, he responded matter-of-factly that if he went to jail for thirty days, or thirty years, nothing would give him greater pleasure than to take Elmyr with him.

While Elmyr anguished over the infernal agreement he made with Legros concerning ownership of La Falaise, it now became a battleground in their mutually destructive struggle. The private contract that allowed him lifetime residence and use of the home also stipulated that it be in Legros's name. He in turn had no legal right to sell the property without Elmyr's accord. This did not stop him from relinquishing ownership to his former companion to settle a stack of IOUs he held from Fernand. Whoever held the strategic high ground of the villa could then conceivably dump vats of boiling oil on the other two assailants below its stone ramparts.

Elmyr once again fled the island in desperation. Despite Fernand's quixotic thought processes and behavior tailored to his personal design, his view of life was uncomplicated. There were no ambiguous shades of gray; everything was black or white. People were either with him or against him. The agility of his mind was perhaps never as evident as in the inventiveness of retributions against his enemies. As if on cue, to aggravate Fernand's growing sense of isolation and pugnacious nature, his longtime lover showed up to claim Elmyr's home. He climbed the stone steps to the front door with his notarized contract transferring the villa to him. Within moments of arriving and brandishing his document, Fernand jumped on the interloper like a territorial tomcat. In the ensuing struggle, Fernand demonstrated he had not forgotten his cabaret kicks. A scratched, bruised, and bitten man fled down the steps and into his car. Grabbing for a souvenir lock of his hair, Fernand reached in through the partially opened car door window and chased him down the driveway before stopping in a cloud of road dust behind the fleeing vehicle.

The battered escapee drove directly to the police station to file a criminal complaint for assault. When the two appeared before the local judge, Fernand, in his own defense to the charges, told the sober-minded court official, "He used to love it when I bit him." The humor of this might have disappeared in translation as he was sentenced to two to fifteen days in jail for disturbing the peace. While Legros dutifully reported to the local jail to serve his sentence, his battered victim returned to his hotel to pack his bags and hastily took a cab to the airport rather than share a cell with Fernand.

Ibiza's prison, located within the old citadel of Ibiza town, was actually a quaint old building with a sun-filled courtyard. Its incarcerated guests could bring personal effects from home as they liked such as beds, sheets, clothing, chairs, books, etc. They could also have friends or family bring meals into the prison for them. Fernand brought Elmyr's stereo, records, cashmere sweaters, and tableware from La Falaise to use during his stay. In a seemingly out-of-body experience, he dignified himself as a model prisoner, so they consequently released him two days before the end of his sentence for good behavior. Waving a fond farewell to his fellow inmates and new recipients of his largesse and Elmyr's belongings, he walked back to La Falaise. His early and unexpected arrival set off a chain of events more in keeping with the real Fernand Legros.

As he entered the house, he immediately spied some young women sunbathing nude around the pool. Like an unleashed greyhound after a hare, he dashed through the sliding glass door, emitted a blood-curdling scream that caused everyone else to shriek in unison, and chased terrified naked girls around the pool. In an effort to escape the rampaging maniac, one unclothed creature flew through the open front door and down the steps with Fernand in hot pursuit. She had managed to get into her car and start it before Fernand pulled her out, pushed her away, and released the vehicle's hand brake. Then, happily watching it roll down the driveway, it careened off the road and down a steep hill—crashing into a military barracks and exploding in flames. Thinking they were under attack, soldiers burst out of their quarters and charged up the hill like Marines on Iwo Jima. Sirens from fire trucks racing to the scene brought dumbfounded spectators from their homes in amazement to view the Sunday morning spectacle occurring at the house where Elmyr tried in vain to live discreetly. Enraged by Fernand's one-man assault on the hung-over poolside guests, the young American, who abetted his escape from France and found himself implicated in the Pontoise scandal, unaffectionately threw the berserk Legros down the steps. Fernand's screams of rage turned into screams of pain as he grabbed his now-broken ankle. Following the Spanish infantry and fire department were the police and an ambulance. His coming-home party could not have had more panache if he had planned the whole thing himself.

It would not have surprised Elmyr if Legros set an unbroken record for the shortest time between the release and re-arrest of someone for criminal activity in the lengthy history of Ibiza. Besides the speedy reunion with his somewhat stunned cellmates, the unamused judge seized his portside bar and a $12,000 Chris-Craft speedboat he had brought to the island for compensatory damages.

It was understandable that his former lover thought it better to be a fugitive from Spanish justice than be incarcerated with his unhinged and combative partner. He nevertheless had the documentation to right-fully assume ownership of the villa and was not about to surrender his claim to the expensive piece of real estate. Despite the daunting pros-pect of jousting again with Fernand and paying the price of fleeing the long arm of the law, he returned to the island in November. With con-siderable apprehension, I imagine, he drove up the hilltop road to La Falaise, nervously climbed the stone stairs, and knocked on the door. When Fernand opened it, once more finding his favorite sparring part-ner standing there, he immediately looked past him for any loitering witnesses and then invited him in.

Tucked down below the front of the villa in a cluster of trees was the small home of a German woman named Manon. She was one of the earliest foreign residents, lived with about thirty cats, and drank incessantly. According to Elmyr, she had little else to do than lie about drunk and call each of her cats by name all day long. She was also well within earshot of anything occurring at the house and apparently called the police often while Fernand stayed there. Like the haunting refrain of a children's lullaby, Manon soon heard the familiar strains of The Concerto for Untuned Screams emanating from the villa next door. It was more painful-sounding than serenading alley cats in heat and occasionally punctuated with a crescendo of breaking glass, definitely one of those atonal, dissonant modern pieces that real music lovers abhor. She politely waited for the performance to conclude before calling the police. When they arrived, they seized their fugitive from justice. Fernand stood like a haloed Russian icon pointing his finger at his bleeding but alleged attacker. The two police officers already knew Legros well and received lovely cashmere sweaters from him.

His friend made the acquaintance of his fellow prisoners in the town jail while serving his previous fifteen-day sentence. Fernand, feeling perhaps a bit remorseful after their scrap the day before, strode confidently into the prison to see how he was enjoying his new accommodations. He arrived not alone, but with a nearby restaurant owner who carried a large pan of paella. His glowering friend stood in the courtyard below. Fernand displayed his charming, toothy smile and shouted down, "I thought you might like a little lunch, so I brought you something. Unfortunately, I changed clothes and left all my money in my other pants. If you could send up three hundred pesetas he says you can have it." He put three rumpled hundred-peseta bills in a basket, and the food was then lowered to him. "Hope you like it!" Fernand shouted as he left. An echoing riposte of "Screw you!" followed.

The following day, Fernand left for London. Only later, after Elmyr returned, did he get the staggering bill for all of Fernand's long-distance phone calls. The most frequent and lengthy conversations were between Legros and his Paris attorney, who kept him apprised of the steadily deteriorating situation in France. His apartment with its red-flocked walls and gold faucets was now gone. His Mid-Eastern affectations and life style of a pasha, so intertwined with his image and ego, vanished. The police had confiscated the artwork and issued an international warrant for his arrest the day he departed the island. What items of Elmyr's that he did not care to take, he gave away to others. This included a West Highland white terrier given to Elmyr by a friend. None of the material goods stolen from him was as dear as his dog that he left in the care of his housekeeper whenever he was away. It was Fernand's way of exacting revenge on the man who helped make him rich. His vengefulness did not stop here.

In a London warehouse, Legros still had a crate of artwork left over from his trip to South Africa. He had his shipping agent send it on to

Cairo, his new destination, where he would be safe from extradition. He then flew from the UK to Egypt where, for the next three months, he divided his time between Cairo and the city of his birth, Ismalia. If the French government wanted to cause him problems, he could claim Egyptian citizenship. It was his international safe house.

For the almost seven months Legros appropriated his island home, Elmyr wandered through Europe. It seemed the newspapers in Switzerland, Germany, and France insistently refreshed people's memories periodically by publishing the story of the Pontoise scandal, the notorious art dealer Fernand Legros, and discoveries of fake art cropping up in renowned public and private collections. The sensational revelations haunted him wherever he went. The bad news was inescapable. While he had little money left from what his friends had loaned him, he did not dare sell anything. He would have better luck selling matches in the middle of a forest fire. Now, the conflagration Legros's greed ignited threatened to consume him. He felt trapped in a nomadic limbo, at least until Fernand left Ibiza. During his absence from Spain, Elmyr engaged a Parisian attorney to negotiate with Fernand to vacate La Falaise. All the letters and pleading phone calls were unsuccessful, until one day a friend informed him that Fernand had left the house and the island. At last, he could go home.

In late October, Elmyr once more showed up at the Alhambra Café and Hotel Montesol terraces to catch up on the local gossip. Only now, he was at its center. The French newspaper *L'Aurore* identified him by name as the painter who had done all the fakes that had the whole art world buzzing. Everyone was eager for more details, but he was suffering an unusual bout of reticence.

I suspect few places on earth provided as fertile ground for the counterculture values of the swinging sixties as did Ibiza. However open and transparent its atmosphere appeared, the local authorities were every bit as curious about what its residents were doing as was its loquacious café society. Spain was still a very well-informed and organized police state under its omnipotent dictator, Generalissimo Francesco Franco. Elmyr's activities and growing reputation did not pass unnoticed. One point he consistently stressed for the home crowd was that he never did any fake paintings in Spain and sold nothing there. This was a mantra he uttered repeatedly. I have my suspicions about its veracity, but I cannot be certain. It was more accurately the keystone of his defense to avoid prosecution for criminal activity and expulsion from the country. If the courts could unequivocally disprove his assertion, they would send him to prison. The State, however, could not prosecute him for those crimes without a preponderance of evidence and perhaps, most glaringly, they could produce no witnesses who would corroborate those charges.

For a brief moment, Elmyr waltzed through the radioactive fallout from the scandal that pegged the needle of any Geiger counter in Fernand's vicinity. His temporary luck was about to change. In June, officials in Madrid initiated an investigation of Elmyr and determined that he had not broken any laws. Since his association with Legros was well established, his link to a known criminal brought his case to a court for *Vagos y Malientes*, meaning "vagrants and undesirables." His circle of friends in Ibiza rallied round him. A number of actors, writers, artists, business owners, and local government officials signed a letter attesting to his good character. Other influential people in Madrid did the same. The indictment against him consisted of three accusations: consorting with known criminals, having no visible means of support, and homosexuality. The collective display of support of so many people bolstered his confidence. For him, it was, after all, that social network of those he liked and respected that was his psychological and emotional safety net. His reliance on who one knows never seemed as crucially important as it did at this time.

His lawyer vigorously defended him on all counts. It was the unwitting testimony of his friend Princess Smijlia Michalovich that took the inadvisable tact of admitting that Elmyr *was* homosexual, but "so was Julius Cesar, Michelangelo, Leonardo da Vinci…" However delighted she may have been with her grasp of history, this rationalization apparently did not favorably impress the judge. He consequently sentenced Elmyr to serve two months in jail. While the court did not expel him from Spain, he had to leave Ibiza for one year. Amazingly, none of this had anything to do with his fakes.

With a gesture of lenience, the judge allowed Elmyr a few days to put his affairs in order before he reported to the jail to serve his sentence. An appreciably dispirited artist elected to give a dinner party for his friends who demonstrated unflagging support throughout his travails. That evening each of his guests assured him they would continue to assist him however they could during and after his incarceration. One comforting thought dulled his depression: his prison term was only eight weeks, not eight years. He would somehow get through the difficult two months ahead. Together, he and his steadfast friends dined around his massive mahogany table, savoring his famous Hungarian chicken paprika and drinking robust Spanish red wine. The conversation was understandably less animated than usual.

One of his many daily visitors later captured a vivid impression of his sojourn in Ibiza's jail. According to Irving's account, he said, "Around the periphery of the courtyard, many of the prisoners, young people mostly there for drug possession, sat listlessly in the shade. Elmyr sat in one of his patio chairs in the bright sunlight, wearing white shorts, short-sleeve polo shirt, and dark sunglasses, reading yesterday's copy of *Le Monde*. The only thing missing was his morning coffee and croissant." He once more proved he was not only a survivor, but also a gentleman, displaying his irrepressible class despite his current predicament. His visiting friend also reported that Elmyr cheerily exclaimed, "My dear, can you guess how many visitors I had yesterday? Fourteen!"

Shortly after his liberation from jail, Elmyr arranged to lease La Falaise to an American woman during his imposed twelve-month exile. Life was not as bleak as this suggests. His new notoriety prompted an international interest in him and his art. As Clifford Irving worked on his biography in 1968, the American magazine *LOOK* published a lengthy article about his exploits. The world's curiosity about Elmyr de Hory was not yet satisfied.

A few weeks after he returned to Ibiza in September 1969, I met him. That chance encounter changed my life, and from my perspective, things were about to get a lot more interesting.

Part Two

Elmyr introduced me to his world and his friends. Well, his world *was* his friends, a Jackson-Pollock splash of people, and he collected them in the same way static electricity attracts all forms of matter, though, he thought their presence in his life was the result of a conscious act, the product of free choice to admit those individuals into *his* private realm. This perception served his ego, but a history of dicey choices should have taught him differently. He was charming, articulate, well educated, and easily convinced of his own rationalizations. This last part was not immediately apparent to me. However, as my emotional commitment to him grew, I tried to maintain some clarity in the shadow of Elmyr's influence and help him avoid the tiger traps of his misjudgment. And that wasn't always easy to do.

Meeting a stream of new people every day became as predictable as breakfast. One evening we drove to Santa Eulalia, a small town where some friends of his owned a restaurant. There, a group of people joined us. With pride in his voice, he said, "Mark, I would like you to meet Princess Smijlia Michalovich." Elmyr was good enough to prime me on court etiquette earlier, as you never know when you might need it. She extended her right arm toward me. At the end of her rigid limb dangled

163

a limp hand in a way I might otherwise have thought injured in a farm accident. I was then supposed to bend from the waist and *pretend* to kiss her hand. No puckering or drooling, just swoop in like a bat going for a mosquito. Oh, in order to give the impression that I was *way* used to doing this in Minnesota, Elmyr had me practice on him a few times before we left the house. "No problem," I thought, just like that toy duck that repeatedly dips its bill in the water glass and bobs back up. Well, it worked.

Smijlia was a forever-blond woman of self-ordained royalty with the blue blood of Queen Latifa. She claimed to be a princess, a Montenegrin Anastasia of sorts. After years of practice, affected body language revealed her idea of regal carriage through deliberate and self-conscious movement in a weird kind of Central European Tai Chi. A rumor, most likely started by her, that she had been the lover of "Peter of Yugoslavia," made her believe, according to Elmyr, that she had been impregnated with royal blood. Everyone humored her and treated her with the respect accorded her title. Even though I was used to Elmyr's enthusiasm for aristocratic name-dropping, "Peter of Yugoslavia" sounded like a Beverly Hills hairdresser.

In one of the newer high-rise apartment buildings near the Bay of Figueretas, she held court, receiving her tolerant friends, and was always elegantly dressed and well coiffed. Her exalted charade and pretense to a station beyond her birthright, while accepted with a wink and a nod by others, was not all that sustained her many friendships. Underneath the mask of theatrical artifice was an inherently warm and caring person, and it was these qualities that held those in her entourage close to her. When greeting guests at her small but chic apartment, and commonly wearing a form-fitting gray velvet pantsuit with a white blouse, she would, with a slow sweeping gesture of her arm, invite visitors to take a seat. The only catch was there was nary a place to sit for the small tables everywhere overflowing with collected objects in polished silver. They were, I thought, given her modest means, the most affordable symbols of stately comfort within her reach. Her livelihood, however indistinct, was the product of her wits. In keeping with her high social standing, she would insinuate herself in organizing various civic functions as a kind of Chamber of Commerce plenipotentiary and fund-raiser.

In contrast to her carefully stage-managed image, Smijlia deigned to take on a French lover barely taller than a dwarf, who seemed better cast as her court jester. His only redeeming quality, we all assumed, was his wealth, which, as Elmyr liked to say, was "a good explanation but a poor excuse." He was nouveau riche and a Latin version of a used-car salesman who frequently forgot which direction of his trouser zipper meant "closed." Once invited to lunch at Elmyr's for no reason I can remember, he demonstrated the same table manners as participants in a State Fair pie-eating contest. He then proceeded to suck clean every metacarpal of every finger as though they were stuck in a cow-milking machine. We sat dumbstruck, as silent as the prairie. After he left, we all agreed that your average cannibal would look like Emily Post next to our departed guest.

These entertaining theatrics were a part of everyday life on the island. There, the characters performed without charge, unscripted, as walk-ons in each other's plays, and no one suffered from stage fright. Everyone, or so it seemed, was used to role-playing, not just Elmyr. This was one reason his parties were so fun. They were like Venetian masquerade balls, difficult to distinguish the actor from one's real identity, which likely increased Elmyr's comfort zone, blurring reality and fantasy. They also provided me with opportunities to practice all my lessons of social etiquette "expected of a gentleman," as he reminded me. Despite feeling an inner discomfort with some of these newly acquired affectations, he beamed at my apparent mastery of these maneuvers in the same way the stage mother of a talentless child is blind to imperfections obvious to everyone else.

Since in Elmyr's company I was learning about all things Hungarian, perhaps I shouldn't have been surprised to discover more of his fellow expatriates cropping up on Ibiza. Another Hungarian friend of his was Ançi Dupres. "She started life as a *putain* [whore] as he described her colorful past. It was still easy to see how this diminutive blond woman with limpid blue eyes attracted admirers. One seduced by her beauty was François Dupres, owner of Paris's three premier hotels, the George V, Tremoille, and Plaza Athenée. Their marriage conferred a respectability that often accompanies wealth. She, along with a close-knit group of friends from Avenue Foche, bought summer homes on the island.

They flew down from Paris to Ibiza each summer like a flock of Canada geese. Never tiring of each other's company, they took turns entertaining their clique in their seaside cul-de-sac in a sort of incestuous conviviality. I thought their enchantment with themselves a bit bizarre, as though they felt compelled to maintain the purity of the gene pool. Ançi's being Hungarian, however, made her a member of an even more exclusive tribe, so she and Elmyr automatically enjoyed a hometown familiarity, quacking away in a language indecipherable to everyone else. Although, in contrast to Elmyr's spontaneous largesse, she was as avaricious as she was rich. When her husband died, she not only inherited his hotels, but a home in Deauville, a stable of 125 thoroughbred horses, and a private house in Paris with museum-quality furnishings and an impressive art collection. Her adopted interest in art animated long conversations in their cryptic Magyar tongue with Elmyr.

The degree of familiarity with callers was evident in the fake hand-kissing or the cozy French cheek-pecking. One day Ançi arrived with the usual gaggle in tow. I rushed downstairs, opened the front door, and promptly forgot which cheek to kiss first. I lunged into her headlong. She parried, avoiding a bloody collision. We weaved and bobbed like two flamingoes in courtship until I finally kissed her forehead as the Holy Father might a supplicant.

Elmyr prepared his famous chicken paprika for lunch that afternoon. "The secret," he confided, "is the paprika. You must use the Hungarian sweet paprika. Nothing else will do." Everyone knew his prowess as a gourmet chef, so an invitation to dine with him and enjoy his charm, hospitality, and conversation was a coveted treat for those invited to the house. He also sensed any opportunity to sell his artwork. Ançi was a bargainer, a master of getting what she wanted and paying as little as possible. "Leave it to an ex-whore to know the value of a franc," he once said after a down-market haggling session with her. Their body language needed no translation while the two discussed a tentative transaction. After much eye rolling and head shaking, punctuated by an emphatic "yes" or "no" in Hungarian, they reached an agreement on a price that seemed to satisfy both. Their verbal sparring concluded before we sat down to eat. Elmyr later used his own favorite malapropism to describe her reaction to their negotiation, "She looked like the cannery that swallowed the cat."

On one of her visits to Elmyr's studio, she noticed a portrait Elmyr had done of Simone Vogue. She resembled Catherine Zita-Jones and Elmyr had captured this in a head-and-shoulders painting. It was a sensuous tour de force, revealing her long neck, bare shoulders, large brown eyes, full lips, slightly cleft chin, and silken hair that rested on her shoulders. Her beckoning regard captivated the viewer. It thrilled me. Like Gainsborough's portraits, she wore an oversize flowered chapeau, a colorful counterpoint to her English rose complexion. The picture remained in Elmyr's studio, rejected by her husband as too romantic. He returned it, and Elmyr did something entirely different. This time a scarf covered her hair, the colors bold in wide brush strokes. Elmyr was happy to keep the first portrait. Ançi then asked Elmyr to paint her portrait. He told her he could do something similar. "No," she insisted that he use *that* painting, probably thinking it would cost less, as he merely needed to paint in her face. They argued in Hungarian and, predictably, he conceded. The result was a disaster—George Washington in a bonnet. She of course hated it and refused to pay for it. Wealth, power, hubris, self-indulgence, and vanity trapped her in a Dorian Gray perception of her past beauty, although not even Elmyr's cosmetic brushwork could mitigate the forty years' difference in age between her and Simone.

We first met Ançi at the home of David Stein. His brother Jules owned MCA, Music Corporation of America. David, apparently, had also been involved in the business, but was now retired. Some years before, he discovered Ibiza. The little known island was unspoiled by tourists then. He and Elmyr met there in the early '60s. Elmyr told me, "At that time everyone knew me as an art collector—of independent means," he said through a smile. "I asked David why he wanted to live in such a remote area." He found a lot on the waterfront in a pine-covered cove. "Because no one will build out here," he told Elmyr. The parcel of land he purchased was slightly bigger than the house he wanted to build. "David," he questioned again, "why don't you buy more land? You can afford it." The reason was the Achilles heel of many wealthy people I began to observe. David was cheap. When Elmyr and I made the trek to his distant home, we drove down an alleyway, as the house was now sandwiched between two large hotels. Elmyr laughed at the poetic justice of it all and was giddy knowing his suggestion was a rare instance of precognition.

The house was a Spanish-style Beverly Hills transplant. David cheerily greeted us, opening the paneled mahogany door to the home's cavernous lobby. Now a suburban requisite, it was then showy and ostentatious, a stagy expression of an entertainment mogul's ego and architectural opposite of the spatial economy of Elmyr's villa, La Falaise. Like a car salesman kicking the tires, David pounded on the stucco wall, claiming that he was the first to introduce reinforced concrete on the island—"a solid epitaph for his headstone," Elmyr thought. He whisked us through a house tour. The white walls, ceiling, polished marble floors, and furniture caused instant snow blindness relieved only by a large bouquet of silk flowers atop his white grand piano. His bathrooms boasted gaudy gold faucets, all done in a Vegas Revival style.

We met David's other lunch guests on his terrace just meters away from the aquamarine Mediterranean. At that time one could not buy the land right to the water's edge, so as we sat and chatted, a constant stream of tourists from the adjacent hotels peered at us with the same proximity and curiosity of the lowland gorillas in the San Diego Zoo leering at an endless parade of weirdly dressed humans. David looked unfazed by the ringside spectators and rather like the giddy matchmaker, introducing Elmyr to the Count and Countess de Chabrol, and the Marquis and Marquise d'Harcourt, Mme. Dupres's fellow colonists. Their family names littered French history. David immediately added, "There were seventeen Marshalls of France between their families."

Given Elmyr's rapture with aristocrats, that afternoon I thought he would faint, or, worse still, start explaining the connectedness of us all from early man to present tense. He stored a mental file of every genealogical detail associated with a world obliterated by transformative events of the twentieth century. His manners and values often seemed closer to 1870, not 1970. It may have been the fragrance of rank and privilege that he found so intoxicating. All this banter about who was related to whom by this or that marriage made my eyes wander in random orbits. Family trees looked like an invasive ground-covering weed without beginning or end, which just happened to be his specialty. I imagined the sun/moon cycles spinning around us, Day-Night-Day-Night. Thankfully, the subject of art came up to redirect the conversation. "Which of the impressionists are you most drawn to?" Count d' Harcourt asked him. Off we went on a stream of consciousness while

Elmyr opined on the French colorists, and they seemed as impressed by his knowledge as they were starstruck by his celebrity.

Elmyr was especially pleased to meet a fellow Hungarian in Ançi Dupres. He had a special view of his compatriots. Even though Prosky, for example, was everything Elmyr was not and the least likely guest in his home, the fact that they both were from that small Central European country made them members of the same club, like Freemasons without the secret handshakes. One symbol identified him as Hungarian, though. He always wore a pinky ring—two, actually: one in platinum and the other in yellow gold. Each had a row of three round-cut gems, separated in their settings. "Whenever you see someone wearing a ring like this," he said, "it means that person is Hungarian."

They all seemed cordial to me that afternoon. Countess de Chabrol asked where I was from. I said "Minnesota," evoking the same blank stares as when you forget what you wanted to say—in mid-sentence. I try to recover in these moments of awkwardness by offering some factoid like "Minnesotans own more reindeer per capita than any other state." This is probably not true, but I trust its uniqueness redeems me from early onset of Alzheimer's or at least from imparting that notion to others. I then mentioned that I planned to visit my family back in the States in a couple of weeks. First, I was going to visit my sister in Detroit. "Do you know the Fords?" she asked. She was dead serious. After checking my memory banks for any missed recollection, I replied, "No." I couldn't help feeling that I was playing Eliza Doolittle to Elmyr's Henry Higgins. The chasm between their lifestyles and my working-class upbringing seemed unbridgeable. While this was my impression at our first meeting, the more I came to know them, the more endearing they became. They were upper crust, for sure, but warm, charming and genuine, I discovered. The d'Harcourt's daughter, Lesline, was an unassuming brunette beauty around my age, and one I quickly fell in love with. Elmyr gave any such liaisons his approval, as long as I set the bar high enough. This reflected his standards, which I was supposed to adopt as well.

At one of their breezy August night soirees, I met Brigitte Bardot, the Bad Girl Sex Kitten of the French cinema. She lived up to my fantasies. Elmyr later told me she asked him, "Who's the beautiful boy?" It was ego polish without equal. What further made the evening memorable was the party's location, a seaside grotto. One had to climb down an impro-vised path that would inspire caution in a mountain goat. Illuminated by flickering candles, danger and death flirted with a wavering sense of balance along the precipitous descent. Bardot, I imagined, expected a stand-in to take such risks and expressed her dismay in emphatic *"C'est pas possible... mon dieu"* (It's not possible, my God) on the way down. Only after the trek back up without the aid of a Sherpa guide did she regain her sans souci demeanor. Elmyr chatted with her while I fixated on her pouty lips and gorgeous body. He asked if she could come to La Falaise for a lunch or dinner. She said she would love to but was return-ing to France the next day.

What I began to observe was that even the privileged few blessed with fame or fortune were not so different from other people. They sought validation, acceptance, and love the same as the rest of us. It was on this emotional plane where I gained an equal footing, allowing me to be comfortable with people I formerly thought unapproachable. However, that first summer was my novitiate, becoming acquainted with many of the island's French contingent. All my private lessons at the Alliance Française made perfect sense to me now.

Ançi entertained us at her home in this enclave of the French Foreign Legion. When she invited us to lunch or dinner, one knew not to ask for seconds. If there were eight people at the table, there would be eight meager portions. No more, no less. God couldn't save you from her serial-killer glare if you asked for more. One conclusion I made early on remained unchanged: she was difficult, spoiled, self-absorbed, and likely capable of harboring grudges that could clog the Bay of Naples. I know she consistently challenged Elmyr's diplomatic skills.

In her home, scores of Haitian primitive paintings hung on her walls. She loved collecting these colorful naïf works for their irrepress-ible cheeriness. Haiti was then, and still is, the poorest country in the Western Hemisphere. Life is near the bone. I have no difficulty imagin-ing her glee at bargaining down the prices of these pictures amid their dire living conditions. She was used to getting whatever she wanted and paying as little as possible for it, even in Haiti.

Once, while I was driving her somewhere, she expressed her upset with Elmyr because he refused to paint a recently acquired "Modigliani" on an authentic period canvas. Anger contorted her face for two reasons;

she was unused to not prevailing in a test of will, and it cost an extra $150 to have the new painting glued to an old canvas. I offered the unacceptable defense that the sum sounded cheap. Her rage was instant and unequivocal. Only twice during those years with Elmyr did I feel my sphincter heat up as it did at that moment.

When she came for her summer getaway, her sister and brother-in-law came along. She gave them a stipend that was probably less than stable costs for one of her horses. She was, in her brother-in-law's words, *la reine des enmerdeuses*. Hard to translate, but the key word there is *shit*. On a solo trip to Paris, she invited me to lunch at her home. Expertly framed and hanging in her stairwell was Elmyr's Modigliani. Again, Elmyr's signature vanished. It bore the signature: Modigliani. She once came to London when Elmyr and I were there and asked if I would help her. For a few hours I was her personal valet, carrying her packages while on a shopping safari at Harrods. After my putting them in her chauffeured Rolls, she said thanks and drove off. Offering me a ride back to where I needed to go didn't occur to her, but I knew her by then, and it didn't surprise me.

Perhaps the most interesting thing about Ançi was her involvement with a society dedicated to the teachings of the mystic philosopher G. I. Gurdgieff, which promised her immortality. Apparently, she intended to leave the bulk of her estate to this group that would thaw her cryogenically preserved body at a future date, thereby allowing an unsuspecting upcoming generation the opportunity to rethink the virtues of life after death.

La Falaise

My first exposure to modern architecture in any meaningful way was my introduction to Elmyr's villa, La Falaise, French for *the cliff*. It sat atop a saddleback hillside at the edge of a precipice. A paean to radical, early twentieth-century design, it seemed oddly placed in this ancient setting. They called the hill where the house stood, *Los Molinos*, "the mills." You could see windmills, perhaps a half dozen, in various states of ruin, reminding one of those formidable foes of Don Quixote in the pages of Cervantes. The remaining foundation of one of these round stone towers just meters from his bedroom terrace was converted to a barbeque pit. Along the spine of the hill was a dirt road, little more than a two-rut goat path. The Romans, who ultimately became the island's governors after displacing the Carthaginians, said of Ibiza that "it was the right size for man," meaning that no part of the island was beyond a human's gait. I have no doubt that for thousands of years every dominant Mediterranean culture trod upon this primitive thoroughfare.

Mark, Elmyr, and Ursula Andress at La Falaise

Historians credit Ibiza as the birthplace of the father of Hannibal, the famous Carthaginian general whose elephants were a precursor to modern tanks and who nearly defeated Rome for supremacy in the western Mediterranean. A British woman who lived nearby once showed me artifacts such as coins and pieces of jewelry she found in the vicinity, reminders of former glory and transience of the flesh. The next hump along this pathway was the necropolis or burial site of toga-wearing residents. My interest in archaeology made it easy for me to become distracted for hours at this timeworn cemetery in hope of finding my own physical remnant of history. A few weeks after meeting Elmyr, I became a regular itinerant on this road, walking daily to the Alliance Française for my French lessons. It was at his urging that I began studying French. He explained its importance in a way that any opposing point of view was inconceivable.

La Falaise faced the old walled city of Ibiza, with its appearance of impenetrability due to its massive, high, and thick stone walls. This looming monument is one of the finest intact fortresses of Europe, dating from the reign of Phillip II, when Spain was in its golden age and the dominant superpower. Its geographically endowed location, overlooking a natural harbor the Romans called "portus magnum," with a commanding view of the surrounding countryside and translucent blue sea, it offered a superbly strategic site along well-traveled trade routes. Consequently, its heritage and continual habitation dates back to Neolithic times.

Ascending stone steps to his front entrance one stood before a late seventeenth-century decoratively carved panel door. The wood's distressed appearance was the authentic by-product of age and use. (I later found out it was another source of conflict between Elmyr and the architect who wanted something simpler, more industrial.) Strangely juxtaposed to the slightly recessed entrance was the home's exterior facade, a whitewashed flat plane interrupted by a large glass window bisected by a thin black vertical line. It was twice the width of the door and about a half-meter above it, but still left one clueless as to its interior space.

This visually chaste style of architecture had a name—Bauhaus. At the time, this meant little to me. I just thought it was a cool house to live in. Today, its minimalist lines send shivers through me, this invention of ascetic German shut-ins, intellectual sadomasochists wearing pince-nez glasses and peach fuzz haircuts, deprived of sunlight and human contact and able to drink cod liver oil without wincing, I suspect. This, however, may be an overly sentimental view. La Falaise's creator, Irwin Brauner, a German architect, was a student of Walter Gropius, the founder of the Bauhaus school of design.

It is easier to understand and appreciate the thrust of this minimalist aesthetic in its historical and cultural context. In a kind of academic revolt against the visual gluttony of nineteenth-century art and design, early twentieth-century creative activists thought an emetic was needed in order purge this corpulent excess and Victorian hangover. Their response, as in Gustav Stickly's furniture, George Braque and Pablo Picasso's cubist paintings, the Japanese idea of "less is more" gathered currency. "Simplicity rules!" was the mantra that animated the Bauhaus philosophy.

More than forty years after entering La Falaise, I think of it as an expression of predominantly straight-line architecture, a paradigm of simple geometry—its right angles rarely punctuated by a curved line but, perhaps, only then by testosterone-deficient effetes unable to resist the feminine side of their nature. Brauner, being a good soldier of this rigid mind-set, came prepared for battle. Armed with the self-righteous dogma of a fundamentalist, those not in agreement with his design notions he dismissed altogether. This set the stage for Olympian clashes between two strong-willed individuals. It was easy to imagine the echoing, thunderous cracks of head-butting Alpine rams, challenging each other in territorial dispute.

Elmyr's world was that of figurative art, interpretively rendering nature and the human form based on reality. Reading schematics was not part of his visual vocabulary, so deciphering Brauner's blueprints for La Falaise was not easy. Therefore, he was compelled to express his design wishes in oral arguments in vociferous German before his unmoved and stone-faced architect. Looking over the house plans one day Elmyr noticed a small square with WC, indicating water closet or toilet printed on it. It was the quintessential, no-frills-needed room in the home, to Brauner's thinking. Questioning him about its phone-booth size, Brauner responded, "You need it for one simple function. It doesn't have to be *big!*" Elmyr's rejoinder was, "When I'm there I don't just want to read *Reader's Digest*; I would also like to read the *New York Times!*" Another unwelcome assertion followed. The master bathroom was absent a bidet. Brauner's retort: "*You* don't *need* a bidet!" After considerable verbal arm-twisting, Elmyr prevailed. He enlarged the room to accommodate one. I am sure Brauner was greatly chagrined seeing his precious spatial economy sacrificed to petty whims.

(Hitler, by the way, was none too keen on his contemporaries advancing what he deemed "degenerate art." That included Gropius's Bauhaus group. Since Hitler had only one testicle, he knew a thing or two about what was abnormal. Having been a house painter along with producing a handful of landscapes and still-life paintings, and a self-ordained avatar of Teutonic culture, he was also unequivocal about what art was supposed to be. He chose the architect Albert Spear as his paladin to realize a redesigned Berlin in a classical Greek style and would have nothing to do with avant-garde thinking. His taste in art also reflected his own swivel-eyed vision of Aryan taste. Judging from the many officially sanctioned commissions by good Nazi artists, they strongly suggested that the new Reich's inhabitants felt no compunction to wear any clothes at all!)

When the villa was nearing completion in late 1964, Brauner approached Elmyr, soliciting a design change. He not only considered himself a world-class architect but also a world-class artist (a widely held view among, well, him and his wife). He thought Elmyr should buy some of his large abstract oil paintings and prominently display them in his home. This epiphany simply required more wall space. The plan originally called for a wall-to-wall bank of windows in the second-floor living room. Through these south-facing windows, shafts of sunlight would cascade in, filtered by the branches and leaves of two ancient olive trees just a few meters from the side of the house. The clarity of the air and quality of light was what attracted artists like Picasso, Matisse, Dufy, Delacroix, and others to the Mediterranean region. Beyond the trees lay the garden, the freshly excavated site of the first swimming pool on the island and an expansive view of a blue sea. With the whisk of a pencil eraser, it could all be gone, replaced with a solid wall on which to display his architect's "wretched art," as Elmyr described it. His response: "Are you mad?"

The austere, enigmatic exterior did little to prepare one for the shock that accompanied opening the front door. Immediately, the angular planes and crisp lines of the foyer directed one's attention, as if looking through an open-ended box, through a wall of glass, into a verdant oasis of semi-tropical plants, succulents, fig, mimosa, carob, olive trees, yucca, agaves, and hanging geraniums, sunlight and water everywhere. The stark construction, an invention of man's mind, was no longer in competition but in harmony with nature. One felt at peace—spiritual.

Frank Lloyd Wright coined the term "organic architecture," a concept advocating a compatible coexistence between fabricated structures and their environment. While Wright's Prairie School philosophy shares some common threads with the tenets of Bauhaus design, such as hard line geometric minimalism and spatial economy, Wright dismissed any comparisons between them. His stand-alone genius and accompanying megalomania compelled him to suggest that any stylistic similarities to him—i.e., Le Corbusier, Gropius, Mies van der Rohe, et al.—was the product of also-ran imitators borrowing from a cannon of design principles he alone had invented. Then, Wright was likely to think the chap staring back from a mirror was not as clever as he was.

I believe what made the overall design of La Falaise work so successfully was that it reached a treaty between abstract thinking and a gracious acquiescence to the natural beauty of the home's setting. Brauner remained faithful to his teacher and executed a clean-lined residence whose spaces were functional, unpretentious, and simple. He even softened its appearance by introducing rare but strategically placed curves: a short, rounded wall on the second floor above its open stairwell and a semi-circular wall for a rooftop solarium. Apart from its low, flat ceiling and off-white ceramic floor tile that gave the house a seamless continuity as it covered the expanse from the front door, through the garden to about the pool's edge, the structure became essentially a three-sided shadow box. The abundance of glass and openness to its southern exposure, however, made one feel more like an actor on stage under nature's powerful spotlight. Heavy, double-lined, pale gold draperies that glided easily along a small track attached to the ceiling diminished summer sunlight and heat.

Under the living room's south-facing windows was a bookshelf, a meter high and wide as the room itself. In the middle beside it were two matching natural leather easy chairs facing each other. Elmyr began selecting reading material from these shelves, compiling a must-read list of great authors. It became my new college course, "Introduction to European Literature."

Separating the chairs was a cushion-height trestle table, nothing fancy, just a plain wooden table a little darker than the chairs, the kind that invited you to put your feet on it to relax. Perpendicular to that seating area was a long, raised stone hearth approximately a half-meter high. A full-view glass door at the southwest corner accessed a second-floor terrace and balcony that wrapped halfway around the south side of the house. Adjacent to where the hearth stopped and thin metal door frame began, a flat, steeply angled, white stucco-textured fireplace hood about two meters wide vented large wood fires during the mild but often damp winter days and nights. The heat from those fires warmed and comforted us as we read, lounging like country squires.

It was this home and its friendly atmosphere, with a caring mentor to guide me that made an education gain an appeal it never had for me in school. And what an education it turned out to be.

Island Life

By the summer of 1970, life with Elmyr began to assume a recognizable pattern. His rise to fame made him a local supernova and there was little evidence of any foreseeable burnout. The path to his house was like the runway of a Paris fashion show, with callers eager to bask in his glow. Many were rich, glamorous, famous, titled, and fashionable—or not. Some, like Prosky, hoped to capitalize on his celebrity. I soon learned that good judgment is not an inherent trait like eye color. For Elmyr, its absence made each day a game of chance whose risks were unpredictable. For all the good people and true friends he attracted before or during the time I knew him, it had more to do with luck and happy accident than design. He liked to say, "Friendships are easy to make, hard to keep." Those who stuck with him remained faithful for the same reasons that form the glue of any relationship—generosity, kindness, empathy, common interests, reliability, etc.—and the success of those friendships were due more by virtue of their appreciation of his humanity, not his fame.

Since he became a recognized personage, people knew where to find him. He had a postal box he checked each day. The volume of mail often exceeded its available space. One day he picked up an envelope addressed: *Elmere, pintor, España.* Despite the lack of any specificity of address, the bulk of letters found its way there as dependably as in a small town where everyone knows everyone else. This is not to imply that expediency was part of the equation. Sometimes delivery took months. This quaint feature of the Spanish postal service was also certainly the product of some personal touch automation could not replicate.

Once, Elmyr and I went to pick up his mail after an absence of several days. The postal director came out, gesticulating with great excitement and urgency, and exclaimed, "Señor Elmyr, Señor Elmyr, thank you for coming to get your mail. A number of my people have been very upset and threatened to go home if I did not do something about your package!" We had no idea what the distraught fellow was rattling on about. We collected the amassed correspondence along with a brown-paper-wrapped box and placed everything on the car's backseat. The package seemed battered from its journey. While driving away I looked at the rearview mirror. It was odd, I thought, to see the director standing in the dusty road, waving a fond farewell, or maybe waiting to see if we would leap from the moving vehicle—an unsurprising possibility with Elmyr's little clown car. A smell of putrefaction engulfed the car's interior. We shared a look of horror as I floored the accelerator, racing the short distance home as though the car were in flames. Arriving at the house, we leaped out, stood away from the vehicle, and wondered about the source of this smelly assault. I picked up the carton and held it at arm's length like it was my first day on the bomb squad. (I am sure instances like this justified my presence.) The last time I whiffed anything comparable to this disgusting odor came from a commercial hog farm in Minnesota, a smell so repulsive it must damage the central nervous system. It seems Elmyr's friend Eugene Weinreb, while unmindful of the Ox Cart Express mail delivery system the Spanish Post Office sometimes employed, was nevertheless thoughtful to send him a gift. Inside was a collection of Switzerland's deadliest cheeses that, even when fresh, would send cadaver dogs fleeing with their tails between their legs. Unfortunately, the well-intentioned offering meandered along a circuitous and halting path on its way to the island, leaving, I suspect, an ever-growing contingent of misfortunate victims in the wake of this natural disaster.

Elmyr liked to say, "Le fromage n'est pas bon si ça se promene pas." (Cheese is not good if it doesn't walk!) This lot was definitely at a gallop. He dutifully opened the various foil-wrapped delights with brown liquid oozing from their seams. Like a desensitized surgeon who lost his nose to leprosy, he judiciously whittled away at the decaying matter. I no longer recall if the tears welling up in his eyes were because of the noxious fumes or his lost hope of salvaging some edible remnant. Alas, we had to discard every bit of our comestible variety pack shortly after its long-delayed arrival. The recalcitrant odor, however, lingered like a guest who didn't know when to leave. We each, like Lady Macbeth, washed our hands with OCD vigor, all to no avail. For having touched the organic goo, we could rid the stench from our hands only by using some of Elmyr's mineral spirits, no longer used uniquely for cleaning the oil paint from his hands and brushes.

Disposing of the aromatic surprise was another matter. The early seventies might well have been an ecological awakening of sorts for some people, but it was not the widely embraced cause célèbre we know today. In Ibiza, at least, it was not. Garbage collection was selective, and outside the towns it had changed little since Roman times. People burned or buried their refuse. When I began living at La Falaise we were scrupulously neat and clean. The house had every civilized amenity for which the twentieth century had shamelessly spoiled us. When household debris filled the white plastic bags in their small containers, I would remove them, tie them closed, take them outside down the steps, and casually throw them over the cliff. Some of their contents were jarred loose from their sacks and became lodged in clinging cliff-side vegetation and rocks, creating a giant collage of multicolored garbage. The sort of thing the artist Cristo might do if he were a slob.

In many ways Elmyr was like the proverbial absentminded professor. Shortly before my arrival, he made the trek to the short stone wall that encircled the house, making it a kind of medieval rampart for pygmies. At its lowest point, below the swimming pool, he stood with the bag of trash in one hand, his eyeglasses clenched in the other. Then, with the deliberate move of a shot-putter, he launched his glasses into space, only for them to plummet downward among other errant reminders of conspicuous consumption. Upon hearing his account of the incident, I thought it was enormously funny. Enjoying my laughter less than I did, he reminded me that if I had been present two weeks earlier, he would have had me go look for them. Far from being an annoyance, his occasionally spacey lapses of concentration were part of his charm and, though unwittingly, a source of amusement. For example, one ritual of personal hygiene he regularly enjoyed was washing his feet in the bidet. He had just finished filling it with warm water for his footbath when the phone rang one morning. Rushing to answer it, he then became engaged in a long, distracting conversation. When he finished his animated dialogue, he promptly returned to his bathroom and then immersed one foot into the toilet.

When I began helping him with the ever-increasing demand on his time by responding to requests from people for his paintings, he often asked me about sentence structure, spelling, or other mystifying quirks of the English language. There were some things that I would repeatedly tell him, but they defied his remembering. Although he was fluent in the language and possessed a wealthy vocabulary, there were just some things that would cause a cerebral hiccup for him. For no apparent reason he would consistently refer to the "kitchen" door as the "chicken" door. After a few corrections, I thought the little malapropism was too cute to change. When feeling overwhelmed he would also say, "I can't scoop with it" instead of "cope." He would then turn to me for affirmation, asking, "Is that right?" to which I always said yes.

His French, German, and, of course, Hungarian were flawless. He basted English in a slight Hungarian accent but not appreciably. I forever marveled at the ease of transition with which he moved from one language to another. With no forethought or notice, he glided effortlessly among them. Spanish was the outstanding exception to this rule. They commonly say younger minds more easily learn languages. I am not sure why this linguistic skill failed him when it came to Spanish. Maybe it was due to his age, or brain fatigue, when he went to Ibiza. More likely it was because the island boasted a large contingent of foreign expatriates with whom he could already converse in English, French, German, and even Hungarian. Most of his Spanish friends spoke first French and then English as second and third languages.

After nine months of intense study, I spoke French fluently. Knowing a foreign language goes deeper than simple communication. It is a key to unlock an entire culture and vehicle to transport you easily within it.

When we would read in the evening and chat about things, the conversation could migrate to French. My accomplishments were his accomplishments, and, with noticeable pride, he asked me to talk to his friends in French. Along with my French lessons, Elmyr gave me his books to study. They, with his constant insights, eased me into the world of visual arts, a world enlivened in his company.

Mark, Elmyr, and Fernando Madurga at the gallery

Given Elmyr's newly acquired high-profile status, a friend suggested he open his own art gallery in Ibiza town. The idea held considerable appeal and would afford him the civic benediction he had always struggled to attain. It made sense. It would offer him a personal forum in which he could not only promote his own work but also the sizeable community of artists on the island, many of whom he had already helped. He found a suitable location. It was a first-floor space (meaning second floor) that was formerly a small residential apartment about a block off the end of the Vara de Rey, Ibiza's principal boulevard and pedestrian thoroughfare. Over our morning coffee at the Montesol, he turned to me and asked what I thought of his new adventure in business. His face signaled what seemed an irresistible billing on the old marquee, "Elmyr—Galeria de Arte Contemporáneo." In his mind's eye he could see himself garnering the same cachet as those Mayfair mavens with real Monets in their gallery windows. While Elmyr thrived on the flurry of social activity of an art exhibit, and he fancied the notion of further legitimizing himself in everyone's eyes, he was really looking to give me a raison d'etre. My new job would be running the gallery, organizing the exhibitions, and seeing if we could make money conventionally and—honestly. It was what he was grooming me for, and, just as important, he wanted to elevate my status from personal aide/bodyguard/gardener to something more respectable. After all, appearances were important to him. Moreover, it worked for the next four years.

As Elmyr juggled success and its side effects, I moved easily between two disparate worlds, one of glamorous society, the other of earthy simplicity and counterculture values. While I smoked hashish with Elmyr that first evening at La Falaise, it was not a routine indulgence for him. Given the precariousness of his past, he thought it wise to avoid blatantly illegal activities. I, on the other hand, was not much inclined to curb my hedonist impulses, being a child of the '60s' psychedelic lifestyle I embraced while in college in California. There was a huge colony of my contemporaries on Ibiza, and I soon made friends with many of them.

Most rented *fincas* (farmhouses) in the countryside. These primitive dwellings starkly contrasted the luxury and creature comforts that quickly became second nature to me. Traditionally, fincas had no indoor plumbing. One fetched water from a well and calls from Mother Nature led one to a latrine away from the house. It is as precariously close to camping as I have ever been and a bit *too* earthy for my liking. Some friends had family money cushioning their back-to-nature forays; many were artists, artisans, or writers who, to my great admiration, demonstrated a self-sufficiency of mind, body, and spirit. All, I believe, thought the trade-off of modern conveniences for a more rustic lifestyle was more than worth it.

This is what they gained: once off the narrow and sporadically maintained ribbons of blacktopped highways, one drove over potholed, switchback roads through pine-covered countryside. Ancient stone terraces followed the contours of the hillsides up to or beyond the paths that ended at the small, secluded houses. Grape vines, and almond, apricot, fig, olive, orange, or lemon trees stippled stair-step swaths of cultivated earth. The fincas often had domed bread ovens covered with chalk-based whitewash resembling layers of phyllo dough. The always-white structures had flat earthen roofs laid on a combination of reeds and wood base, supported underneath by large hewn timbers spanning the room's width and darkened over centuries from fires on a stone or earthen hearth. If one lived in a valley or a plain, the soil had a distinct rust-colored hue. This was the desirable land for cultivation and handed down to the first-born males of the family. Those farther down the pecking order often inherited the useless waterfront property. With the advent of tourism, that didn't seem to be such a raw deal after all. Without exception, every one of these homes offered uninterrupted views of pastoral tranquility and, frequently, vistas of the Mediterranean. We felt privileged having the camaraderie of our friends and a spiritual sense of peace and unspoiled nature around us.

In an uncanny act of natural defense, wild asparagus grew within the root base of thorny thickets—tricky to pick but a succulent organic delight. Rosemary, fennel, garlic, and other herbs grew wild. Many of my friends, with the aid of composting, had organically raised kitchen gardens. All this presaged the mainstream acceptance of these formerly funky notions. They read *Mother Jones Magazine*, the *Whole Earth Catalogue*, and lived off the land. Joni Mitchell visited Ibiza in the early '70s and referenced the island in the song "California" on her album entitled *Blue*. The lyric is, "Went to a party down a red dirt road, there were lots of pretty people there readin' *Rollin' Stone*, reading *Vogue*…" While the counterculture thrived then, it has been supplanted by more materially minded folk, but it is still known as the party capital of Europe. I just do not know if drugs are as prolific as they were then.

Elmyr was tolerant of my foibles and simply asked that I exercise a modicum of discretion and do nothing to reflect poorly on him. It was our understanding, so I tried to be mindful of his wishes. By most appearances, I succeeded. If not, I kept them out of view. While I felt a natural gravitation to my less-formal friends, I gradually absorbed his old-world standard of how a young man should conduct himself. I therefore observed Queen Mary's famous maxim as my guiding rule. She said she didn't care what anyone did so long as one didn't do it in the street and frighten the horses.

There were occasional lapses and my incaution had its consequences. After a summer night fling with a young French woman, I contracted lice. Upon discovery of this, I went directly to the pharmacy. In simple, unambiguous Spanish, I whispered, *Yo tengo peqeños animales abajo*, simultaneously pointing to my genital area. A knowing, Mona Lisa smile fell across the pharmacist's face. He returned with a small bottle of liquid, *Aecete Inglais*—"English Oil." This abhorrent new adventure worsened when I lavished my pubic region with the medicinal-smelling stuff (not at the pharmacy of course). Its blowtorch sensation prompted a spontaneous war dance. Directions on the bottle suggested using it more than once a day and I am sure their author, probably familiar with the manufacturer's laboratory tests, had good reason to smile as he penned them.

The curious product labeling also spoke to the high regard the Spanish had for the English. It was then apparent why a friend of mine and I had such difficulty getting rides when hitchhiking to Barcelona. He had a Union Jack flag on his backpack that was akin to wearing a "kick me" sign on one's back. I was oblivious of the longstanding antipathy between Britain and Spain. Sure, we all knew about the defeat of the Spanish Armada in 1588 in their miserably failed attempt to invade England to get that lot of bandy-legged heretics back into the Catholic fold. Oh, and that Henry VIII was unforgivably nasty to his first wife, Catherine of Aragon, but still feeling chippy after 380 years? Never mind that they also helped lighten the Spaniard's ships of some very heavy New World gold and silver. Furthermore, that little issue of the Brits stealing Gibraltar from them was still working through their system like a Tabasco enema. In addition, weren't the British gracious enough to admit countless Spanish laborers into the UK to seek work as nannies, house cleaners, chauffeurs, and the like? Truly, it was difficult to understand why they were still so miffed.

Writing these recollections, especially when I revisit my less-than-prudent behavior, it is remarkable that so many of us survived our youth. Perhaps because Ibiza was an island with a constantly moving tide of people, a subculture of illegal pursuits flourished in the midst of an Orwellian police state. Franco's dictatorship was rigid and unforgiving of those who broke the law. Drug possession of, say, a pinch of hashish could be punishable by six years and one day in prison. They added one extra day to demonstrate an institutional sense of humor, a gift from the Spanish Inquisition, I suspect. Our abject disregard for the dire consequences of immediate arrest should we be caught by the police for getting a little high, has now been better explained by recent research into brain function. Apparently, the frontal lobe that governs emotional development and behavior like risk-taking and impulse control does not mature until one reaches the age of about twenty-five. This would explain my own blunders in judgment—before that age, anyway.

Café Society

For as small as Ibiza was, I marveled at the variety of its inhabitants, this species we call Homo sapiens. If someone told me a carnival caravan of sideshow oddities overturned somewhere on the island, releasing them to procreate with the local population like rabbits on Ecstasy, I could better understand the confluence of this human circus. The only difference was that the sexual activity of many I knew made the furry critters look less libidinous than geriatric monks. However, instead of paying for a peep at these Barnumesque curiosities of nature, one only had to occupy a chair at any sidewalk café or bar and they would inevitably parade by. It was great entertainment for the price of a beverage. There, gossip was the common currency, and the exchange rate generous. One of Elmyr's favorite haunts was the terrace of the Hotel Montesol. It occupied a strategic corner on the Vara de Rey. It was like the pass at Thermopylae, where almost everyone was obliged to pass by on the way to the port, old city, or the heart of Ibiza town. "Here," Elmyr explained, "everyone minds everyone else's business very intensely. They read each other's mail, their love letters, and they tell who slept with whom and how they did it"—ever the champion of an open society. One of the island's best conduits of this vital information was one of Elmyr's friends, Arlene Kaufman.

Like Elmyr, Arlene exhibited a thirst and salacious curiosity for the tawdriest current news. She was Jewish, a feisty former public school-teacher from Brooklyn who, like many diminutive and inviting-looking creatures, when irritable, could remove your face like a wolverine. She was smart, articulate, and favored rude language for emphasis. We thought her remorseless candor and bare-knuckle invective were part of her charm. In any event, Elmyr savored the intellectual nexus in her company. While sipping a coffee during their morning rendezvous at the Montesol, their conversation topics careened from Kierkegaard, Spinoza, Hemingway, Proust, or world politics to a subject for which she demonstrated untiring interest and personal experience—ORGASM. Never before, or since, have I heard someone so compelled to expound on this bodily function with the same wonder and respect. Furthermore, Elmyr had no difficulty following the focus of their chat as it headed south. I always listened, hoping to improve my mind. Maybe it was the deliberate cadence and polished *haute* Brooklyn accent that intoned a note of unimpeachable authority in what she said. She reminded me of Eliza Doolittle in reverse. As owner of La Tierra, the island's most popular bar, Arlene was a celestial body around whom all manner of Ibiza society orbited. In her role as queen of the night scene, she took herself seriously. Consequently, it may have been this perception of self-importance that imparted an oracular flair to her diction. Nevertheless, amour was a domain where most everyone possessed predictable expertise.

Ibiza was a lively Petri dish where people enjoyed sex first and asked for names later. From Elmyr's garden at La Falaise, one could see the flat profile of Formentera, Ibiza's neighboring island. When showing visitors his villa, he often pointed it out from his poolside and asked if they knew what it was. Most responded with a bewildered no. This set up his delighted reply. "It is a secret laboratory where they are trying to develop new strains of venereal disease unresponsive to antibiotics," he informed his guests. We all laughed, impervious to the truth in his joke. Ibiza remains a training camp for hedonists and, I suspect, the least likely place to see an apparition of the Virgin Mary.

At a party one night at Elmyr's, I met Arlene's soul sister, Renee Cohen, a buxom woman who delighted in shocking the locals by showing off her tits with imperturbable pride. She was rumored to be a lover of the Dutch-American artist Willem de Kooning, and, according to Lanny Powers, a longtime Ibiza resident and artist, was the "woman" in de Kooning's *Woman And Bicycle* in the Whitney Museum in New York City. Renee was another expat Brooklynite whose colorful personality matched her profession. She also looked like Bette Midler's twin, and Elmyr loved her company. Renee had been an exotic dancer who preferred a python to a boa. Still, he reveled in rumor-mongering, telling anyone who would listen that "her snake died a mysterious death." He never said it without a twinkle in his eye or an absence of emphasis on the word *mysterious*. Since departing the crimson lights of the catwalk with her serpent, she was ever vigilant and opportunistic about exploring any prospect that looked like a moneymaker. I never saw her fail to engage the attention of any man she wanted, but this probably had more to do with her cantilevered chest than her powers of oratory. Naturally, she tested out a variety of schemes on Elmyr. He may have been irrepressibly gullible, but, fortunately, he demonstrated uncharacteristic restraint in following the investment counsel of an ex-stripper.

One day I ran into Renee in town. She pulled me into a recessed building entrance away from pedestrian traffic and the midday sun. Clutching my shoulders to engage my full attention, she stared into my eyes like an ophthalmologist looking for some defect. I was not used to her serious demeanor and found it a bit creepy. It was more what one might expect from Charles Manson awakened from a deep sleep. Nor could I avoid her mesmerizing gaze. As her grip on my shoulders tightened, I wondered if her snake experienced the same rising sense of alarm as it drew its last breath. Then, figuring the moment ripe with dramatic anticipation, and with all the portent of Lady Macbeth, she uttered, "CEMENT." Since I did not immediately grasp the Delphic significance of what she said, thoughts began to ricochet in my head, looking for that part of my brain that sent a signal to my face revealing comprehension. Instead, I feared I was assuming the vacant look a cocker spaniel might have after electroshock therapy.

I once heard Howard Sackler refer to something "achieving gravitas." I wasn't sure what it meant, but I deduced that it was something grave or hugely important. Then, I twigged to why her otherwise genial personality morphed into this somber other person. Renee, I bet, had been screwing the eyebrows off some Wall Street commodities broker. That's why her cryptic pronouncement possessed the surety of insider trading. While her foray into the world of high finance and market prognostications may have seemed like a right-angle career move, we often needed to shelve our disbelief with the people we knew. In any case, it was clear that I should speedily convey her hot tip to Elmyr lest he lose an opportunity to pad his investment portfolio. The premise of her timely advice was of course sound, if Elmyr had not spent a lifetime demonstrating his slippery grasp of money management.

It was a Dali-esque moment, conveying all the solemnity and import of her announcing she was just designated keynote speaker at a convention of the National Academy of Science. I suppose it would then be as easy to imagine Sir Issac Newton as a pole dancer.

The outdoor tables in front of the Montesol filled each day with all the locals and foreign imports from Central Casting. Another of this group was a charismatic figure that could light up a room like Joan of Arc. Vincente Ribas was one of a handful of native Ibicencos admitted into Elmyr's inner circle of friends and frequent companion at the Montesol. He possessed an all-weather smile, like a beauty pageant contestant's, only toothier. Combined with an unnervingly buoyant personality and Miss Congeniality enthusiasm, Vincente always seemed on the verge of announcing the funniest thing on earth but not quite able to bring himself to share it with others. Although his demeanor accompanied a naturally cheery disposition, the reasons for his effervescence were not always apparent. Moreover, I'm not sure his face was capable of any other countenance. I wondered if he looked any different at night, sound asleep. I suspect this constancy was probably more disconcerting for grieving friends and family members at funerals. Nevertheless, his friendship was steadfast. On numerous occasions he offered Elmyr any assistance he could. Again, loyalty was the mark of those Elmyr could count on without fail, and this quality above all others separated the best from the rest.

Vincente wore jaunty polo shirts, white trousers, Italian-style loafers, and a sweater draped over his back, its sleeves loosely intertwined across his chest as though he were stepping from a yacht in Capri. Working as a travel agent, his impeccable English and *GQ* dress allowed a seamless fit with the growing and well-healed foreign contingent on

Ibiza. He and Elmyr enjoyed the universal pastime of people-watching from the sidewalk tables in front of the Montesol. One morning Vincente joined us there for coffee. Within moments of his arrival, a young male backpacker sat down at the table next to ours, placing his guitar case on a nearby chair. He wore the uniform of a hippy: a tie-dyed shirt, ragged jeans, round wire-rim glasses, and red bandana headband holding back long tresses of unwashed hair. Almost instantly, surprised horror replaced the insouciance of Elmyr's face. With nostrils widened, he raised his head in alarm, wincing from an unfamiliar odor assailing him as though a gust of air announced he was standing downwind of a cow pasture. Then, with a tortured expression on his face, he began sniffing like a hunting dog in the direction of the hippy. "Tell me," he said to the stranger, "do you have three feet?" After a moment of indecision, he replied, "No." "Impossible," Elmyr shot back, "you couldn't stink that much with only two." For Elmyr, personal hygiene was de rigueur, not an elective.

Elmyr's blitzkrieg quip drew a stunned silence and frankly shocked me. Rather than voicing his instant disapproval, I had witnessed far more instances where he was likely to reach into his pocket and give people money to help them out. His response also suggested his defense of a laissez-faire lifestyle had its limits. Certain democratic notions he embraced often collided with the values learned in his youth, and they were commonly clothed in a social decorum that justified the summary judgment passed on the less-than-fragrant hippy. Far from his thoughts at that moment, I suspect, was the ease with which others condemn those who violate some rigid precepts of acceptable behavior, say, by homosexuality.

Another permanent fixture at the Hotel's sidewalk tables was an American writer, Steve Seley, grand-prize winner of the Norman Mailer Look-Alike Contest, I imagined. Unlike Mailer, Steve long ago ridded himself of any pretense of working at his craft after a publisher printed one of his books. I guess he saw no further need to prove himself. Once emancipated from his creative slavery, he felt at ease whiling the years away sipping coffee and cognac at his usual table. He lived on Ibiza from a time when its small coastal towns were actually fishing villages, and consequently was a witness to the island's transformation from quaint to hip. Like many seasoned drinkers, he rarely appeared drunk, and his sidewalk orations sounded logical if one could follow his ribbons of thought that flowed quickly, but not always in ordered sequence. At least, this was my take on his chats with Elmyr.

He and Elmyr shared a common acquaintance. That was April Ashley, whom I met at La Falaise. At that time, April competed with Elmyr for print space in some of the London newspapers. Her official title was Lady Ashley. Some most likely viewed her marriage to a British lord as somewhat surprising. None more than Steve Seley, not because she was American, but because he knew her from when she served as a merchant marine. She was a man at that time. As I recall, Elmyr said she/he was one of the first gender-change operations in the early '60s. Except for her Adam's apple and voice that descended an octave or two, depending on how much she drank, she was strikingly attractive. Not so attractive that I responded to her dance-of-the-seven-veils for me on Elmyr's coffee table. Lord Ashley, however, according to the press, appeared surprised and dismayed that their three-year marriage ended. For a while anyway, he thought there was nothing problematic about their union. Elmyr recounted how April ran into Seley at the Montesol one day. "He kept calling her George. I thought April was going to deck him," Elmyr said. "April was no lady, and still could probably kick the crap out of a lot of men—balls or no balls." She soon after opened a popular restaurant in London called April and Desmond's. There, she was as convincing and entertaining a hostess as her title and past suggested.

I saw April again in London when she sublet the King's Road flat of a good friend, Guy Munthe. Guy was just a couple of years older than I was and a frequent guest of Elmyr's in Ibiza. It wasn't surprising that Guy and April were friends, as he was at least as interesting as she was. When April moved into his Chelsea apartment, he moved to a house on the south bank of the Thames River directly across from St. Paul's Cathedral. Its East End location was far from gentrified southwest London in more than distance. It sat in the shadow of a giant smoke-belching power plant and industrial warehouses. Still, it possessed a heritage that appealed to Guy. On the building's facade was a plaque stating "Sir Christopher Wren lived here" when he was designing St. Paul's and much of London after the Great Fire of 1666, Guy told me. It had been an inn, a brothel, and finally the object of Guy's passion and restoration efforts. Apart from its fireplaces on the ground and first floors, it had no central heating, and when I stayed there as his guest I better understood the common image of the English wrapped in wool sweaters and tweed jackets. Guy's maternal grandfather was a leader of England's Liberal Party. His paternal grandfather was the Swedish doctor and writer Axel Munthe. He wrote a best-selling memoir called *The Story of San Michele* about his life in Capri. The book's success enabled him "to collect houses," as Guy expressed it.

Guy entertained Elmyr and me there when we came to London. Candles illuminated the high Jacobean oak paneling, the creaking wooden stairs whose treads looked like carved-out chair seats from centuries' wear. Floor-to-ceiling bookshelves lined his dining room walls. Heavy draperies pooled on floors flanking tall windows. Once we enjoyed a dinner at his home with the British ballet star Anton Dolin, formerly a principal dancer in Serge Diaghilev's *Ballet Russe*. After dinner Guy felt comfortable enough with Dolin to fashion his hair in an upward swoop, crowned in a question mark. His new look destroyed any notion of haughtiness. On another occasion Guy enlisted my help in liberating a casket he found in an abandoned warehouse. How we managed to carry it home after the wine and hookah-smoking that evening remains a fuzzy recollection. I'm not sure if he wanted it as an extra bed to sleep in a la Sarah Bernhardt, but getting it up his narrow stairwell was a comic challenge. He was inventive at earning money. Often, he rode a Moto Guzzi motorcycle with his parrot on his shoulder back up to Chelsea, and as a street performer played the musical saw.

On one of his visits to the island, we went to a new restaurant opening in the Ibiza countryside. It was formerly a finca but its new owners decided to turn it into a fashionable eatery. I think we toned down their efforts to create a cachet of pastoral elegance when Guy and a fellow dinner guest started a food fight at the table. He then felt inspired to pick up our waiter and carry him around the restaurant like a groom carrying his bride across the threshold. It was the only time in my life—and, I'm certain, in Elmyr's—where the owner kicked us out of a place and said, "Never come back!" Guy was of course contrite the next morning, after the wine's effects wore off. I think Elmyr's fondness for him was the only thing that saved him after trampling inviolable laws of social decorum. However, Elmyr laughed as much as the rest of us at the burlesque performance that evening.

When Elmyr received letters or phone calls from people wanting to meet him, the Montesol was a landmark everyone could find. Consequently, he often sent me there in search of those people to bring them to the house, or he came himself. To make sure they recognized him, he liked to say, "I'll be wearing a green carnation." He never did, of course, but he liked that line, something he lifted from a Graham Greene novel, I think, but he wasn't beyond appropriating authorship if it suited him. That was typical Elmyr. "Why obsess about the truth if it neither amused or amazed?" he once told me. This might be an appropriate motto in Latin under his coat of arms, I thought. I realized that he was prone to exercising a little artistic license from time to time when he could not remember every detail, explaining away inconsistencies thus: "I am not a court stenographer!" Still, there are things I would refuse to believe about Elmyr's life if I had not been there to witness encounters and events as I did. "Fantastic" best describes his saga. We soon learned how his biographer, Cliff Irving, tried to make his own life as fantastic as Elmyr's.

"Imagine my lack of surprise," Elmyr later said to others, recounting the morning we sat at the Montesol, sharing the *International Herald Tribune*. Again, he did a convincing impression of someone with a thyroid disorder, his eyes bulging as he read the newspaper that sunny day in 1971. The article enthralling him at that moment was about Clifford Irving, Elmyr's former friend. Their association started to disintegrate almost from the first day I began living at La Falaise. He told Elmyr's story in *Fake*. It was an instant success, shooting to the *New York Times* best-seller list, and, thus, a departure from anything he wrote before. His earlier works of fiction "better demonstrated his prowess as illusionist, as each unremarkable novel made him invisible," Elmyr later remarked, with a tincture of resentment still on his tongue.

Apart from Cliff's alleged failure to give Elmyr final approval of the manuscript as their contract stipulated, according to Elmyr, the prospect of seeing any future profits from sales of the book looked even more precarious. After receiving an initial payment of ten thousand dollars from the publisher, McGraw-Hill, for the rights to his story, Elmyr told me he signed a private agreement allowing Irving to collect *all* royalties. The author was then to give Elmyr his share of the monies. I never saw any evidence that Elmyr got a nickel from Irving. Again, he invested in an expectation that Irving would feel some compunction to do the right thing. Elmyr characterized his efforts to get first an accounting from Irving, and second, his share of royalties, in a streetwise pragmatism: "It makes no sense in chasing a bus that's not going to take you."

By Irving's own account, Elmyr gave him three drawings—two in the manner of Matisse, and one by Modigliani—for him to show curators at the Museum of Modern Art in New York after the scandal involving Elmyr exploded in the world press. Irving claimed the curators thought the works were authentic. Elmyr said their agreement was that Cliff would return the drawings to him when he came back to Ibiza. Elmyr claimed he repeatedly asked Cliff for the drawings but "he told me he destroyed them."

When he first asked me to help him with some of his correspondence, he dictated a frustrated letter to a recalcitrant Irving, asking for an accounting of sales proceeds from the silent writer. His overdue answer was continued silence. It left little doubt about the future of Elmyr's benefiting from his own life's story or that of the ill feeling between Irving and his former protagonist.

I remember that morning on the Montesol's terrace as we shared the day-late issue of *International Herald Tribune*; it was different from any other. Elmyr and I were both stunned to read the *Tribune*'s account of billionaire Howard Hughes selecting Clifford Irving to write his biography. In an ocean of writers, he landed Cliff. What were the chances? Could Cliff really charm the eccentric recluse out of hiding? Alien abductions far outnumbered credible sightings of Hughes. From what everyone knew about this secretive man, this revelation was as incongruous as a cockroach basking under a sun lamp. A huge smile instantly displaced the look of shock on Elmyr's face. He started laughing, handing me the paper to point out the punch line of the joke. Apparently, after much thought, the publicity-shy tycoon selected him (over all others) due to his integrity and great talent. We knew that assessment could have come only from Cliff himself or his mother. Our mutual laughter infected those sitting nearby in a way that spontaneously happens even when the source of mirth is unknown.

This news immediately became the topic du jour for Ibiza's sidewalk gossip vultures for a few weeks. Others, not just Elmyr and I, were scratching their scalps bloody, trying to figure out what was wrong about this picture. Cliff produced handwritten letters from Howard Hughes to him attesting their collaboration. Forensic handwriting analysts confirmed their authenticity. Based on the say-so of these experts, Cliff's publisher, McGraw-Hill, advanced him four hundred thousand dollars for his forthcoming manuscript and coup the rest of the publishing world would envy. Not long afterward, friends spotted Edith Irving at Ibiza's airport—in disguise. Her ruse was less than convincing. It would be like my blond third-grade teacher coming to school wearing a black wig and expecting no one to notice or say anything. Oh, come to think of it, this was exactly what Cliff's wife did. She did not even acknowledge her bewildered audience in the airport's lounge, even though they could not take their eyes from her, trying to figure out her Halloween persona. Within hours, she opened a bank account in Geneva in the name of Helga R. Hughes. Then, she deposited the check from the duped publisher in her newly opened account, made out to H. R. Hughes. Howard Hughes, like Elmyr, never saw the money. The outcome of this charade was delightfully predictable to us both. When Cliff's short-lived foray into the annals of literary infamy ultimately earned him a rent-free sojourn in a federal prison, Elmyr enjoyed some righteous and poetic justice. In the same week that Nixon traveled to China in a historic rapprochement of superpowers, *TIME* magazine elected to grace its cover with a portrait of Clifford Irving—by Elmyr. He was their pick for "Con Man of the Year." (In 2007, the story of Cliff's misadventure became a feature film starring Richard Gere, Alfred Molina, and other accomplished actors. National Public Radio critic Bob Mondello, called *The Hoax* one of the year's ten best movies. Cliff did not much care for it.)

Elmyr may well have inspired Cliff's hopeful but miscarried scheme to perpetrate a literary fraud. When I asked Elmyr about this possibility, he said that "Cliff would have been wise to not have targeted Hughes, one of the richest and most powerful men in the world, and especially as he was *still alive*." Clifford Irving prefaced *Fake* with a prophetic observation by a twelfth-century writer: "If fools did not go to market, cracked pots and false wares would not be sold." Cliff attributed this quote to the author Jean Le Malchanceux, whose name roughly translates to "Jean the Unlucky." He, as it turns out, was not only a literary invention of Irving's but an apparent role model for him as well.

One who knew of Elmyr's problems with Irving nevertheless became a victim of Cliff's allure. Nina van Pallandt was one of the first people I met in his circle of longtime friends. Nina was Danish, tall, beautiful, blond, intelligent, and a template for what a good friend should be. Her longstanding friendship with Elmyr preceded his fame, and she remained a pillar of support through all his troubles. Elmyr said, "When I was in prison in Ibiza, Nina came to see me all the time. She is also a marvelous cook and brought me wonderful things to eat. I'm lucky to have her as a friend." She exuded at once class and an unassuming approachability. Together with her equally attractive Dutch husband, Frederick, they became a successful and popular singing duo in Europe for a number of years.

Later, when their marriage dissolved, Nina had a brief affair with Irving. It was during their romantic interlude that Irving announced to the world that Howard Hughes granted him exclusive rights to author his biography. When he claimed that Hughes was personally relaying his story to him during clandestine meetings, he tried to implicate Nina in his hoax by insisting that she had witnessed these sessions with the billionaire. Nina, however, refused to be drawn into this imbroglio and simply told the truth—that they had been vacationing together in Mexico at the time of the said rendezvous with Hughes.

After appearing on the cover of *LIFE* magazine, Nina had offers for singing engagements in New York. Starring roles followed in Robert Altman's *The Long Goodbye* with Elliot Gould, and *American Gigolo*, Richard Gere's breakout film. Her career blossomed.

When I think of all the characters and memories associated with Ibiza's café society and especially the Hotel Montesol's terrace, I only once went there to visit someone staying there. That was Ursula Andress. She and Elmyr were old friends from their time together in Rome. By the early '70s, she, too, fell in love with Ibiza and decided to build a house there. It was during its construction that she decided to stay a while at the old hotel.

Life with Elmyr immediately catapulted me into a thin-aired world of high society jet-setters and glamour, all which had previously been isolated to movies or the pages of magazines. This culture shock was never as striking as when I met Ursula. After all, few film stars experience that magic celluloid moment and instant stardom she enjoyed in those breathtaking seconds when she emerged, bikini-clad, from tropical waters in the first James Bond film, *Doctor No*. Back in Minnesota I saw the movie with friends from school. Yeah, Sean Connery was cool as Bond—but she was the one young boys, and probably old men, dreamed about. Three weeks into my new life with Elmyr, Ursula came to the house. She was not only the most perfectly beautiful woman I'd ever seen, she was, I soon discovered, totally without guile, little impressed with her own success or status. Her humility most likely found its origin in her no-nonsense Swiss upbringing.

A French land speculator made her an attractive offer of a piece of seafront property. Contrasting her unassuming nature, he was one of those self-possessed entrepreneurs, bloated with Gallic pride, and probably wore his Legion d'Honeur medal in his pajama lapel. What appeared to be a choice location for her intended new home became a disaster. The waterfront land was at the bottom of a steep, vegetation-free hillside prone to erosion. Horror stories of incompetent builders abounded in Ibiza. After spending more than $100,000 for a beautiful new home, not only did its unstable terrain begin to crumble, the architect and builder together managed to overlook putting in a proper foundation under the house. Cracks in walls and floors grew over time. The septic tank twice migrated downhill after heavy rains. What began as a dream home quickly turned into the house from hell.

Before her Mediterranean sanctuary went the way of most wishes, she and Elmyr formed a glue-like bond. As a by-product of their friendship, it was one of the greatest privileges of my life that she considered me a friend as well. On my twenty-first birthday, she sent a telegram with birthday wishes from Beverly Hills. How thoughtful that *she* would do that for *me*. How extraordinary is that?

That first night Ursula came up to La Falaise, she was radiant, her blond hair characteristically swept back from a high forehead. High cheekbones, soft brown eyes with a fine aquiline nose—she possessed all those individual features that made her a timeless beauty. I found out that she and Elmyr had a history going back a number of years, to before she became a movie star. When they knew each other in Rome, she was married to John Derek. She sat in the leather easy chair opposite Elmyr. Stories and laughter flowed. The conversation jumped from French to English and back to French. I sat quietly in a corner listening and working on homework from my French textbook, conjugating the verb, *to be*. Amid the animated banter, Elmyr seized a thought. "*Whatever happened to Dimitri?*" he asked, as though hoping to satisfy a long-standing curiosity. Ursula's face became serious. She raised her arm in a dismissive gesture of disgust. "Oh!" she exclaimed, "he was impossible, always screwing around. I told him I wouldn't put up with it any longer. When he didn't stop—I had him castrated." I dropped my pen, instantly realizing that infidelity warranted an Aztec-style retribution and unthinkable pain. When they noticed the horror on my face, they started laughing. Elmyr announced that Dimitri was her Afghan dog. Throughout the following years, Ursula unfailingly showed the depth of her friendship toward Elmyr. Each was generous beyond convention or expectation.

As popular as the Montesol or Café Alhambra were for a mid-morning rendezvous, it was Ibiza's teeming bar scene where all of God's creatures, or so it seemed, congregated when the sun went down.

In Ibiza, beautiful people were fifteen to the dozen. Young gods and goddesses strode through the streets after sun-filled days at the beach, spilling into portside restaurants, bars, and outdoor terraces each evening. The air was pungent with pheromones. One night Elmyr and I were entrenched at La Tierra. Arlene was stage-managing the scene when a young woman walked into the bar through the whitewashed, arched doorway, emerging through long strands of Moroccan glass beads that reminded one of Ibiza's Moorish past. She wore a wispy white dress with a plunging neckline; her bronzed skin contrasted her pale blue eyes and shoulder-length blond hair. She possessed a physical perfection that commanded everyone's attention. The Saturday night saloon silenced as the crowd allowed her through, separating like the Red Sea for Charlton Heston.

With the flourish of a circus ringmaster, Elmyr stood up and gestured to her to join us as though he were hailing a longtime friend. We had eaten at a favorite French bistro earlier and were now enjoying a cognac and socializing a bit with Arlene. The after-dinner brandy made him even more talkative than usual. Always attracted to people for their looks, brains, or pedigree, this siren's allure piqued his curiosity. Amazingly, she made her way to our table as if it had been a prearranged date. Elmyr rose from his seat, as did I, introduced himself and me, bent courteously over her outstretched hand, as a well-bred man would do, and then embarked on polite small talk.

Brittany was her name, from Pompano Beach, Florida, a fashion model on vacation. A photographer told her about Ibiza, and she wanted to visit this much-talked-about island before returning to work in Milan. When Elmyr mentioned he was a painter, her face flashed incandescent. She thrust her hands upward, palms toward her, fingers apart, inches from her face as though she were going to have him guess how many fingers she had. Then, wiggling them in case he hadn't noticed, she proudly exclaimed that *she* applied the new nail color, implying, I guess, that this creative endeavor surely ought to put these fellow artists on a first-name basis.

It became apparent that her brain had declared its independence from her body around puberty, so while her centerfold looks would prompt nocturnal emissions in Baptist ministers, her frontal cortex was still earning babysitting money. At the same time, she exhibited a frothy self-confidence from all the attention directed her way. She thought, mistakenly, this made her interesting—a delusion she was comfortable with. Despite her sensuality and adolescent mind, she was living proof that the gods also have a cruel sense of humor, for she possessed a whiny, glass-shattering voice that would make one long for the dulcet sound of a cat that caught its tail under a chair rocker. Hence, it was not her beauty, or chi-sucking prattle, or brain activity with toe tag attached, or having the depth of a tea saucer that was most memorable about this encounter, but her withering voice that would induce scabies in anyone within earshot. It was the singular most effective defense mechanism conceivable, one that guaranteed her unsullied virtue among the horniest of buccaneers, I thought.

Elmyr conducted himself like a gentleman and displayed unusual composure with our ill-chosen guest that evening. I admired him even more for his feigned interest in her vacuous chatter knowing full well he would have preferred being sprayed by a skunk than endure her a minute longer. When a brief lull occurred in her self-absorbed monologue, Elmyr rose, stating he had to leave as his grandmother died in a tragic motorcycle accident that day and the funeral was early the following morning. On our way home I imagined a row of leather-bound, tattoo-titled bikers on chrome machines rumbling to Granny's gravesite to pay tribute to their hundred-something-year-old club member. It wasn't unusual that Elmyr unleashed his agile wit as in his impromptu exit strategy from the bar. Nor was the funereal imagery beyond the realm of possibility on Ibiza. We accepted the surreal with a shrug. Furthermore, he had a knack for making the unbelievable believable. He possessed a natural theatricality that often turned conversation into performance art, ever aware of the audience and delivering his lines with the timing and conviction of a seasoned actor. After all, when Elmyr created his pastiches of the modern masters, he also transformed fine art into a performing art, a grand impersonator at his craft of deception, blurring the distinction between what was real and what wasn't.

Every day held some adventure in Elmyr's company. Just a few kilometers from Santa Eulalia, Robin Maugham lived in a home of ever-increasing size. Like his more famous uncle, W. Somerset Maugham, Robin was also a writer, attempting, everyone thought, to live up to Uncle Willy's success—and talent. Elmyr introduced Robin to the island. He even completed writing one of his books while he stayed in the guest room at La Falaise. His time there apparently inspired him to find a house of his own. One day Robin invited some friends to lunch. Comfortably seated on a feather-cushioned sofa before a fire in the fireplace on a damp winter day, Elmyr reached for a book among many stacked on a large square coffee table in front of him. The book on Modigliani was one he had not seen before. Typical of these editions, beautiful colored illustrations filled the book with an accompanying description, history, and scholarly analysis of each painting on the opposite page. Watching him leaf through the book with curiosity, his face seemed to register a look of déjà vu when he stopped abruptly, his ennui displaced by shock and surprise. Our friend Sandy quickly asked, "Is that one of yours?" He said, "Yes!" We all laughed. He then explained its illegitimate birth. It was a portrait of a seated woman with eyes conspicuously absent and characteristically in Modigliani's style.

Just to illustrate my point that most of Elmyr's fakes still rest inconspicuously in collections, this book places this Modigliani comfortably in the cannon of his works. The description reads as follows:

PORTRAIT OF YOUNG GIRL
recognized as a Modigliani,
but done by Elmyr

"In many cases, Modigliani's sitters are known to us. In other cases, the first name, or the sitter's occupation (e.g., *la belle epicière, la marchande de fleurs*) or only her nationality (*la petite japonaise, la belle polonaise*) has come down to us. **Here we know nothing about this young girl, a casual acquaintance whom chance put in the artist's path.**" (Bold italics are mine.)

It goes on to describe the virtues of the piece in terms only authentic works would elicit. These adulatory reviews undergo a speedy reassessment when they are found to be less than authentic. Here, the writer documents the work's unexplained origin and, despite its unknown pedigree, offers a flattering synopsis of the painting. Elmyr's explanation was that he had painted it in a YMCA in St. Louis. He then consigned it to an auction house. They sold it, but shortly after the sale, the auction house declared bankruptcy. Elmyr was in no position to begin any kind of legal action or do anything at all that would draw attention to him. The relatively youthful painting has received its proper christening with its inclusion in a book by a respected publisher; it is unlikely that the picture's current owner would care to revisit the question of authenticity.

This glimpse into Elmyr's past was unforeseen, though not unusual in the sense that there always seemed to be an endless supply of anecdotes or observations related to something he knew and thought noteworthy enough to share with me. However, my daily lesson was not yet over. Like Elmyr's villa, Robin's home was a reflection of him, his ease and comfort, surrounded by the elegant trappings of culture and refinement. Elmyr helped Robin find his seaside villa, and under our friend

Sandy Pratt's guidance, he turned his garden into an oasis of palms, rubber trees, pines, mimosa, and succulents. Lavender, white, and fuchsia-colored bougainvilleas climbed the stucco exterior, ever higher as he added a second and third floor to the home. Inside, his wingback chairs, Chippendale dining table and chairs, camelback sofa, Spode china, and Georgian silver transplanted the gentrified casual elegance the British achieve without breaking a sweat. A painting in a hand-carved gilt frame hung above his fireplace and was a focal point of pride. It was a portrait of a seated fair-haired woman wearing an oversized hat. English oak trees in the background were a counterpoint to her blue and white silk dress. Robin claimed Joshua Reynolds, the eighteenth-century portraitist, did the painting. I later remarked to Elmyr that I liked the painting. He rolled his eyes and gave me his "You've still got a lot to learn" look. "Reynolds was a great artist," he said. "If that woman stood up, her right arm would hang down below her knee. It has *nothing* to do with Reynolds." Elmyr of course never expressed this anatomical impossibility to Robin. He simply didn't want to deflate him in any way. It was, again, the kind of aside and perspective he shared as generously as his friendship, and one that no classroom experience could replicate.

Elmyr—The Artist

A s I came to know Elmyr, I understood why Ibiza was a perfect setting for him. The bohemian lifestyle of the island suited his artistic sentiments, resonating with his creative nature. At that time, it was becoming the Mediterranean's new San Tropez, since the French Riviera was an ancurism bulging with people. Some of its upper-class habitués now elected to turn the small Balearic isle into their new destination. Elmyr was comfortable with people of far-ranging interests and social credentials, and many of them frequented his parties at La Falaise. While the diversity of these people may have resembled a big tossed salad, Elmyr knew exactly the kind of person he allowed through his front door, and his guest list derived from a simple formula. This meant that if you were beautiful, you didn't have to be titled. If you were titled, you didn't have to be beautiful. If you were interesting, you didn't have to be titled or beautiful. I'm sure these events appeared thoroughly democratic, but that perception would be inaccurate.

It always fascinated me how he was with people, a kind of social chef and they were his ingredients. Add a cup of culture, the zest of beauty, a little color, and stir until interesting. These gatherings also provided a forum for everyone to exchange gossip about everyone else, and Elmyr was in the center of it all. In the BBC film, he says, "When one tells naughty stories about someone, you do it much more enthusiastically than when you reluctantly talk about yourself." In such moments his wit was lively, without constraint, but rarely self-deprecating. At one point in the documentary, for instance, Elmyr beatifically looks heavenward and quotes what a friend said about him. With radiant self-pride, he exclaimed in French, *"Mallorca a eu Chopin. Ibiza a Elmyr."* (Mallorca had Chopin.* Ibiza has Elmyr.) The film's producer, Richard Drewitt, later recounted how it lost some of its adulatory punch when a Shepard's Bush transcriptionist gave it a fish-and-chips twist: Mallorca has champagne. Ibiza has beer. Elmyr found this substantially less amusing than did everyone else. (*Chopin briefly sought a winter retreat on Mallorca with writer and paramour George Sand—a woman. That particular season's weather was unfriendly enough to just about kill off the fragile composer.)

When it came to his art, however, he took himself seriously, and expected others to view him as nothing less than a serious artist. He always felt his work merited respect, and each retreat into his studio was a sacrosanct communion with his muses. I therefore respected his time there. In the movie *Grand Hotel*, Greta Garbo uttered her famously parodied line, "I want to be let alone," and then spent a lifetime fulfilling her desire. Elmyr never needed to make that request. I just knew the routine. Once he disappeared behind that closed door, any reason to interrupt his work had better be life-threatening, so unless something unimaginably important occurred, I knew I'd better just not disturb him.

I had seen him create works of art, each time inspiring a sense of wonder in me. Whenever he stood before his easel or his sketchbook, his arm, hand, pencil, or brush formed a communion with his breathing. It was as though this autonomic function stopped while his hand was in motion. Since his normal respiration "was loud like a horse," I once told him, it was discomforting to listen to him. At times, I found myself adopting his halting pattern of inhalation and exhalation and then gasping for air when the pause seemed too long. He was oblivious of this after decades of habit. When I asked how he managed to hold his breath like a Polynesian pearl diver, he laughed and said he learned it when he first started taking art lessons as a boy in Hungary. I told him I thought it was creepy and unnatural. He laughed again and explained how the controlled breathing steadies the hand. His lines and brushwork attested to this. They were sure and unwavering—constructed by design from an unconscious act.

This was not the only anomalous movement associated with his creative process. His concentration apparently flowed smoothly if, in conjunction with his asymmetrical breathing, he positioned himself just right in front of the easel. He frequently looked to the floor in search of some invisible black shoe silhouettes like those used to teach the dancing-impaired certain steps or like an unsure stage actor constantly looking for his mark indicating where to stand. With one leg positioned behind the other and knees slightly bent like a relaxed fencer preparing for his next duel, he engaged his unresisting adversary, a blank white canvas. His never-divulged strategy showed only as much as he wanted his incremental strokes to reveal. In his left hand he held a clutch of paint-daubed brushes, perhaps a dozen at a time, ranging from those with a few fine bristles to stout ones about an inch wide. Their shafts emerged perpendicularly between the webs of every finger, their bases held firmly in a clenched fist. These were his arsenal of interchangeable tools. Only he knew the proper sequence of their use, all of which conformed to a vision unique to him. The sound emanating from this colorful birthing process was a scratchy, crisp staccato as the brush moved quickly across the tautly woven fabric. A hush fell over the studio when he required a delicate adagio of fine brushwork. For added fidelity of line, he would further steady his hand by balancing it on the canvas with his smallest finger.

He was a fine art engineer of sorts, no less cerebral than an architect was, but at the same time given an emotional freedom of movement that a wealthy spectrum of color permitted. As any builder tends to dwell on the importance of foundation, his skill as a draftsman was the skeletal structure that supported everything he did. It is what convincingly held together all the musculature and connective tissue of form, line, color, movement, expression—basically all those building blocks that construct figurative art.

On a table beside his easel was a splattered disarray of semi-crushed tubes of oil paints. He would grab one he wanted and with spontaneous largesse squeeze a dollop of the expensive substance on the interior flat plain of his large wooden palette. Around its edge was a miniature mountain range of dried, age-old paint, now rock hard. From, say, a flea's perspective, it would look like the Himalayas in psychedelic Technicolor splendor. According to his desire, he amalgamated contrasting colors in that mystical visual alchemy that would mysteriously yield something entirely new that had nothing to do with its original ingredients. It was inspiring magic, and, witnessing the emergence of these works of art, I felt privy to something special. Again, these up-close and personal viewings were generally in conjunction with those moments when he asked me to model for him. Otherwise, my presence in his studio was as unwelcome as the arrival of the police.

I continually marveled at each visual tour de force he produced with apparent ease. From all his tutelage, volumes of art books, and museum and gallery tours, he showed me that one common thread weaves its way through the history of painting. "Great artists display a facility and command of their métier that make it look simple," he explained. "If you examine the work of Rembrandt, Titian, Rubens, Goya, Hals, Homer, Delacroix, Lautrec, Monet, and many other masters, you will see in every one a tremendous economy of brush strokes that conveys a powerfully expressive image." This was his teacher voice, and I was his only student. Elmyr was quick to point out that "their work became increasingly fluid," the continuity of movement interrupted only to replenish an exhausted brush with more color. This sense of perpetual motion was "most evident in their later works." Unlike many other pursuits that require a physical rigor, old age was for many of these great artists the culmination of talent, training, experience, and endurance. "Look closely and you will see how transcendent their art becomes when they have completely exploited the potential of their medium," he told me when viewing a painting by Rembrandt. Their creative spirits overcame physical frailties so these irrepressibly productive periods not only became dramatic exclamation points in their oeuvre but the pinnacle of their careers as well.

An anecdote he repeated more than once was about one of his favorite artists, John Singer Sargent. In the late nineteenth century, John D. Rockefeller was reputed to be the richest man in the United States. He commissioned the great painter to do his portrait. With considerable verve and speed, Sargent completed the work in one sitting, taking perhaps an hour, according to Elmyr. Upon completion, Rockefeller was amazed that he had done it so quickly and asked his portraitist how much the picture was going to cost. When Sargent replied with something like $40,000, which at the time was a king's ransom, his sitter was shocked. Only one thing exceeded the industrialist's reputation for wealth: his stinginess. "Forty thousand dollars for one hour's work?" the old man asked. Sargent unflinchingly responded, "Yes, but it took forty years to learn how to do it in an hour!" This story illustrated Elmyr's point about heightened ability that comes with age.

Elmyr would be the first to admit that not everything he did was perfect. Even extraordinary people have moments of normalcy or something a tad below that water line. Any professional athlete, for example, knows when one is not "in the zone" or not performing at the top of one's game. With more than a tincture of irony, Elmyr liked to quote the German painter Max Liebermann, who thought the only reason to justify the existence of art experts was that "after an artist's death they could declare his bad work forgeries." He commonly vacillated in his blanket condemnation of those who might wear the title "expert." He readily acknowledged there were genuine scholars out there whom he respected, but through experience and a rare grip of reality recognized the imperfect nature of people and their propensity to make mistakes. While he was no stranger to ego, he could not abide the power, pretense, and self-importance of those whose depth of understanding and expertise was shallow.

One important factor that contributed to his displeasure when talking about those paladins of the art establishment was the lack of success he'd encountered when trying to sell art in no one's style other than his own. Those barren efforts weren't due to an absence of talent, obviously. Nor was there great stylistic difference between his work and those works of artists who enjoyed a commercial success. It left him upset, although he recognized various reasons for his continued frustrations. He and his art were products of "The School of Paris," an appellation of broad scope encompassing a variety of art movements that were largely centered in the French capital in the first half of the twentieth century. By mid century, tastes in art had changed with the advent of abstract art or abstract expressionism. Dealers championed the exponents of these styles. They were viewed as exciting, new, and fertile ground for greater commercial exploitation and profit margins. Elmyr quietly slipped through the cracks of fad and fashion.

The shadow of an object near a light source appears larger than the object. Such was the aura of irony surrounding Elmyr, forever larger than him. When he was finally able to bask in the public attention and recognition he always hoped for, it came with a price. As someone expressed, "Expectations are premeditated resentments." With his fame he expected acceptance of his worth as an artist. With recognition of his talent, he would at last fulfill the awaited requests for his artwork—in his own style. Sadly, these requests were infrequent, almost negligible. I witnessed the crush of interest in his creations—in the manner of others, those works that originally brought him his notoriety. He realized it was what people wanted most, and it was a bitter pill to swallow. His celebrity, like his art, may have appeared authentic to the world, but to Elmyr, it fell short of the vindication he sought and thought he deserved.

This outward image viewed by others became an impressionist work of its own. A loose association of media hype, shreds of reality, and colorful story allowed one to paint a picture portraying a tale of success. It was not only a skewed perception, but beneath the surface was a disturbing truth. Like a Shakespearian tragedy, his life's tribulations would ultimately demonstrate that fame and fortune counted for naught. The trajectory of events that affected his life for the better also put him directly in harm's way.

From Elmyr's perspective, things improved appreciably from the financially uncertain existence he had known most of his adult life. While a sense of self-worth may be inseparable from self-sufficiency and a universal impulse rooted in human nature, its construct may be fragile as well. The impact of job loss, for example, can be psychologically devastating. Knowing the frustrations he endured trying to establish himself professionally and having to resort to fakery that demanded the same high level of skill he brought to his own work, simply to make a living, was psychically corrosive. At one point in his life, he probably became clinically depressed. When living in Washington DC he attempted suicide by an overdose of sleeping pills and was rescued before it was too late. It was the ultimate act of desperation but not his last.

After the publication of his story, his public profile rose along with his bank account. Both these recent phenomena cheered him up considerably. With this newfound stability, he was able to create his art with a freedom he hadn't enjoyed since living under that umbrella of parental protection and bourgeois comfort of his youth. One truth that slowly manifested itself during those years in his company was an observation I had not suspected or had any reason to deduce. His life seemed to have no rapport with that assumed inner voice and spark that are not only supposed to be inherent, but also the spiritual engine that propels one to create something—anything. Instead, I noticed that these moments of artistic impulse in Elmyr sprang from an almost working-class, lunch-box ethic that had nothing to do with his rose-smelling, satin-covered sensibilities. The impetus that prodded him into his studio was far earthier than attaining any apotheosis of art for art's sake. The ego polish the sale of his work produced was about—money. It became his yardstick for success and motivation.

When this revelation occurred to me I realized two things; one, he may have felt passionately about art but it was not his *passion*, and two, it had nothing to do with his talent. His skill was beyond reproach, but I could now see more accurately that art was his *craft*. While I was disappointed to learn that art was not his raison d'etre, I was even more encouraged to realize that what truly fueled and animated his life was not academic at all but was real-life relationships. That's where his heart was. Never completely comfortable with solitude, it was the love and acceptance of others that he valued most. Friendship was his life's blood, and his need for the companionship of others was what brought me into his life and world. For those whose lives he touched, his most lasting legacy may not be his art at all, but the cherished memories of the man who touched the lives of those around him.

It is important to remind one that his love of others was not dressed in any Benedictine mantle of universal love and forgiveness. It was more normal, more selective. Elmyr was utterly childlike in his inability to mask his emotions. He was effusive and demonstrably affectionate with those he liked, and his uninhibited generosity and charm rarely failed to earn him friends. Even his critics, outraged over his perceived acts of sabotage against the art establishment, mellowed greatly after meeting him. I witnessed an exchange between Elmyr and a particularly acerbic British interviewer, Ludovic Kennedy. His opening question was, "Mr. de Hory, how does it feel to be a second-rate artist?" Elmyr calmly responded, "Well, Mr. Kennedy, it depends on what you call second-rate. If you talk about artists like Leonardo, Rafael, or Michelangelo, then artists like Picasso, Matisse, or Modigliani can only be considered second-rate...in which case I'm happy to be in their company." The tone of questioning softened considerably afterward. For many others, Elmyr's story assumed a kind of David versus Goliath folk hero status. In fact, the public spotlight shining on him at first caused considerable discomfort until the attendant notoriety translated into a demand for his artwork.

No one knows how many of Elmyr's fakes are in permanent collections around the world and may forever be deemed authentic. Estimates range from the hundreds to the thousands. It's impossible to tell. One thing is certain, as Elmyr always insisted: "If it hangs in a collection long enough, it becomes real!" However, even *he* was fully aware of the "greed factor" that played a role in his success. Long after his "outing" as the author of so many of these spurious masterpieces, people still flocked to his doorstep to buy his creations and still tried to pawn them off as originals. I saw this occur, and he knew it was happening. He also knew it was impossible to interdict them or always forecast their intentions. At the same time the lure of cash often stifled his curiosity, as it had done so often in the past with Legros. While art forgery is an ancient profession, human disposition toward larceny may be an inherent trait since walking upright.

Elmyr made a living from a body of work that bares the names of other artists. Now he is the model for countless forgeries that bear his name, but are not by him. He didn't experience this one irony during his life. In fact, the subject of fake Elmyrs was brought up only once in passing, as I recall, and the prospect seemed so far-fetched that he dismissed it immediately. Since his death, I have the distinct impression that works purportedly by Elmyr have proliferated at a rate that exceeds sexually transmitted diseases. The value of these works, as in authentic artwork by Elmyr, should be based uniquely on the pleasure they give to their owners. However, in most cases the artistic merit of many of the alleged "Elmyr" paintings makes refrigerator art look good. My, how incestuous this world of forgery seems to be.

While on the subject of forgery, there was a book published, astonishingly enough, but appropriately entitled *Enigma*. It purports to add a little something to Elmyr's story as it was "retold to Ken Talbot." All

I can say about this is that Elmyr had been quietly minding his own business for about seventeen years in his casket when, for no reason I can discern, he elected to recount his life's story from the grave to the author. While as startling an event as this might be, I could not bring myself to order the book, as it could not be corroborated by any credible supermarket tabloid at the time. Nor were any two-way communication devices placed in his coffin. Talbot also alleged to be in possession of Elmyr's personal diaries. I can't wait for their publication! Some publishers are evidently as tolerant as the paper upon which anything can be written.

I saw some photos of paintings supposedly by Elmyr reproduced in Talbot's book. The chances of them being by Elmyr are, in my opinion, neutrino slim. Talbot (who resembled Michael Cane), however, knew Elmyr and even bought some of his artwork. I was present when they first met. At the time, anyone who Elmyr thought might be a possible buyer earned an invitation at his dinner table. Ken came to buy.

He had retired from a successful career as a bookmaker in London, and then, comfortably set from a life in gambling, decided to take on the challenges of a new life in Ibiza. His most attractive physical feature was his Caribbean blue eyes, although I thought they more closely resembled giant olives in the bottom of a martini glass, only slightly better lubricated. The olives, however, had a better chance of moving in concentric orbits. He also had a sloshy affability buttressed by an unrestrained love of gin and tonics. I also had the impression that he thought he and Elmyr were kindred spirits of sorts, each just on the wrong side of social acceptability due to a phony moral priggishness. Nothing could be more inaccurate. Elmyr was, by nature and inclination, a snob, and recognized Ken for what he was, a nouveau riche bit of rough trade from London's East End. He would not be unique in having made a cottage industry from his acquaintance with Elmyr; others have done it with much less of a connection to him.

Elmyr knew the inherent risk of others' using the formula learned from his saga to replicate similar schemes for easy money and that he was powerless to do anything about it. In my view, it became a kind of pop-up how-to book for others wishing to test their skill at larceny. The number of fake Elmyrs floating around like visual flotsam attests to this, and the upshot here is yet another irony. What many of these would-be imitators undoubtedly count on is the assumption that phony fakes don't register at all on the sin list—hence, considering it, I imagine, a rather innocuous pursuit. Like Shakespeare said, "A rose by any other name would smell as sweet." Conversely, any bad art remains bad art, under any name. However, I will concede this: if it comes down to eating or not eating, then more power to them. After all, not everyone has a critical eye to tell the difference between what's good and what's bad. Some experts have been fooled, too.

Elmyr's frame of reference in judging art was representational or figurative art. For non-representational art, conceptual, or abstract art, he was not dismissive of it entirely. It was outside his comfort zone, but he attempted to understand it. He respected artists like Lichtenstein or Oldenburg, whose works he found clever. I remember accompanying him to an exhibition of contemporary art at the Royal Academy in London. Judging by the scowl on his face, he was at a loss to fathom how it came to be enshrined within the walls of that institution. Indeed much of it appeared to be assemblages from garage sales or constructions from the contents of one's kitchen junk drawer, all without the wit of Rube Goldberg. He opined that it was "some sort of bad joke or a kind of ode to anarchy."

For a while, Elmyr's existence on Ibiza was an edgy one fraught with uncertainty; he thought that art, with its aura of respectability, might just be the right avenue to ingratiate him to the local authorities. He contributed a number of paintings to Ibiza's Museum of Contemporary Art, works of his own and those he collected from various artists who had some connection to the island. These gestures of generosity and civic endowments were accepted graciously and duly noted in the local newspaper, but were quiet useless in the sense of granting him any preferential treatment vis-à-vis the law, which they were ostensibly designed to do. They were, in fact, much less effective than the direct payoffs to the right people, as he previously had done. Despite his disingenuous motives, the museum still possesses some wonderful examples of his work.

Money Barks

One truth became immediately apparent to me in Elmyr's world. First, money was the axis around which we all rotate as unavoidably as the law of gravity. Second, one could not ignore the fact that it did not rule his life, which seemed to defy the first immutable law I just mentioned. Perhaps it was due to his unconscious disregard of money learned from the bourgeois comfort of his upbringing. When he had it he didn't give it much thought. It was about as far from his mind as Louis XIV looking at his palace at Versailles, thinking, "Well, there sure are a lot of windows. Who's going to clean them all?" Again, Elmyr would enjoy any simile connecting him to the King of France. Still, since the days of crossing borders, using the gems sewn into his coat lining to ease his path back to Paris, he respected the power cash gave him as a tool to survive. Yet its acquisition was never his end goal.

During the last two months of 1969, my eyes remained dilated from the flurry of social activity. In early January 1970, I accompanied Elmyr to Madrid. It would be the first of many trips there, and these visits were a mix of pleasure and business. One obligatory pilgrimage, however, was to the apartment of Nini Montiam. She was one of Elmyr's circle I met who influenced events in his life, both good and bad.

One room she converted into a bar. It was red with smoked mirrors on the walls, tropical kitsch everywhere. It was what hell might look like with a Polynesian theme. Behind the bar, two large brandy snifters filled with matchbooks from her travels anchored each end of a shelf with liquor bottles. It was in "Bar Nini" that Elmyr and I met Lita Trujillo. The dark-haired beauty had recently lost her husband. She married Ramfis Trujillo, son of the longtime dictator of the Dominican Republic. Banner headlines covered the story, reaffirming that reality trumps invention. On a fog-shrouded highway outside Madrid, he crashed his Ferrari head on into the Jaguar driven by the Duchess of Albuquerque. She died instantly, he later in a hospital. That evening his bereaved widow stood before us in her black, spaghetti-strapped, low-cut cocktail dress, relaying the tragic events. Placing her clenched fist below her left breast, she pressed her chest, administering a mini-Heimlich maneuver, almost jiggling free her ample bosom the dress could barely contain. Then, maybe forgetting which side of the body her heart was on, moved her hand underneath the other breast, again attempting to free it from her garment. She repeated the somber burlesque motions a few more times before another guest captured her attention. Elmyr then turned to me and asked, "Did you know it was a Duke of Albuquerque who led the Spanish Armada?" Incidental but apparently important lessons in genealogy lurked around every corner, I thought. Nevertheless, his subsequent reenactments of our encounter with Trujillo's widow were both accurate and funny.

Nini retained a curly mane of auburn hair, a reminder of her youth but long past what nature intended. Her appearance was exactly what a casting director would desire for the role of a red-light district madam. Heavy makeup, mascara, and lipstick, designed to hide her age, just accentuated it. Her time in front of a mirror was more than simple narcissism. As a stage and film actor, she was accustomed to the glare of bare lights surrounding her image. One silver-framed photo of herself on a piano shawl in the living room revealed her association with Eva and Juan Peron, another of her and jaw-jutting Mussolini. In fact, she was the daughter of a general, well connected in certain circles of Spanish society, and made a good living as an influence peddler. Her calling card should have read, "Friendship for Hire." When visiting her at her apartment, filled with portraits, gilded Rococo armchairs and settees, every available niche suggesting the marshal pomp and mustiness of a bygone era, favor seekers waited patiently in anterooms. She and Elmyr had more than a cordial relationship, she helping him negotiate the labyrinth of Madrid's bureaucracy and making sure bribes went to the right people. During the Franco regime one's ability to avoid problems with the police depended on having the right signature and officially stamped document. Apparently, she had not yet exhausted her passion for men in uniforms when I knew her. A colonel in the army called on her regularly. According to her, he had romantic designs on her, although I think it was more likely another link based on mutual interest. "He has dreadful table manners. He eats his peas with a knife," she said. Now, if he managed to balance whole peas on the flat side of the knife from his plate to his mouth, then that feat alone should have earned him a promotion, I thought.

Nini was an efficient procurer of whatever one needed. In a moment of prophetic candor, Elmyr once said to me, "God help me if Nini ever became my enemy!" In about 1973 that's precisely what happened. Her self-serving instinct prompted her gravitation to the dark side and an alliance with Fernand Legros. Forever bent on Elmyr's demise, with her help they orchestrated his incarceration for three months in a Palma jail. While the manufactured charges against him were bogus, the gears of Spanish justice moved imperceptibly before the accusations were dismissed. This temporary success, however, provided the pathway that would ultimately guarantee their goal. Their clever manipulation of the legal system vividly illustrated that the law and justice are very often incompatible.

However, while Elmyr and Nini were friends, she devised a plan to help ingratiate him with the Spanish authorities. As his existence on Ibiza always had an edgy uncertainty that brought him uncomfortably close to the justice system, they thought that a little positive public relations spin would be helpful. They agreed that Elmyr should establish an art foundation in his name and leave an endowment that would promote art and the enhancement of cultural life on the island. This would entail making La Falaise the foundation's new home. The fact that it was not in his name or power to give away was an inconvenient detail that became conveniently fuzzy when his monocle fell out because of relaxed scruples. This little bit of stagecraft was again more show than go, as so much PR actually is.

Never mind that the insincerity of this ploy was utterly calculating to bend public perception and do a little image-polishing at the same time— it worked. The local newspaper, the *Diario de Ibiza,* duly applauded the altruistic gesture and acknowledged him as a great artist but also a generous benefactor. Truth is apparently expendable as long as one's approval rating gets a boost. Knowing him to be generous, the idea was not incompatible with his character. However, as was so often the case, there was a slight reality gap that didn't bridge between idea and fact. So long as the winds of fortune seemed to blow in Nini's direction and her relationship with Elmyr worked for her, she was willing to assume those duties of publicist and protector. While I was too young and unworldly to see through that curtain of artifice that really masked her vampire instincts, Elmyr more presciently demonstrated a rare insight into her character when suspecting more accurately her mercenary nature.

She may have quite enjoyed her duplicitous nature; after all, she honed her ability to deceive through her profession as an actor. I shudder to imagine if her treachery that reached Biblical proportions with Elmyr had proven to be as venomous to others. I often thought but for Legros's being gay and considerably younger than Nini, they would have made ideal bed partners. I just don't know who would have eaten whom after sex. There was a little story, however, that Nini often recounted with a sparkle in her eye. Her father was in Cuba in the days when they had a revolution about every eighteen months. She explained that he offered amnesty to some of the rebels if they would turn themselves in and stop their insurrection. A number of peasants accepted the peace overture and surrendered. He immediately ordered their executions. His justification was simply, "What do you think they'd have done with us?" Her glee never diminished with each retelling. It also disclosed a lack of hesitation and obvious subscription to the notion that the end justifies the means. Even if I'd grasped the implications of this queasy and gruesome tale, I'm not sure anything would have changed. Events seemed to gather momentum and their eventual deep impact suggested disaster.

Elmyr never needed to travel far from home to witness deceit. There were plenty of people on the island, as I've already suggested, whose ability to deceive ranged from harmless to dangerous. One of these was his lawyer. He was a rotund man. It looked like someone drew his facial features on a balloon inflated beyond its capacity. His thinning black hair slicked back with gleaming pomade did little to disturb this impression. Still, dapperly dressed in a gray suit, white shirt, and black tie, and black Buddy Holly glasses, he was an imposing figure. Nor was he devoid of charm. Moreover, he was intelligent, loved Italian opera, possessed a sonorous baritone voice, and spoke fluent French, which helped him pick up hookers in Paris.

Once, before leaving for France, he cheerily announced, "This will be my sixty-fourth trip." Always before departing, he came up to La Falaise and presented Elmyr a hastily concocted bill for services not rendered. I suspect he passed the collection plate among other clients, as well. Elmyr knew these minor extortions were similar to the periodic payments he made to Nini. In other parts of the world, this custom is called "baksheesh." It's a widely accepted practice and cultural norm. Elmyr's lawyer also understood the notion of money as a tool. He was well connected and familiar with bribes and under-the-table payoffs. For probably a good two thousand years, this small island of traders and merchants knew this marketplace tradition, and it was certainly alive and well among the current batch of residents. Unlike the mafia, there was no fraternity, or secret society bound together by oath or arcane rules. It was a more laissez faire, individualist kind of banditry. In a collective gesture of civic pride, they erected the largest bronze statue on the island in Ibiza town, dedicated not to a national hero, but to a pirate!

Another visitor who made the pilgrimage to Elmyr's villa also had a reputation as a charlatan. They said, "Be careful. He doesn't pay his hotel bills—or any bills. He's charming, but don't trust him." The French called him a *"monstre sacré."* That was Orson Welles.

Intrigued by Elmyr's story after seeing the BBC/Reichenbach documentary made on him, Welles used it as the basis for his 1973 film *F for Fake*. Filmmaking, according to him, was another art form that is as unabashedly illusory as Elmyr's canon of fake art. In this respect he felt well qualified to draw intersecting lines between these two visual media to illustrate how each relies on a degree of duplicity or trickery to manufacture a "truth" that is more a product of stagecraft than a reflection of reality.

Orson Welles and Elmyr – 1972

In the opening scene of his movie, Welles is dressed in a black cape, performing sleight-of-hand magic tricks before a small boy in riveted wonder. He introduces his audience to his subject with his hypnotically sonorous voice. "This is a film about trickery and illusion..." For the rest of the picture Welles goes on an escapade questioning what is real or not and the value society attaches to their perceptions of art. The notion of tweaking the nose of convention or propriety becomes a joyful idée fixe and underlying theme that he squarely embraces and of course counts himself as a contributing iconoclast as well.

He revels in recounting his 1938 radio broadcast of H. G. Wells's story "War of the Worlds," with its simulated reality and impending doom that caused widespread panic, instances of suicide, and claims of abduction and rape of innocent victims by the invading Martians. A contrite Welles made a public apology the following day for his program's too-lifelike and sporadically tragic consequences. I am sure he felt especially devastated for those cases of brutal Martian rape. It also cemented his reputation as a hoaxster that he afterward never entirely disavowed nor shunned. He also shares an admission that he curiously started his professional life as a young painter in Ireland. When his artistic endeavors brought him to the brink of starvation, he told his Irish hosts that he was actually a famous American actor and thereafter tried to make good his lie. By virtue of his own dubious beginnings, his treatment of Elmyr's chicanery is perhaps understandably lighthearted and generous. He is also acutely aware that Elmyr's skill as an artist is close to his own, an interpreter of art.

Welles was what the French describe in a shudder of awe and respect as a "sacred monster." Prior to his visit to Ibiza, his reputation of course preceded him. The temperamental nature and easily ruffled sensibilities of this star were already common knowledge. Rumored to have a taste for only Titinger champagne, we dared not risk incurring the wrath of

Zeus by not having any. Elmyr delegated me to seek out the expensive and rare ambrosia on the island. After several stops at various bodegas, I found a bottle. That was it, one lonely bottle. We all were queasy, apprehensive in advance of his arrival.

At La Falaise the BBC crew of technicians readied the house as an improvised sound stage. I had seen the blindingly brilliant lights used before and wondered if they would be unnecessary, as his star power might be sufficiently luminescent by itself. After all, he had that incandescent status of "living legend." That evening he entered the house looking surprisingly mortal, casually dressed in a traditional Spanish shirt with fine pleats running vertically from symmetrically matched breast pockets to its bottom and worn outside the trousers about hip level. Elmyr, by comparison, was dressed for a night at the opera and was lost in Welles's shadow that further contrasted their different appearance and stature.

He and Elmyr needed no introduction; instead, they bounded into a friendly banter that suggested a comfortable familiarity or merely a reconnection only interrupted by the passage of time rather than a first-time encounter. Taking my cue from Elmyr for being an attentive host, I asked if he would like a glass of French champagne. He replied, "A glass of *vino tinto* would do." OK, a little red wine, I thought, was not too godlike. When he later asked me where I was from and I said Minnesota, he informed me that he was from Wisconsin. He not only proved to be entirely human but my respect for this fellow Midwesterner grew even greater. His approachability and charm were unaffected, and his inimitable voice was as soothing as the sound of a purring cat. I no longer saw him as some fearsome temple deity and object of worship, but as someone who would cordially pass you the jam across the table if asked.

It was indeed an edifying glimpse of a unique meeting between two remarkable men. For about three hours Welles and Elmyr exchanged views on life, spirituality, love, religion, philosophy, and art. Both were thoughtful, erudite, and appeared to enjoy their spontaneous conversation. I only wish I had kept a private recording of the dialogue, as it all but vanished on the editing room floor. My impression throughout their metaphysical expositions was that while Welles was clearly an intellectual titan, Elmyr proved to be at least his equal. After the filming concluded, Welles stayed the night as Elmyr's guest. Early the next morning we expected to breakfast together; however, he disappeared, leaving only a long three-page letter on his bed thanking Elmyr for his hospitality and excusing his sudden departure. I do not recall the reason given for his abrupt flight, but he succeeded in maintaining an air of mystery about him.

The film debuted at the San Sebastian Film Festival in northern Spain in 1973. For seven days, the city became a cultural wormhole attracting an interstellar array of celestial bodies. I could only compare the teeming carnival atmosphere to what I had experienced at the state fair back home in Minnesota, but for the absence of the gleaming new farm machinery, corn dogs, and cotton candy. Those attention-grabbers, however, paled next to the glittering human confetti of the film world. Festivals, as the name implies, are fanciful, joyous occasions, in this instance an international swap meet designed to promote, display, buy, and sell movies for the pleasure of a visually voracious public. Just beneath the glamour of these tony events is a hardscrabble world of the marketplace. Along with a plethora of actors, directors, screenwriters, producers, distributors, et al., an army of paparazzi, tabloid journalists, television reporters, and even representatives of the mainstream press were present to record and interpret their every word and movement on and off screen. It was a colorful, entertaining zoo.

Elmyr and I went to a number of the premiers that week. Festival organizers probably lobbied long and hard to capture Elizabeth Taylor to inaugurate the event, which may have been a misplaced effort. She arrived two hours late, sweeping across the stage in a bolt of sari fabric à la Isadora Duncan to boos and shrill whistles from the audience, whose patience was long spent. Elmyr took the occasion to lean into me, saying, "You see, it doesn't matter who you are, never be late and never waste people's time." There was a lesson in most everything.

Madrid

In 1972 I bought my first Nikon camera. A romance ensued. The schools of visitors to La Falaise offered me opportunities to create a visual logbook of famous people coming to see Elmyr. One of his friends was a Catalan woman, Juana Biarnes, who owned a small press agency in Madrid with her French husband, Michel, a correspondent for *Paris Match* magazine. While visiting one day, Juana suggested that during the off-season when we closed the gallery, I should come to work for them in Madrid, and they would teach me everything about photography. I accepted her offer and flew to Madrid for a few weeks' internship that would open my pupils to a wide aperture. Someone I met gave me the address of a cheap cold-water pension with meals included. Its style was basic military, but I had my own room.

To my amazement, two Japanese students inhabited the room next to mine. They were there to learn Spanish cooking, a novel idea, I thought. In the thirty-plus years since I lived there, Spanish cuisine has sprinted past its former unremarkable simplicity, I understand. During my time there, international gourmets were not tripping over one another queuing up "to do Spanish." No one confused it with French cuisine. It all seemed rather modest fare, with much generously fried in olive oil and garlic. It therefore appeared both bold and mystifying that the two Japanese fellows were keen to proselytize it back in their homeland.

The person who recommended the pension also resided there. He was Moroccan and unusually tall, about six feet four inches. Being over six feet myself, I wasn't used to feeling short around anyone, especially since I could easily survey the tops of heads during my subway rides each day to and from the agency. The press agency was not what I expected, not at all. It was actually a small house in a residential area. It possessed no furniture other than a couple of folding tables and chairs and a dark room for developing film. It looked more conducive to conducting clandestine interrogations. Juana treated it as the War Room. What also eluded me prior to my arrival was the exact nature of what they expected me to do. Their principal customers were Spanish illustrated weeklies and daily newspapers. They bought their photos and articles, and this was my baptism in photojournalism. The impression from my first day on the job is indelible.

About eight a.m., the phone rang. Juana listened like a squadron commander awaiting details of the day's target. She hung up and pointed at me, entrusting me to accompany Carlos, a veteran staffer, to a location outside Madrid. The hot tip led us to monastery in the mountains. Juana told us film director Louis Buñuel was there. Our mission was clear: get photos and an interview with the elusive recluse. For years, his anti-Franco sentiments earned him non grata status, forcing him to live in France, a country proud of its robust leftist sympathies. His surreal film classic, *Un Chien Andalou* (Andulusian Dog) and association with Salvador Dali made him a living icon in Spain. More importantly, perhaps, the embers of rebellion cooled sufficiently to let him back into the country.

The monastery was now a hotel, although no less austere in appearance for its secular conversion. The chill at that altitude made our necks recoil into our shoulders. The scarcity of cars suggested there were few guests this time of the year. Three-meter-high wooden doors with steel hinges resembling crusader's swords opened easily in the rounded arch. They separated in the middle, allowing us into a stone-floored foyer. We approached the reception desk and asked the concierge if Señor Buñuel was staying there. He said he was. Was there any chance we could call his room? Carlos asked. "No," he said, shaking his head in a way that allowed no appeal. Then, with the anticipatory look of someone expecting a reward, he added, "He does go out for his daily constitutional between three and four…" My companion's face remained inert, impenetrable to the custom of tipping for the information just given us. I soon found out why.

Like a bored housecat patiently waiting for a mouse to emerge from under the refrigerator, we sat in our car for more than two hours watching the hotel entrance. Buñuel finally came out alone for his walk. Carlos said, "Now"—as though his prey were at last in the cross-hairs of his scope—"grab your camera." I followed Carlos, who took off as though we were chasing a departing bus. Buñuel cast a casual glance over his left shoulder when he heard our gallop over the gravel path. Carlos stepped in front of a small man wearing a black leather jacket, stopping his advance. He looked annoyed. Apologetically introducing himself, he begged the director for a moment of his time. We simply hoped to get a few photos and ask him some questions about his current film project. I stood back, quietly snapping a few headshots. Buñuel folded his arms across his chest; his jaw muscles rippled. Extending his right arm within inches of Carlos's face, he raised his index finger from a closed fist. "You can take *one* photo, no interview." Carlos raised his camera to frame his subject in its viewfinder for a full-face portrait of the interdicted filmmaker. He then depressed the button, sending its motorized body into a serenade of incessant clicking while moving in a close circle around his stationary subject. I continued photographing the now lemon-faced Spaniard. The director-turned-action hero then leaped like a pissed panther at Carlos, short arms rigid reaching up to snatch away his camera. Wow, their struggle was straight out of the movies. My shock was complete but superseded by my companion's excitement. "Did you get it?" His eyes were a prospector's twenty-four-carat gleam. "Did you get it?" he asked again. "I'm not sure," I uttered in a somnambulant daze. "It happened so fast," I added. Buñuel threw out some Spanish invectives demonstrating the language's richness. We went on our way, he on his. When we reached the car he explained how a photo of their little dustup was worth more than any stupid interview.

I better understood why celebrities struggle to recapture the tranquility anonymity gives the rest of us unknowns and how precious that imperturbable peace is. Juana's expectations were also clear. She was grooming me to be a paparazzo. During our ride back to Madrid, I contemplated the contempt for this profession. People viewed sexually transmitted diseases with less scorn. They, at least, were curable. It was also an upside-down world from what I was learning from Elmyr, the gentility of social decorum and good manners. The notion of purposefully making myself a hateful outcast ran contrary to my values and natural desire to be liked and accepted.

When we returned to the barren agency, Carlos took our cameras into the darkroom to develop the glossy strands of 35-millimeter film. When he came out, his face wore the disappointment of failure. Neither of us had proof of the scuffle, no fabric on which to embroider fantasy around fact as on a medieval tapestry. Afterward, I confided to Juana that I could not bring myself to the level of social detachment needed to succeed in this business. I waved a conciliatory flag, assuring her I would be happy to send her photos of noteworthy people and stories as opportunities occurred in Ibiza, contingent on their consent and cooperation, of course. For the rest of my time there I covered local events, conferences, beauty contests, and offended no one. Juana taught me how to use a darkroom, and it ended up a worthwhile experience

My photography lessons however, enabled me to learn more about a visual medium I respect for its ability to capture truth and transform a craft into an art form. Later that summer I put some of my newly acquired skill to work. I met Georgianna Russell. She, like so many others, arrived one day at La Falaise unannounced. She was attractive, vibrant, with a lively mind, and Elmyr loved her pedigree. She was a great-niece of Bertrand Russell, the English writer, philosopher, and pacifist. Her father Sir John Russell was then British ambassador to Spain. Once, while visiting her at their residence in Madrid, I met her mother, who was Greek, a renowned beauty. Naturally, Georgianna spoke Greek and several other languages. On top of the grand piano in the living room were various photos of Sir John with Churchill, Stalin, and others. Georgianna worked as a contributing editor for *British Vogue* magazine. She told me about an article she had just written about Salvador Dali. She interviewed him by phone, asking him, I remember, to concoct some summer drink. The ingredients he offered better demonstrated the elasticity of Dali's imagination than remotely resembling anything one would dare consume. According to her account, he first suggested using water from the Guadalquivir River in southern Spain, then some extinct bird guano, and then the recipe became strange. Anyway, it was a Daliesque flight of fancy. The bird poop was unsurprising, as it reminded me of an anecdote Elmyr shared with me. Apparently, when Dali was trying to lure away Gala, his future wife, from her then lover, French writer/poet Paul Eluard, he smeared his naked body with shit. He went to Gala and loudly proclaimed, "Je pue d'amour pour vous!" (I stink of love for you!) Now, with sincerity like that, what mother wouldn't let her daughter go to the prom with a person like him?

Georgianna was heading to Mallorca after her stopover in Ibiza. She had another assignment there, to interview British writer and poet Robert Graves, author of *I, Claudius*, among numerous other books. Graves had lived for decades in Deya since before the Spanish Civil War. The village rests in the island's coastal hillside, and is an artist's enclave, probably in no small part due to Graves. I told Georgianna of my photojournalist stint in Madrid, so she asked if I wanted to accompany her to do the photos. "*Vogue*," she assured me, "would pay for the pictures." Elmyr gave his benediction and we left two days later.

In Palma, we rented a car and followed the two-lane roads ascending into the mountains. It was the 24th of July 1973, a special day, Graves's 78th birthday, and we were about to attend the celebration. His house was a typical Mediterranean farmhouse of mortared stone. His wife greeted us when we arrived. Although Georgianna had not yet met Graves, her family name assured us a warm reception. A short distance from the house, the author sat in a rattan chair under a carob tree. Rays of sunlight hit his back through its branches. Others scurried around the patio preparing a long table and smaller ones for the party later that afternoon. He didn't stand when we approached, a formality dismissed some time ago due to age, I imagine. Spain may have been his retreat for health reasons, too. During the First World War, he suffered the effects of "shell shock" or post traumatic stress disorder. In any case, it assured his discharge from military service.

Georgianna introduced herself and me. She sparked his interest. They talked about her "Uncle Bertie" and her father. Then, she explained my weak reason to live, my connection to Elmyr. Well, it sounded like that, sort of. He turned to me and asked, apropos of nothing else, "Were you in the hussars?" I understood the question, but briefly taken aback, responded, "I beg your pardon." "Did you serve in the cavalry?" All I could think of was Custer at the Little Bighorn. "No...no, I didn't." Nor did offering that I rode a pony in a circle when I was five reach the threshold of noteworthiness to continue in this equine vein. It was still morning. Afternoon looked far off. Sensing, I think, that this topic looked fruitless, he vaulted into another realm. "I've been dreaming a lot lately," he said, "but it has nothing to do with sex." This declaration was bewildering, but at least promising. It was at once strange for this man with thinning white hair scattered by wind, flesh cascading in neat crescents around his elbows and knees, to still have libidinous thoughts. Great expectations suddenly buoyed my future old age. Before that moment I did not think at all about whether or not I would be doing it at that advanced stage. Today, I have a favorite photo I took of Graves that day. The sage is backlit with those shafts of light. He appears lost in thought—or thoroughly bored by my company. No matter.

On the hillside below where we sat, he built in the land's contour a semi-circular amphitheater. There, that afternoon, he recited poetry he recently wrote in Latin and Greek. I took photos while he spoke. I understood none of it, but remained quiet and polite as I learned in my youth, especially in moments of cluelessness.

Palacio Liria

In the center of Madrid lies a treasure chest disguised as a private home called Palacio Liria. It boasts a Baroque-style facade and stone columns within a walled, parklike setting. Considering the home burned to the ground during the Spanish Civil War, it is a remarkable reconstruction, attentive in every way to period detail, a paean to its owners' wealth, status, and sense of their own historical prominence dating back to the Middle Ages. It belongs to the Alba family, Grandees of Spain for centuries—and through aristocratic marriages they are even on the short list as successors to the British throne, as their family name happens to be Fitz-James Stewart. Did I mention they were rich in an incalculable way? Really. They possess vast property holdings throughout the country and one of *the* most important art collections in the world, including hundreds of works by the great Spanish masters Velásquez, Goya, El Greco, Zubarán, Murrillo et al.

A friend in Madrid introduced us to the son of the Duchess of Alba. He then offered Elmyr and me a private tour of the family villa. He explained how Italian and Spanish artisans painstakingly replicated every original element of the palace. Its rectangular floor plan echoed many of the great country houses of European nobility of the seventeenth and

eighteenth centuries. Inlaid marble floors displayed intricate multicolored designs like those reserved for the tops of tables or finest cabinetry.
Far exceeding its value was the extensive art collection that mercifully
moved to the vaults of the Banco de España during the three years the
country devolved in its internecine civil war.

Life-size Greek statues flanked the wide marble stairwell to the second-floor salons, past the spacious family chapel with its gold leaf reli-
giosity. Besides the paintings in their ornate gilded frames in an endless
procession of rooms, Goblain tapestries and museum-quality marquetry
furniture added to their pomp. Our stamina withered under the visual
onslaught. We returned to the ground floor to their library. It was a large
room. I remember its ceiling perhaps six or seven meters high, fifteen
meters wide, and about thirty meters long. Spaced evenly around the
perimeter of the library, near its ceiling, were brightly painted escutch-
eons, each signifying one of their duchies. I imagine the hypoxic condition afflicting the winded major domo having to recite *all* their titles.
It was difficult envisioning the surprises contained within this library.
Waist-high glass cases contained beyond-rare documents. Among them
were letters from Louis XVI and Marie Antoinette, the marriage certificate of King Ferdinand and Queen Isabella, their last will and testament,
the Alba Bible, an early fifteenth-century illuminated translation of the
Old Testament from Hebrew into Spanish, and, stunningly, letters from
Christopher Columbus, including the first map of the New World drawn
in Columbus's own hand. (Now this is the best part.) We staggered forward zombie-legged. The Duchess's son threw an over-the-shoulder
caveat. "Of course, we keep the valuable things in the safe." I added,
"Do you have one of Moses's tablets in there?" He laughed, but didn't
specify what those treasures were.

The Grand Tour

Visitors to La Falaise often seemed like a trail of ants winding their way to a mound. With each new set of claps from the black iron doorknocker, I would scurry to see who arrived to see Elmyr. One of my appointed tasks was resident major domo, greeting, admitting, and announcing those wanting to meet Ibiza's celebrated artist. Elmyr relaxed his observance of social protocol for these unexpected callers. Not everyone had a phone, so it was often easier to make a personal visit, an informality we all accepted.

At that time, the island's telephone system was a bit more effective than using an empty can at each end of a taut string, but only slightly. When attempting a call to his friend Sandy in Santa Eulalia, a village about eighteen kilometers away, he had to go through a local operator. Often he sat on the edge of his bed; his face went crimson when communicating with her, shouting as though he were trying to raise the dead through a mostly deaf spiritualist. These blood-pressure-raising events were somewhat successful as he made himself audible a good part of the way in an imperfect Esperanto that Elmyr mistook for the Spanish equivalent of the Queen's English. The odd thing is that his linguistic gumbo stew became perfectly understandable to anyone spending much time with him. After learning French, I studied Spanish and only then realized his notion of Castilian Spanish was his own hybrid of Latin, Italian, Portuguese, and smattering of the native language thrown in to be polite.

On a sunny morning, responding to the familiar sound at the front door, I opened it to find a middle-aged British couple eager to see Elmyr. Informing them that he was in his studio working, and by custom, did not wish to be disturbed, I welcomed them to wait upstairs. They had come from San Antonio, the more modern resort and hotel area on the other side of the island that catered to the ever-growing influx of tourists.

Before long, Elmyr emerged from his bedroom suite, where he had transformed its sitting room into his atelier. Speckles and streaks of oil paints of various colors on his hands and fingers suggested a less fastidious relation with his brushes than with his table flatware. He wore a gray-blue smock to absorb the splatter from his palette, and it was always a roadmap of his creative journey. He possessed scores of brushes, consisting of every conceivable thickness and width, all of the finest quality from his favorite supplier, Windsor and Newton. They were expensive, highly prized, and cared for with motherly attention. In his left hand was a clutch of freshly used brushes. Washing them carefully was a never-ignored routine afterward.

Hearing strange voices emanating from the second-floor living room, he asked, before coming into view, "Who's here?" I replied, "You have two visitors who've shown great perseverance in tracking you down." I introduced Ian Major and his wife, Cynthia. His hands still bearing the traces of his morning's work, he cordially greeted them, but excused himself to wash up and clean his brushes. Returning within minutes, he then warmly engaged his guests. Ian, a tall, stout, jovial man comfortably bore a retirement-age weight gain stretched over a once-athletic frame. He also displayed that self-assured ease that wealth breeds, a look I became familiar with in Elmyr's world. His wife, Cynthia, imparted the class of those whose speech was associated with the landed gentry. She was warm and gracious. Her past was anything but a life of uninterrupted privilege, as her accent intoned. On the contrary, her history was marked with the hardship of a generation emotionally and physically scared by war. Her personal story was as unique as it was unexpectedly harsh. She was previously married to Hoar-Belisha, a member of Churchill's cabinet, his war minister and a Jew. Hugely unlucky, Cynthia was in Germany at that unpropitious moment when England declared war with Nazi Germany. The Gestapo gave her accommodations in Auschwitz as personal guest of the Führer. When she shared this background with Elmyr, visibly overcome by grief, he broke down and cried, unable to hide his upset and sorrow. He told me his father, a Hungarian diplomat, died at Auschwitz, one of the most horrific sites of mass exterminations.

Ian was interested in buying some artwork. He and Cynthia disappeared into Elmyr's studio for more than two hours. Besides his technical skill as a painter, Elmyr had the profound knowledge of an art historian, so he could speak about his work and his profession with an unchallengeable persuasiveness and authority. His convincing banter usually secured a sale. He was a "closer" par excellence, and watching him was an inimitable experience.

They bought over six thousand dollars' worth of paintings, watercolors, and drawings, which they split between their homes in Geneva and the Virgin Islands. It afforded Elmyr a comfortable life for the next several months. Ian earned a fortune buying and selling property in the islands and exhibited no second thoughts about spending his money. His casual largesse mirrored Elmyr's own generosity, and this common trait drew the two men closer to one another. Their friendship grew quickly. Cynthia, Ian, and Elmyr felt a kinship that became apparent over their weeklong stay on the island. Elmyr threw a party at the house to have them meet some more of his friends. He was an attentive host during their visit. Before seeing them off at the airport, they had coaxed a promise from Elmyr to visit them at their home in Geneva at summer's end. He said we would come.

As September neared, we arranged to visit our new friends. With some additional sales of his work during a socially hectic summer, Elmyr wanted to extend our itinerary into a grand tour. It would include Vienna, Salzburg, Venice, Rome, Capri, Milan, Florence, Geneva, and London.

It is hard to imagine under any circumstances how any stop in Italy would not be fantastic. I visited the country on my own during my backpacking and youth hostel days. Now, accompanying Elmyr, I traveled first class and stayed at five-star hotels.

VIENNA

In Vienna, we went to the Sacher Hotel, home of the internationally famous chocolate tort. There, the clerk informed us that there was no record of our reservation and it was unlikely that we would get a room, as the hotel was full. Elmyr then pulled a woven gold cigarette case from his suit pocket. The case's sides each had forty uniform, bevel-cut, deep-blue sapphires. With a slow-motion gesture, he opened the jeweled case and offered me one of his unfiltered Turkish cigarettes from Abdul's of Jermyn Street, knowing I did not smoke. The hotel manager gave a look of a conquistador eyeing Aztec gold. An instant later, he excused himself and said he had found *one* room available after all. Elmyr did not smoke, but when a Madrid jeweler offered an exchange of the 18k objet d'art for a painting, Elmyr felt compelled to give the impression he did.

He generously tipped the hotel concierge for hard-to-get tickets for the renowned Vienna Opera across from the Sacher. That evening we saw *Cavalaria Rusticana* by Pietro Mascagni. To my ears, his *Intermezzo* remains one of the most beautiful orchestral pieces ever written. Excursions through Europe's grandest temples of art commenced with a tour of the Kunst Historiche Museum and the Albertina that houses perhaps the largest collection of old masters' prints and drawings. Elmyr shared insights into European art with his personal viewpoint in gallery after gallery, always revealing details unnoticed by the casual observer.

Vienna was the capital of the Hapsburg Empire, consisting of the Kingdom of Hungary and the Austrian Empire. In 1867, they joined to become the Austro Hungarian Empire. Elmyr was happy to make clear the complex history, geography, and political spheres of influence via a dizzying organizational chart involving marital alliances, accessions, concessions, treaties, battles, coronations, borders, ethnicity, and cultures, all of which he kept neatly in his head and made perfect sense. His endurance was Herculean and a product of his passion to impart his knowledge even long after he sucked all the oxygen from the room.

One luminous morning, we visited Schönbrunn Palace, one of those cheek-slapping wonders that makes Buckingham Palace look like some down-market digs. It had a bazillion bonus rooms, all nicely appointed by the Royal Family Furniture Warehouse, most likely. Inside, a game of hide and seek might well prove fatal. The Royal Mice could nibble away at your remains before, with any luck, they found your gnawed-clean bones at all. From my modest working-class background, this kind of pharaonic wealth and power was unimaginable. Elmyr identified portraits by Winterhalter and then shared not-too-brief histories of the people in them, for the genealogical pleasure of it all.

SALZBURG

This city, nestled among the snow-capped Austrian Alps, challenges the imagination to rival its scenery. Everyone should make a pilgrimage there at least once in one's life. Here, we followed a performance of chamber music of Mozart the first evening, with lodging in a fourteenth-century inn. Just to attest to its authenticity, its ceilings and doorways were low, its wood floors slanted and squeaky, like the beds. While the peak tourist season had waned, it was surprising how bourgeois this city was. Around eight in the evening they seemed to "roll up the sidewalks," as they say in the Midwest. It's as if all the residents responded to some inaudible dog whistle, shuttered their windows, locked their doors, donned ankle-length nightgowns, night caps, and dutifully went to bed—a quaint custom for a large European city, I thought.

Some friends who were also clients of Elmyr's invited us to visit them in the Tyrol region of Austria, where they lived. Through some quirk of geography and location, this area is a blessed climatic sanctuary in the mountains, offering lush forests and weather mild enough to support semitropical plants in much the same way as the Gulf Stream warms the southern coasts of Ireland and England for their gardening-obsessed residents. The region also boasts the oldest (or largest) grape vine in Europe. Heavy gauge wire supports its fruit-bearing canopy, covering hundreds of square meters. The viticulture there dates back to Roman occupation, and the fermented juice from the pressed grapes is probably as delicious today as it was to the Latin forebears who introduced it.

VENICE

Traveling then to Innsbruck and through the Brenner Pass into Italy, one could savor the majesty of the Italian Alps and better appreciate how formidable a feat it was for Hannibal to move his army and precious elephants over this intimidating snow-capped mountain range twenty-two centuries earlier. We were on our way to Venice, the splendid city of the doges. This would be my third time back, but first with Elmyr, although now it was not the low-budget adventure it was twice before. Au contraire; we were booked into the Gritti Palace on the Grand Canal. From our room we had the unusual opportunity to see the city welcome its first visit from a reigning pope (Paul VI) in over two hundred years. The city spared no effort or colored banner to celebrate the occasion. This former maritime superpower brought out every seaworthy craft imaginable for this papal regatta. They orchestrated the Holy Father's naval welcome with all the adept Italian stagecraft and pomp fitting the event. One was not only awed by the visually rich pageantry but also by its historical significance.

Here, fittingly, Elmyr personally introduced me to the school of great Venetian colorists, Giovanni Bellini, Giorgione, Titian, Tintoretto, Veronese, Tiepolo, and others. The city's famed Italian Gothic architecture, with its onion-shaped arches, commonly outlined with stone ornamentation resembling braided bread, are a ubiquitous reminder of its glory years of the late Middle Ages. The eighteenth-century paintings of Francesco Guardi and Canaletto visually document the decay to which the once glorious city had succumbed, but at the same time suggest its haunting grandeur. Its narrow streets and arterial canals still infuse a timeless romantic appeal without equal anywhere else. Elmyr wanted to introduce me to "Harry's Bar," an institution to savor. The famed landmark attracted Hemingway, Fitzgerald, and other illuminati, also any other aspirant who wished their name connected to the word *class*.

One morning a couple of days into our stay, I woke to a knock at our hotel room door. It was a young man in a crisply starched white jacket, carrying our breakfast tray. A large divided window opened to the cloudless sky; sunlight glistened on the blue-green Adriatic waters of the Grand Canal. It was a morning of promise but for an uncharacteristically dour look on Elmyr's face. "What's troubling you?" I inquired. He explained that he had gone to the casino at the Lido the night before and lost the equivalent of seven hundred pounds sterling, or about $1,400. This was a time before the ubiquity of credit cards, which, in fact, he never owned. It represented a large portion of cash he had left until he could access a Swiss account in Geneva. We spent most of the day trying to reach a Hungarian friend of his in Geneva, a retired investment banker, who had helped him open the account. It was a complicated process involving international bank transfers. This challenging monetary maze seemingly required some divine intervention. By late afternoon the requested funds had been wired to the Italian bank, Banco di Santo Espirito—Bank of the Holy Spirit; a fitting redemption for an earthly sin—gambling.

It was not Elmyr's first flirtation with games of chance, or his last. He liked the thrill of the game with its adrenalin rush. Strangely, despite his propensity to lose money practically all the time, he would return. Instead of it becoming a compulsive addiction (and curse to many), it was the glamour, ambiance, and battle of wits that beckoned him. Skill was another matter. The only two games that interested him were chemin de fer and baccarat. He always dressed for the occasion: black velvet jacket, tailored shirts from Jermyn Street, silk tie in a Windsor knot, gold monocle, and a suitable amount of jewelry. What he unfortunately never twigged to was that he had the bluff of a newborn. For his lack of a poker face, he would have been much better off, and richer too, to wear a Venetian Carnival mask. It was always painful to endure the predictably disappointing outcome of what the "gaming" industry inappropriately calls "entertainment."

On Ibiza, Elmyr often got into high-stakes poker games with people with deeper pockets and most often more skill. In these instances, he hadn't the aversion to risk-taking that experience should have taught him or that age should have greatly diminished. This behavior, I believe, really points to the emotional rather than analytical plain on which he operated, and also to his cavalier attitude about money. It was, after all, just a tool—like his paintbrushes, which he could always use to make more money.

MILAN

The next stop was Milan, a largely forgettable city but for the requisite visit to see Leonardo's *Last Supper* in the Church of Santa Maria della Grazie, the magnificent Gothic cathedral, the Duomo, and the elegant Victor Emanuel arcade (if one has shopping in mind).

Standing before *The Last Supper* leaves one awestruck not so much for being in the presence of great art but more so for the Christian iconography attached to this imagine. In the early 1970s, its staggering deterioration was sadly apparent, so it looked more like a painting applied to the sun-baked, cracked mud of a dried-up river bed. Its disturbing condition greatly detracted from the experience. It should be remembered, "da Vinci was experimenting with a new fresco technique that began to fail badly within his own lifetime," as Elmyr pointed out. Consequently, the faded colors and surface loss over the almost five hundred years since its creation invites a liberal application of imagination. The art historian Vasari described it in 1556 "as 'a muddle of blots.'" Another important caveat Elmyr offered was that when viewing these precious works, one should keep in mind they had most likely undergone numerous cleanings and attempts at restoration with sometimes shocking results. Illustrating his point, he asked me, "Did you notice that the Mona Lisa had no eyebrows?" I said that I hadn't. He was right, of course. Their absence is the anatomical anomaly that always comes to mind first every time I see it. He was a cornucopia of these pearls of knowledge that he generously sowed because he needed to share what he had learned.

FLORENCE

We traveled from Milan to Florence by bus. Tuscany echoed the semiarid hills and vegetation of Ibiza. It is easy to see why the familiar Mediterranean topography made many of its sea-going cultures feel at home throughout the breadth of this region. Here, the Etruscan civilization, influenced by colonizing Greeks, thrived for six to eight hundred years before the Romans assimilated them. Tall, slender cypress trees lined the winding roads. Rippled terracotta tiles graced the rooftops, slanting like three-dimensional chevrons in a myriad of directions. When the city came into view, those images so vividly described in Benvenuto Cellini's autobiography raced through my mind. He was a contemporary of Michelangelo, the foremost goldsmith of the sixteenth century. His memoir, however boastful, provides a firsthand account of the crucible that was Florence, the creative birthplace and turbulent center of the Italian Renaissance. The Campanile bell tower designed by Giotto is still the commanding landmark of the city. He, more than any other artist, is credited with liberating the art of painting from the stiff, iconic Byzantine style that had frozen the human form like gilded, vertically stacked cordwood. The writer Bocaccio and poet Dante were his friends. Together, these three giants were at the vanguard of a cultural and artistic awakening that would sweep through Europe like a canyon brush fire. Florence became the navel of the universe for the next 250 years.

Having Elmyr as my guide through the Uffizi Gallery and the Pitti Palace thrilled me. In a condensed, total-immersion, walking art history lecture, I felt my right brain would implode. The depth of his connoisseurship was staggering, but beyond his scholarly expertise was another dimension he was showing and teaching me. They said Balzac was a "seer." Elmyr was also a seer. It was a sense of penetrating what was present, but also developing a psychic sense of what was not there. For some time he was ratcheting up my education. Starting with elementary building blocks, as a surgeon accumulates an increasing familiarity with anatomy, he showed me systematically all the elements of figurative art and what separates the best from the rest. To illustrate what I mean, the following day we went to see Michelangelo's statute of David. It was simultaneously a paradigm of latent power and calm confidence, sculpted by a genius. We studied it together in silent appreciation. Then Elmyr pointed out that "the head is too big for his body." His matter-of-fact announcement was now an apparent observation that it was slightly out of proportion. To this day it is a haunting refrain each time I see it.

I should make clear that these were no judgmental condemnations or carping faultfinding. It was simply a matter of stating what "is." He knew when he was in the company of quality art and viewed it holistically. On the other hand, he knew what was bad and was not usually shy about expressing himself. In no way am I suggesting art is a recondite, elitist discipline understood only by tea-sipping Brahmins. If it were, it would not be the playpen of color and honest and spontaneous expression universally enjoyed by children. It is, nevertheless, a visual language designed to communicate with the viewer. Having an idea of its historical timeline and connectedness to the social fabric simply takes one to a greater depth of comprehension and appreciation. He simply analyzed and explained these things, wanting me to understand.

Often, visitors in art museums appear oxygen-starved, sucking air like a freshly landed fish. With eyes glazed and about forty-five minutes removed from any recollection why they were there, they would wander singularly or in a bovine herd, looking aimless, as though stunned by a Taser. Anyway, my point is that what ought to be a stimulating and rewarding experience too frequently is not. I am not sure it is imagery overload, because people show an impenetrable resilience to countless hours of television viewing without assuming that look of disengaged boredom.

As you will recall, that elfin intergalactic visitor who disguised himself as an architect, Frank Lloyd Wright, found a solution to what's commonly called "museum fatigue" or the symptoms I just described, in his seminal design for the Guggenheim Museum in New York City. His slightly inverted cone-shape tower is open in the center with a wide descending spiral walkway at its perimeter. It is a radical departure from the usual maze of interconnected boxes where even seasoned cartographers wander about disoriented. Visitors start their viewing pleasure at the top of the spiral and casually stroll down. In the event of someone having a sensory short circuit, rather than just melting into a puddle on a flat floor and getting in the way of others, with the help of gravity and incline they can simply roll to the bottom like a spilled sack of oranges.

Anyway, we walked several kilometers that morning, crossing the Ponte Vecchio, the oldest bridge spanning the Arno River. Dating from the middle of the fourteenth century, shops of gold- and silversmiths line the bridge. On one side of the river is another Harry's Bar. Here, we had lunch. Standing next to the bar was a tall, rugged, and handsome Scotsman wearing a traditional kilt and clan tartans. Looking as though he'd become separated from the other costume-wearing trick-or-treaters, he scanned the restaurant. Standing like an old growth oak on a tree farm, he was a head above anyone else. He appeared wistful. Perhaps his deepest fears and worries had come true. Had some cruel wag whispered in his ear that one couldn't find a decent bowl of haggis anywhere in this town? Arrgh! Moreover, what are those white furry dangly things they wear that look like the pelt of a desiccated West Highland white terrier? I suspect he, like many of his kinsmen, found a better than equal trade-off, a wee bit o' food for some single-malt Scotch.

In a book on Boswell, Samuel Johnson's noted biographer, a British wit said of his northern neighbors, "Scotland...a land where half-starved spiders prey on half-starved flies." It should be of little surprise that its gift to world cuisine was haggis. I half believe that contrary to historical accounts, vestiges of the famed Spanish Armada succumbing to violent storms, destroying the rest of their fleet on Scotland's harsh, rocky shores may have actually been an act of sixteenth-century public relations revisionism. More likely, the ships' crews, finding out what there was to eat if they went ashore, preferred to watch their vessels flounder and drown themselves. Even if Scotland was a good Catholic country, a soggy death seemed preferable.

Elmyr, by habit, liked to take a siesta. After lunch, we would return to our hotel. He would take a nap, and I would read or write postcards and letters. After resting less than an hour, he was again ready to resume the intense sightseeing in this cultural treasure chest. Later that day we visited the Italian Gothic cathedral, Santa Maria del Fiore, to view Brunelleschi's Duomo, the largest dome constructed in Europe since the Pantheon in Rome. Nearby, the Battistero di San Giovanni (Baptistery of St. John) and the gilded bronze doors by Ghiberti are beautiful enough to inspire wonder in any viewer. At the Piazza della Signoria, we studied Cellini's bronze statue of Perseus holding the head of Medusa (a mythic precursor to Texas Chainsaw Massacre). Another invaluable book that illuminated this personal domain of the powerful Medici family and their patronage of the arts, also recommended by Elmyr, was Vasari's "Lives of the Artists." Their stories not only imbued life into these emotionally moving works of art, but also grounded them in reality.

ROME

The Eternal City—Rome—was our next destination. For a young Minnesotan, the blasé resignation Europeans displayed in the presence of their rich historical and cultural heritage always amazed me. Excavations for the Rome metro begun in the 1930s immediately pitted progress against preserving its past and haltingly introduced its citizens to the benefits of a rapid, urban underground transportation system. Everyone knew you could not dig a hole in Rome without unearthing some archeological artifact. So ubiquitous, in fact, were these reminders of ancient Rome's patrimony, that the capital city's water supply came from its aqueducts, and only after 1955 other sources exceeded this volume. One senses the rich tapestry of its imperial and ecclesiastical past, the far-reaching legacy western culture has inherited from these dynamic peoples in our Christian religion, language, law, form of government, customs, and art.

We checked into the Grand Plaza Hotel. Its sumptuous multicolored marbled columns and floors, crystal chandelier, and gilded bronze lions at the bottom of its wide Carrara stone stairwell lent the unmistakable mark of old-world elegance. A velvet-lined comfort that Elmyr accepted as a matter of course quickly seduced me. Our room was dripping with brocade curtains, queen-size beds, Louis XV furniture, feather cushioned bergère chairs, and a wall safe in which to store the pearl strands and diamond tiara. The high-ceilinged bathroom was large enough to accommodate a presidential press conference.

Elmyr and I unpacked. He then dragged out his dog-eared, old leather address book with its scribbled names and numbers readable only to him and began phoning some friends. The first to get his call was an old acquaintance, Novella Parigi, (loosely translated as Paris Story). A name of theatrical invention, according to Elmyr, she did whatever she could to scandalize Roman society, which took some effort, and put her on the Pope's short list for excommunication. In the pre-thong-wearing fifties, she wore meager bikinis that were apparently crowd-pleasing and just on the shy side of legality. Just to make the Holy Father go even more squinty-eyed, she affixed over her pubic area on her swimsuit bottom one of those flat tromp l'oeil pictures of a mouth. When moved slightly, the image would change to an opened mouth, just like the Cracker Jack prizes. She was a good-looking blond and darling of the tabloids, a kind of self-generating publicity machine. When we arrived at her apartment, it resembled what a warehouse of stage props would look like. To make even the stuffiest visitors at ease, she had a couple of hammocks strung up where you might find chairs in a more conventional setting. I suspect it's hard to be haughty while looking like a netted bass. She and Elmyr caught up on time past and events in each other's life since they had last seen each other. He recounted his recent notoriety. Hoping to bask in the glow of more camera strobe flashes, she suggested calling in the local glamour vultures. Elmyr politely declined the invitation.

Apropos Novella's stagy but paparazzo-loving name, I want to go on another water-slide descent to explore some thoughts tangentially connected to this story, if only in a slightly gossamer way. Novella chose her name deliberately as writers often use a nom de plume, e.g., Mark Twain instead of Samuel Clemens. Others are less fortunate with their given names. In some instances it may even make some sense when, for instance, a family of innkeepers name their daughter Paris Hilton, after their French auberge, or if some fellow named Wood has a girl named Holly. My best friend's family name is Gray, and I forever admire his parent's restraint in not naming him Earl.

Only recently, my wife picked up a novel on audio disc for a long car trip. It was F. Scott Fitzgerald's *Tender Is the Night*, one of those ignored classics. Written in the thirties, its fine descriptive prose seemed a bit stilted. Harder yet to digest was the main character's improbable name, Dick Diver. Each time I heard it I could only imagine him introducing himself, his sister, Muff, and his gal pal, Pussy Galore. Not only would this name leave anyone in the gay community with cheeks tearstained from laughter but also anyone whose first language is English. Nor can I believe this was lost on a sophisticate like Fitzgerald. Go figure.

Another of Elmyr's longtime friends in Rome was Count Esterhazy, who interestingly played himself, an aristocratic embassy staffer, in *Roman Holiday* with Audrey Hepburn and Gregory Peck. He was from one of the oldest and most illustrious families of Hungary. For twenty-eight years the composer Franz Joseph Haydn was in the personal employ of this family. We met for dinner at a restaurant suggested by Esterhazy. Elmyr was in his element and rarely so pleased as when he could talk about people whose titles preceded their names. The animated conversation spoken in an arcane language sprinkled with heraldic significance gave my eyes the same stunned look of a trout on a dinner platter. I had a slim familiarity with Count Basie and Duke Ellington but that was the extent of my grasp of royalty, until, of course, I met Elmyr.

A Norwegian film crew interviewed me in 1996 to gain my perspective and insights about Elmyr. They were doing a documentary on his life. They went to Hungary in the hope of dissipating the shroud of mystery around him. Their investigation had little success. Many records were lost in the Second World War. What I can say with certainty about him is this: like water that seeks its own level, Elmyr had an ease with those whose backgrounds were genuinely aristocratic. He knew their world and possessed a personal knowledge of the genealogical strands of this complex web that connected this privileged class. It was not a facile affectation designed to deceive anyone. That evening, in fact, Esterhazy gave him a small, thin book of poetry in Hungarian written by no one other than Elmyr's father. On its back cover was his photo;

he was splendidly dressed, more resembling a pasha wearing an elaborately woven silk jacket and ornamental turban-like headpiece, replete with a jeweled cabochon in the center, holding a white egret plume. At his side was a gem-encrusted scabbard and dagger hilt. Nothing about this photo suggested that Elmyr may have been the offspring of some chimney sweep or the like, as his sociopath nemesis, Fernand Legros, incessantly claimed

Between renewing old friendships, we absorbed this forever-interesting city; the Coliseum, Pantheon, Trajan's Column, the Trevi Fountain, the beautifully Baroque Piazza Navona (with its fountains designed by Italy's foremost seventeenth-century sculptor, Bernini) and of course the Vatican. Michelangelo's *Pieta* and Sistine Chapel are powerfully transcendent, emotionally moving and spiritually resonating works of art that, in themselves, merit a visit to Rome. Touring the vast Vatican Museum drew Elmyr's ire. Every magnificent sculpture of the pre-Christian era now donned fig leaves over their genitalia to hide those body parts we see every day, even within the walls of our homes' smallest rooms. These imitation organic codpieces stem from the same Christian-inspired sense of propriety that caused the stormy battles between Michelangelo and Pope Julius II. Since the Pope paid the bill for the artist's commissioned work and it was his house, and his Sistine Chapel, he had Michelangelo's nude figures strategically draped in nicely colored sheets. Never mind that many of God's second-in-command servants were unashamedly sensualists and worldly in ways that would make Rupert Murdoch squirm. Elmyr could not tolerate the church's censorship of Michelangelo's art or any art.

CAPRI

It was a rapid trip by train from Rome to Naples. We did not spend any time in Naples, and I regretted not seeing Pompey and Herculaneum, perhaps some of the most interesting archeological sites in the world. From the train depot, we headed to the city's magnificent bay, taking a Russian-made hydrofoil to Capri. A friend of ours, Guy Munthe's grandfather, a Swedish doctor, wrote an autobiographical account of his life on the island called *The Story of San Michele*. It is a wonderful read and it captures the beauty, character, and history of the place. The Emperor Tiberius built a palace here and ruled the Roman Empire from his sanctuary surrounded by the sea. Gibbon's classic, *The Decline and fall of the Roman Empire*, documents his reign and some, but probably not all, of the naughty things he did here and elsewhere.

The island had two distinct areas, Capri and Anacapri. The village of Anacapri is on a mountaintop removed from the lower elevation of Capri. By tradition, the residents of these respective villages have a kind of Hatfield/McCoy relationship, without the flying bullets. I have no idea if these backyard feuds still exist, but the tendency to view the world through a parochial peephole is a custom that knows no geographic boundaries.

A few trucks, buses, and a handful of taxis that circulate are the rare motorized exceptions to the island's unmechanized charm. The popular Funicular (cable railway) shuttles visitors around as well. Capri's Blue Grotto is a natural rock enclave in which one has the feeling of entering a watery cave with views into the clear Mediterranean waters. Wonderful restaurants offer fine regional or national cuisine with delicious locally produced wine.

Elmyr had us booked into another first class hotel, the Quisisana. The view from our room revealed camelback hills speckled with villas, cypress trees, and a Mediterranean of aquamarine or azure. French doors opened to a balcony where we had a light lunch. After his siesta, we headed out exploring. It is almost a requisite stop for those wearing white pants, blue blazers, and chichi little captain's hats. If they wanted to pretend to be seafaring, they would garner a little more respect and attention if they wore an eye patch, had a hook where a hand might be, a leg missing below the knee, and a parrot on a shoulder with a vocabulary that would make women faint. Instead, they come ashore from their yachts, and for some reason I have not been able to fathom, frequent pricey jewelry stores as though they had never seen one before—anywhere—then come out prepared to enter The Mr. T Look-Alike Contest.

That evening at a restaurant a couple came in I immediately recognized as American. (You can tell.) She, acutely suntanned, wearing a demure white dress, he in his yacht club attire, sat down at the table next to ours. His white trousers had blue anchors all over them. Elmyr remarked how he liked his pants, not meaning it, of course. I immediately followed with, "I saw a pair just like yours in an Army Navy Store in Omaha." He looked crestfallen and told us he had just bought them at a fashionable boutique around the corner. Alas, this kind of impolitic candor has kept me from a career in customer service. Can you believe it?

Around 10:30, we returned to the hotel. The following morning we were up early and went to the main plaza of the town for a breakfast of coffee and croissants. By the third week in September, tourists have thinned out like male-patterned baldness. So, to our utter amazement, practically the lone person there seated at a small table happened to be someone we knew. Her name was Norma Clark, another fellow Minnesotan, curiously. She stood up in shocked surprise, warmly greeted us, and invited us to join her. Here, I am happy to crayon in the background because the story invites telling. She was a longtime acquaintance of Elmyr's. Their paths separated when she lived in Italy and France for many years. At the same time Elmyr had found refuge in Ibiza. About six months before embarking on this trip, we went to London together. Elmyr loved the city and the British. A great friend of ours, Jack Fry, an industrialist who had a fantastic home in Chelsea near the botanical gardens, invited us to stay with him. Jack was a charming, gracious, and intelligent man of multiple interests. One was collecting artwork by Elmyr.

During our stay, we went to one of the King's Road restaurants. It was chic and society-friendly. At a round corner table was a group of animated diners, all elegant. While still perusing the menu, Elmyr began staring intently in their direction. He then rose from his chair and headed to their table. In an unmistakably audible voice he exclaimed, "Norma Clark!" A look of recognition jolted her face. "Elmyr!" she said commensurately loudly. He approached nearer, leaned over as if to give her the customary French greeting of a kiss on each cheek. Instead, he reached out with his right hand and tightly clutched a strand of pearls around her neck. Looking intently at her, he said slowly, in an octave lower than normal, "Norma...I told myself if I ever saw you again I would strangle you!" Now that he had everyone's attention, the man seated next to her, the Honorable John Lindsay, former mayor of New York City, chimed in, "Not here!" Poor Norma's eyes suggested she might be on borrowed time. Then Elmyr mentioned a name evoking a glimmer of understanding, and a smile began to defuse the unexpected drama. It seems that a love interest of Elmyr's ran off with her in Italy.

When he expressed his grievance, he seemed satisfied with his theatrical performance, and his audience began to laugh.

Norma was a fading beauty, slender, statuesque, and with discernable poise. Once a *Vogue* cover model, she married well, twice to men of considerable means. Now, divorced for many years, the cost of maintaining a home in Italy, a flat in Paris, and various paramours, she was in the unfamiliar position of having to live by her wits. She knew of Elmyr's new celebrity and was eager to rekindle their frayed friendship. Norma invited us to tea with her at her garden flat on Eaton Square. In a sort of Victorian overstuffed elegance, she surrounded herself with souvenirs of a life past and wealth that no longer came easily to her. Yet, all the trappings spoke of comfort and culture. Her sitting room looked out to the patio and garden area. A large Chinese Aubusson-style rug covered the floor. A highly lacquered black baby grand piano stood in the corner. On top was one of those giant polished steer horns mounted in an elaborately carved silver stand. Its function was uncertain other than to serve as Odin's drinking cup in Valhalla. (I suppose when people have more money than they know what to do with, they ask for one of these horns—or maybe an ashtray carved from petrified dinosaur guano). Café au lait silk-covered love seats faced each other with a heavy glass-topped coffee table in between. Good original art graced the walls, and bookshelves bulged with leather-bound editions.

She was no stranger to the finer things in life but now had to periodically "sell a piece here and there to make ends meet," as she explained. Elmyr knew her plight. What was unusual about Norma's background was that her married name, Clark, had come from her last husband, the son of Stephen C. Clark, who was one of the most important art collectors in America and former director of the Metropolitan Museum of Art. His hugely important collection included Cezanne's *The Card Players* and van Gogh's *The Night Café*, among numerous other impressionist and postimpressionist masterpieces.

Norma asked Elmyr if he could help her. He then examined some books from her shelves. Reaching up, he took down a large antique-looking volume. Placing it on the piano, he opened its cover. As he had already explained a practice familiar to him, he carefully removed one of its beginning pages—a blank one. It was high-quality paper, thick, discolored by age, and noticeably marked from moisture spots called "foxing." He asked her for a number two pencil. With devoted concentration, his breathing appeared controlled as he proceeded to "invent" a Modigliani drawing, a small portrait that might pass for a spontaneous sketch of the artist's mistress, Jeanne Hébuterne. His lines were sure and graceful, balanced between thin light strokes and heavy shading where it needed to be. Within moments a completed drawing emerged. He handed it to her. She was noticeably pleased. She sighed. He looked serious, for he knew what he had done—he helped someone who needed it. Elmyr did not add a signature to the new Modigliani.

Our wholly unforeseen encounter that early morning in Capri was pregnant with curiosity. Anyway, she seemed happy to see us or just happy. Her broad smile anticipated his question. He smiled too, and asked, "What did you do with the drawing?" "I took it to a friend, a curator at the Tate," she responded. "I told him it was part of my husband's collection, but as it was unsigned, I wanted his opinion. He thought that because it *was* unsigned its authenticity was more probable." With that benediction she put it up for auction at a major London sale of modern masters. She cheerily announced that it fetched thousands of pounds, enough to live comfortably for some time, exactly how Elmyr would phrase his successes. We shared a brief laugh, chatted a bit longer. She said nothing more about Elmyr's new contribution to the dead artist's oeuvre. Norma's newly cautionary spending habits did not relax enough to invite us to a coffee and croissant, as she counted out enough lira to pay for just her coffee.

We left Capri the following day. Norma vanished from our lives when she disappeared from view that morning.

Italy remains my favorite country in Europe, and the time spent there with Elmyr was an astounding experience—one I have, until now, kept largely in the vault of my memory. It's good to air things out.

GENEVA

We landed in Geneva aboard an Alitalia flight from Rome and would soon see those friends who initially made our trip possible. First, we went to the Hôtel du Rhône, located on a street with the unsurprisingly Swiss name rue de la Monie, "Street of the Money." Shown to our room, we unpacked, changed clothes, and were now ready to make our sortie into the city. For Elmyr, the telephone was an indispensable tool.

Recalling the old "Mummy" horror films of the forties, the mummy awakened according to the curse, by the high priest Ananka administering the sacred "tana" leaves—three for life, five for movement. Phoning his network of friends three to five times a day reanimated him.

The first couple to receive a call was Philippe and Simone Vogue. They were among the many waves of visitors to lap up on the shores of La Falaise, buy artwork from Elmyr, and become friends as well. Philippe was an interesting man, a Belgian; supposedly not feeling bourgeois enough, he moved to Switzerland. There, he parlayed a small inheritance, the equivalent of about $5,000. He was not an engineer but had a good idea, so he hired a couple engineers to realize it for him. He invented the electric toothbrush, promptly sold the patent rights for about $35 million. Another $35 million followed his next little brainstorm, the Waterpik. His story doesn't mean that all ideas are good or moneymakers. However, it suggests the importance of conviction and perseverance.

Simone was an exquisite beauty with style, grace, and earthy charm. Warmly welcoming us to their luxurious flat overlooking Lake Geneva, we sat in comfort. She asked, "What would you like to drink?" Together we replied, "A glass of wine." She called someone to bring up a bottle from their private cellar. It was something like a '46 Chateau Margaux, probably the most delicious wine I have ever tasted. No, it *was* the most delicious. My mouth waters in longing memory of the occasion. Now what was remarkable about our afternoon with her was a bit of late-breaking news she had to share with us.

An innocent, "Oh, by the way…" was about to smack us with the life-extinguishing force of those giant asteroids. "Legros," Simone informed us, "was released last week. So you should be careful." Although well intended, her words of caution weren't necessary. Elmyr knew what Fernand was capable of but also expressed his doubt that he would do anything to risk incarceration again. Even *he* couldn't be that stupid, he thought. For Elmyr, Geneva was the one stop of our journey about which he had misgivings. Fernand Legros found refuge there after returning from Brazil, where they had jailed him for various illegal activities. Interestingly, while behind bars he made friends with another prison mate of some repute, Ronald Biggs, a member of the British gang responsible for "The Great Train Robbery" in Britain.

The only reason we made the trip to Switzerland was that Legros for many months had been an official guest of the Swiss government—at a hospital for the criminally insane, finally living up to his potential, I thought. He apparently seduced, with some absence of forethought, the three male children of the mayor of a nearby town. For as odious an act, we felt certain that the conventional and humorless Swiss would not be setting him free anytime soon. Astonishingly, Legros's battery of attorneys, psychiatrists, and constant refrain that he could not go to jail because he was "allergic to prison," however, gained traction. While this ploy defies belief, I tend to think the Swiss realized Legros needed regular doses of Thorazine.

When we retuned to the hotel around five o'clock, the concierge handed Elmyr a phone message. It was from a Swiss television station, requesting an interview. We were mystified how they knew Elmyr was in Geneva and our exact location. Six people in Geneva knew of our arrival: Philippe and Simone, Ian and Cynthia Major, and Elmyr's long-time Hungarian friend, the investment banker Eugene Weinreb and his wife, Andruska. That's all. Back in our room, we tried to penetrate the mystery without success. A phone number accompanied the message. Curiosity overwhelmed us. He made the call. Elmyr reached someone who said he was with Channel Three of Swiss TV and eager to have an interview with him. They would pay him the equivalent of $3,000. It wouldn't take more than a couple of hours of his time. When Elmyr asked how they were aware of his arrival, he said someone recognized him at the airport. He told the man that he needed some time to think it over.

We discussed the proposition at length, weighing the pros and cons. Elmyr was not one to dismiss the prospect of so lucrative an offer for so little work. Besides, he had become accustomed to the public spotlight and enjoyed his new star status. What applied the brakes to his inclination to accept the offer was my insistence that it would be tantamount to a personal invitation to Legros to stir up whatever trouble he could conceive. It would be, in fact, completely opposite of our mission, which was to make our presence as unobtrusive as possible. Reluctantly, he called the fellow back from Channel 3 and declined the invitation. Their conversation continued. I could tell from Elmyr's silence, punctuated with the periodic *oui*, he was exerting some pressure. In pantomime I was gesticulating not to relent. When he hung up, I could tell he was not entirely convinced that he did the right thing.

The next morning, after our tea and continental breakfast, we dressed to go out. We would do some sightseeing. Elmyr had a typical European constitution and enjoyed walking. It really allowed one to have that up-close and personal relationship with the city, its life, and the people. By contrast, I'd gone to college in Los Angeles, a city where, if you walk, you were immediately considered "queer or criminal." Around noon we returned to the hotel. We had a luncheon engagement with Ian and Cynthia. Upon entering the lobby, a group of plainclothes police approached us, displaying their badges. My heart began to pound as though it wanted to burst. Questions came in a flurry. As I was fluent in French by this time, I responded instinctively. Elmyr and I were divided; three people were questioning him, two detectives focused on me: What was my name? What was my relationship to Elmyr? Why was I in Geneva? Where were we going? etc. By the time the questioning ended, one of my interrogators referred to me as "the American gentleman." I somewhat suspected at that moment that I wasn't heading to jail. Elmyr, on the other hand, had neatly vanished. In an instant, I stood alone. The police and Elmyr were gone like a flock of birds responding to a shotgun blast.

I collected my wits and asked the desk clerk where they had gone. With the same nonchalance, as if by any other normally departing guest, he said they'd gone through the revolving doors. Fine, but where? I returned to our room alone, called Ian and Cynthia, told them what had happened and that I had no knowledge of his whereabouts. They urged me to come to their home.

The leaves, in their autumnal zenith, fell like confectionary sprinkles covering a green frosting, reminding me of a fauve landscape. Mornings and evenings were crisp, the days warmed by residual summer sunlight. The serenity and beauty of the scenery all along the lakeshore drive could not distract me from the disturbing mystery surrounding the stealthy abduction of my friend.

Ian and Cynthia warmly greeted me and understandably sensed my alarm. Wealth has its perquisites, and social connections are one of them. Ian assured me that he knew a lawyer who could find the answers to my questions. He phoned him, explaining our dilemma. The attorney promised to investigate immediately. Together, we sat down to lunch, all with a substantially subdued appetite. This crisis revealed Ian and Cynthia's deep concern for their absent friend. The same heartfelt sensitivity would have mirrored Elmyr's response if one of his friends were in jeopardy.

Within an hour, the lawyer called back. He informed Ian the police detained Elmyr at the city courthouse and were questioning him. Ian asked him to represent Elmyr as his legal counsel and to keep us apprised of the situation. We waited several more hours for more details. Shadowy fingers crawled across the lawn as daylight waned behind a row of poplars. Ian lit some kindling, hoping the growing flames under the dried birch logs in the fireplace would displace our feelings of apprehension with comforting warmth. Their home imparted the casual elegance that the British not just easily display, but seem to have this cultured sensibility indelibly stamped on their DNA. A long high tea and candid conversation transported us past the early evening hours. As we talked I admired how superbly framed Elmyr's artwork looked on their walls. Once again the lawyer phoned, this time with good news. Elmyr would be back at the hotel about nine o'clock.

Ian drove me back about 8 p.m. We waited for Elmyr in the hotel lobby. About twenty minutes to nine he came through the front door. Looking exhausted, he said he needed a drink. We went to the bar and all ordered a cognac. He proceeded to recount his ordeal, vividly demonstrating the comic but menacing element that characterized his relationship with Legros. Lamentably, a more insidious aspect underscored the uneasy laughter. Legros's latest scheme once more revealed his megalomania, vengeful nature, and flair for the bizarre. My first direct exposure to his antics made me think of him in movie parlance as Darth Vader meets Liberace.

The morning of our luncheon engagement with Ian and Cynthia, Legros phoned the Geneva police headquarters to lodge a complaint against Elmyr, accusing him of having made "death threats" against him. Elmyr, he claimed, made several phone calls to his home and told him if he didn't bring $100,000 (in small bills) to the lobby of the Hôtel du Rhône that very morning, he would be killed.

Despite Legros's local notoriety and reputation, the police were compelled to investigate the charges. Knowing it was Friday, Legros counted on the police arresting Elmyr and keeping him in jail over the weekend and then arraigning him on Monday. Instead, the magistrate convened a hearing for that Friday evening, which was highly unusual. The judge unexpectedly summoned Legros to appear that evening.

Fernand knew the benefit of good legal counsel, but none of his three lawyers showed up for the hearing. Ian's friend sent an associate to represent Elmyr. Immediately, according to Elmyr, Legros stood up in the courtroom, pointed an accusatory finger at Elmyr, and asked the judge, "Why does *he* have an attorney and I don't have mine?" The judge replied, "That's a good question, Monsieur Legros. I don't usually see you when you're not surrounded by lawyers." Then the magistrate asked him, "These death threats M. de Hory allegedly made…how do you know they were from him?" "I recognized his Austro Hungarian voice!" he responded. "When did he make these calls?" the judge then asked.

Legros: "I am not able to specify the hour when I received a phone call last night, for, under medical order, I sleep, thanks to three Vesper. It is true that I often have nightmares, but as soon as I became aware of it, I changed my psychiatrist! The telephone calls I received in the afternoon were made between two p.m. and six p.m.

Judge: Between two and six is a long time. Don't you ever look at your watch?

Legros (Now this, I am sure, went over very well, especially in Switzerland): I *never* look at my watch. If I want to know the time, I hold out my arm and have my servants *read* me the time. *Why else* should one have servants?

Judge: M. Legros, we have M. de Hory's phone records from the hotel. He made no calls that night or between two and six p.m. We also know that he did not leave the hotel during those times.

Judge: M. Legros, what exactly were you planning to do with those people you hired and the house you rented where you intended to lure M. de Hory?

Legros: Nothing. I just wanted to frighten him, so he would leave me alone—and stop harassing me.

Judge: We know those people you hired are thugs and criminals. M. Legros, if you give me the slightest reason to have you arrested *again*, it is *you* who will go to jail. You have already wasted this court's time and mine. Get out! (This exchange is an official translation of the court transcript.) (Italics are mine.)

The judge then accompanied Elmyr to a private egress from the courthouse. Before leaving, the judge cautioned him, "Legros is a dangerous man, and you should be extremely careful." He then proceeded to explain that Elmyr's detention had been a precautionary measure for his own safety. It turns out that Legros knew our every move since we got off the plane—and so did the police. He, in fact, knew our whole itinerary of the trip, which most likely he came by via some monetary payoff to the travel agent in Ibiza. In a singular but mystifying moment of inspiration, (like the kind that gave us the cuckoo clock), Legros hired a private detective to follow us everywhere we went. He, like Legros, had a checkered past. A once-important functionary—chief of police of Geneva no less—he fell from grace like Icarus in flames for the slight faux pas of putting bugs (listening devices) in the phones of people in high places. The Swiss press enthusiastically covered this succulent scandal, calling it, "L'Histoire des Longues Oreilles" or "the story of the long ears." It sounds better in French. The Swiss, being a sober lot, were not amused. After a stint in prison for his transgressions, he thought it appropriate to open a private detective agency. Therefore, in a kind of human chain like one of those Chinese New Year's dragons, he followed us and the police followed him in a scene à la a Pink Panther movie. The offer from the television channel was a ruse that might well have proved dangerous if Elmyr let ego or greed supersede prudence.

We stayed only long enough to fulfill our luncheon date with Ian and Cynthia and pay a social call to our other friends the Weinrebs. The following day I returned to the Majors' lakeside home with Elmyr. They asked another friend to join us, the Austrian actor Oskar Homolka. His roles in films like *The Seven Year Itch* (with Marilyn Monroe) and *A Farewell to Arms* are less memorable than his hallmark bushy eyebrows that invited trimming with hedge shears. He, like fellow actors Vincent Price and Edward G. Robinson, began collecting impressionist art before it became a popular pastime and shrewd investment. He owned one or more paintings by Cézanne, which became a table topic for him and Elmyr. Elmyr was always curious and delighted to discuss authentic works of art and those artists whose lives he unavoidably came to know intimately. This time the lake's surface was glass-smooth, substantially calmer than Elmyr. The previous day's commotion still weighed on his mind. However, we enjoyed the reunion with Ian and Cynthia, and Elmyr was impressed with how good his paintings and drawings looked in their home. The next day we departed for London in the afternoon. Again, Elmyr expected, or hoped, his brush with Legros would be his last.

LONDON

London was Elmyr's preferred destination in all of Europe. I had the good fortune to travel there with him on numerous occasions. He enjoyed the civility of the Brits, their genteel manners, and had an almost Victorian kind of respect for them as empire builders. It was home to polyglot cultures, and the cosmopolitan air was good to breathe. He loved going to a Hungarian restaurant in Soho with the exuberantly campy name, The Gay Hussar. By my first visit there, I had already received a primer in Central European history that answered more questions than I had ever conceived of asking. Now, Elmyr dressed to the nines in his signature black velvet jacket, tailored white shirt from Turnbull & Asser, silk tie, monocle at the end of a gold chain around his neck, and pinky rings in yellow and white gold, each bearing the three cut gems that denoted him as Hungarian. The music of gypsy violins filled the restaurant. He felt at home chattering away with the maitre d'hotel in his native tongue. One could almost infer from his animated gestures the context of their dialogue. We would have a specialty of the house, a variety of fish from Lake Baloton in Hungary. It would not have mattered what kind of wet fish it was. It was the allure of home cooking he found so appealing.

It was compulsory to have a slice of "real" foie gras from his homeland. The difference between it and all other imitators was clear. It was goose liver in its entirety, not a minced up pâté like those French do in Strasbourg. Elmyr then explained the gruesome process that makes it taste so good. Now, this is enough to make PETA members dizzy with apoplexy: they simply crank back the neck of the poor goose and force-feed it until its liver enlarges to something the size of a football. So grab your knife and fork and eat up!

Soho is an enclave of ethnic restaurants, shops, and strip clubs that make it aggressively entertaining and a human zoo for people-watching. As hospitable and naturally helpful as the British are, they commonly write out the names, numbers, and addresses of places to go and people to see on public restroom walls, in case you didn't get a chance to stop at a tourist information booth. I personally witnessed an example of their alacrity to assist a stranger one evening when Elmyr and I had tickets for a West End theater performance. Standing on one side of Sloane Square in Chelsea, we tried without success to flag down an empty taxi. They ignored our arm flailing and drove to the opposite side of the square thirty meters away. There, a single line had formed. People queued up at a taxi stand like well-behaved penguins before a kiosk sign reading "Free Fish." Fearing we would be late for the play, he voiced his upset amid the silent crowd. One man asked where we were going. Elmyr replied, "Piccadilly Circus." He in turn suggested we take the Tube, as it was only two stops away and probably quicker. Elmyr snapped back that he hadn't taken public transport in thirty years and was not about to start now. There you have it. He also enjoyed class distinctions so easily apparent in their culture. We waited our turn in the silent queue, eyes glaring as though he had farted loudly at a royal coronation.

OK, so his overt snobbism was perhaps his least attractive feature. It was nevertheless a part of who he was, and he was not going to change. Strangely, this class prickliness ran contrary to his more humane instincts, and I often found these incompatible characteristics bewildering as they were housed in the same body. It was an adrenalin rush for him to have the simultaneous stimulation of culture and the company of people every time he went to London. The whirlwind social schedule would make one think he'd been some sensory-deprived creature like Robinson Crusoe, cut off from the civilized world. This was far from the case but illustrated his insatiable need for the company of others.

One visit coincided with an annual theater junket by his New York friends Arnold Weissberger and Milton Goldman. Elmyr had rented a home near Sloane Square and enthusiastically hosted a cocktail party for them one night. Longtime friends of Arnold's came, Douglas Fairbanks Jr. and his wife. For as unerring as he was with people's titles, Elmyr sometimes goofed with their names. With button-popping pride he paraded his newly arrived guests, introducing the gracious couple as

"Mr. and Mrs. Douglas." After each intro I tugged on his jacket, whispering "Fairbanks." My promptings apparently just on the wrong side of audibility, I spoke up. Recognizing his gaff, he apologized. Wholly unperturbed by the mistake, Fairbanks recounted a story about his father. During a transatlantic voyage, a small fellow approached him and said, "You probably don't remember me..." Fairbanks Sr. pretended otherwise. When it became obvious that he had no recollection of him, he relented, saying, "I'm sorry, I don't remember you. I meet so many people..." The unmemorable chap was Marconi, who as inventor of the radio left no small footprint in history. The point was that Fairbanks Jr. was not a stickler about protocol and understood human frailties like memory loss. (A condition I find increasingly forgivable with advancing age.)

Elmyr and I had lunch a couple of days later with Robert Patterson. He was Marlene Dietrich's impresario. Elmyr made his acquaintance and he was kind enough to invite us to Dietrich's performance at the Wimbledon Theatre. I was excited to see this living legend singing in her inimitable smoky voice.

That evening we attended a dinner party in her honor at a fashionable London restaurant, privileged to be among a dozen guests. A kind of round-table coterie, it was an unusual occasion, since she rarely ventured outside the company of longtime friends. She was the last to arrive and took her seat at the center of the long table. Immediately everyone's attention turned on her as though eerily reenacting a tableau vivant of Christ's Last Supper. I sat at the end of the table so as not to disturb the illuminati around her. Elmyr sat opposite her, her impresario to her right, the editor-in-chief of *The London Sunday Times* to her left. She and Elmyr began conversing in a lively manner. Horribly cultured banter broke out like a vile plague. Everyone seemed to speak at once, creating a sophisticated white noise, gliding by me like jets of smoke around something sleek in a wind tunnel. I found listening a wasted effort of concentration, like meeting the new vicar and attempting polite small talk while able to focus only with an acid-trip fascination on his saber scars and eye patch. In person, out of her stage makeup, Dietrich looked considerably worse for wear. She still had those penciled-in eyebrows where hair had been a half-century earlier. More alarmingly, her teeth had discolored as though placed in a water glass each night with a generous dollop of Copenhagen chewing tobacco. When the editor from the *Times* asked where she was going after London, she barked to her impresario, "This man's trying to interview me," as though to evidence why her circle of friends was small. She was indeed proving to be a giant with feet of clay.

The manager of Mr. Chow's, the Chinese restaurant hosting this memorable event, decided we needed a Hong Kong version of the Super Bowl halftime show. So somewhere between the dried seaweed and octopus courses, the pastry chef wheeled out a trolley. With lights dimmed around the room's perimeter, he stood in the theatrical glare of a center spot, juggling globs of floured dough, changing their shapes into sorts of edible balloon animals. He did things few of his audience knew were possible, I imagine, and probably wondered why.

By dinner's end, it was evident that she was unaccountably combative and difficult. Just before leaving, a woman restored my faith in a cosmic balance when she approached Dietrich with a piece of paper and a pen seeking an autograph, surely. We held our collective breath. She said, predictably, "I'm your biggest fan! I've seen all your pictures. Please, may I have your autograph, Miss Garbo?" Melting from laughter, we all began slipping from our chairs. I thought everyone would have to be recovered with a spatula. Now, the surprising thing was, she calmly accepted her request although no one knew what name she wrote down. Some legends and myths, I suppose, cannot withstand scrutiny. Perhaps this is why Dietrich and others purposefully limit public exposure.

On another visit to London, Elmyr and I attended the opening of an exhibition of paintings by Lilli Palmer, an actress and former wife of Rex Harrison. They appeared together in a classic British film, *The Four-Poster Bed*. It was made in a time when censorship was rigid and helped further the notion the English were a sex-free society. Lilli told us, "It was illegal to show anything considered risqué such as two people in a bed. In fact, if there was a bedroom scene you had to have one foot on the ground at all times. Well, in *Four Poster* there were several scenes of us in bed together, so they had to cut holes through the bed in order that Rex and I could each have one of our feet touching the floor."

She and her husband, Argentine actor Carlos Thompson, came to visit Elmyr in Ibiza. Like with so many other first encounters, they became friends. We later visited them at their home in Campo de Mijas in southern Spain. At that time, she showed us various works destined for her upcoming show at the Arthur Tooth Gallery in London. Elmyr thought she was a good painter. He offered advice on composition and technique. It was an interesting exchange of ideas with another artist in her studio that I never before witnessed. Elmyr said we would come to her opening.

Perhaps the recognizable faces circulating throughout the gallery should not have surprised me. I met Sean Connery that night, and Noel Coward. Coward had suffered a couple of strokes by then. His watery eyes and slightly droopy eyelids suggested their effects on him. Nevertheless, he sat on a chair, both hands resting on the head of a cane between his legs. He wore a black dinner jacket and silk tie, and a sly smile graced his face. I suspected his mind harbored some clever witticism he was content to share with just himself. Lilli introduced us to him, and he seemed charmed to meet us. Who knows?

Coward lived at the Savoy Hotel for years. He suggested we visit him sometime. A couple of days later we went to see him. Elmyr carried an improvised cardboard portfolio. Someone accompanied us to his suite. There, one of two men who attended to him led us to the sitting room. Coward greeted us cordially, although his expression conveyed a vacant searching, perhaps trying to recall who we were. Elmyr made some small talk. I don't recall about what. He then got to the point of our visit. He wanted to present Coward with a large pencil drawing of me—nude. Must have thought it would give the old boy some pleasure. As he handed it to him, I blurted out, "Well, this should put us on a first-name basis." Everyone laughed, along with Coward. I was so pleased with myself after that that the rest of the visit remains a blur. Elmyr seemed particularly thrilled when I demonstrated some urbane wit. After all, it could only have stemmed from my association with him.

During the evening of Lilli's exhibition, the gallery's director introduced himself. He knew who Elmyr was. He invited us upstairs, along with a few others. We went to a storage room where he provided us a private viewing of some of their collection. One at a time he pulled out large oil paintings in French frames. First was a Renoir portrait of a young girl. Elmyr said instantly, "That's '82, '83," meaning 1882/1883. Then another slid out from its vertical bin. Another Renoir—"That's '85 or '86." He repeated this perhaps a half-dozen more times with works by other masters. Everyone enjoyed this demonstration of knowledge, none more than Tooth's director. I have no doubt that Elmyr merited the title of professor if he ever desired it.

Through our friend Jack Frye, we met Charles Clore, owner of Selfridges, the London department store. The public knew of his philanthropic donations, and some knew him as a passionate collector of art. As I recall, he wore his ego like actor's makeup on a bulbous face. Smoke from his fat cigars engulfed him like a cornfield after the pass of a low-flying crop duster. When he learned from Jack that Nina van Pallandt and Elmyr were friends, he mentioned his desire to meet her. He invited us to dinner at Trader Vic's in the Hilton Hotel. Naturally, the conversation drifted to art. Thinking my question rhetorical and based in some sense now elusive, I asked, "Mr. Clore, when you buy art, do you consult others?" My impertinence penetrated his considerable ego and pride. "What am I, some kind of schmuck?" he hurled in my direction, his breath pinning back my ears. Turned heads of those around us could have better answered his question. Elmyr rushed to my defense, trying to disarm my gaffe, saying, "Well, I'm sure before you spend a few hundred thousand pounds, you want to be sure about what you're buying." He calmly expressed what I was intimating. I remember enduring Ançi Dupres's fury at my absence of forethought when I said I didn't think $150 sounded too much to pay for gluing Elmyr's Modigliani to an old canvas. Now, once more, I thought my sphincter muscle would fail me at Clore's reproach. It suggested my mind was still unwed to the consequences of spontaneous speech, but also renewed my conviction that wealth does not impart class. A young woman we knew who dated him mentioned how he wanted others to love him for himself and not his money. Easier to climb Everest in ice skates, I thought.

I remained sufficiently quiet for the rest of the dinner for his pique to subside. Afterward, he invited us to his home for a private viewing of his art collection. Every impressionist work he possessed was a masterpiece. Among them were a pointillist landscape by Surat or Signac; Degas pastels, his ballet dancers; and behind his desk was a blue period Picasso, a boy on a horse. There was too much to remember, but it was enjoyable to see Elmyr's reaction to a truly impressive collection. If we had another occasion to see Clore, I imagine him saying to Elmyr, "Leave *him* at home."

The Other Side Of The Mirror

A lmost immediately from the moment I met Elmyr there was more than the patina of glamour and success suggested. Underneath the thin, newly formed crust of appearances was substantial seismic activity, unpredictable and volatile. Neither his recent celebrity nor wealth could completely insulate him from their consequences.

He said nothing of his story the first few weeks after my arrival at La Falaise. Ultimately knowing him as well as I did, I can only say this was an extremely unusual act of reticence. He enjoyed talking, and secrecy often collided with his inclination toward spontaneity and candor. Near the end of November 1969, he showed me a copy of *Fake*, the book about his life written by Clifford Irving. It became an instant success and heralded a flurry of spotlight-grabbing articles in the international press. Offers poured in to do films and documentaries about "the greatest art forger of our time," as Irving described him. While he would later accept public attention with the ease of a born-on-stage vaudeville performer, he greeted the initial crush of publicity with self-effacing shyness. This reaction, I suspect, was because he still felt somewhat uncertain about the legal fallout over his activities.

For more than twenty years Elmyr's life was an insecure, nervous existence; a succession of aliases, phony IDs, fake passports, nomadic meanderings, risky business dealings, terminal relationships, and a questionable future most likely made him dismiss the prospect that any stability awaited him. The shock of something good blossoming from something bad was only slightly less surprising but more of a jolt than a slap with a twenty-pound wet fish. Shadowy cover-ups masked by theatrical pretense morphed into reluctant eye contact and ah-shucks foot shuffling when asked hard, blunt questions by the press. In a Sunday confessional whisper he acknowledged that he *did some* paintings but he *never signed* them. That tight-lipped admission later relaxed to the point where he reminded me of the attention-craving Norma Desmond in *Sunset Boulevard*, where, at the top of the stairs, she declares in a self-absorbed trance, "I'm ready for my close-up, Mr. DeMille." Although, Elmyr's burgeoning romance with the public spotlight never assumed that wide-eyed spooky aspect.

By March of 1970 he had whittled down the various film offers that were cascading in since the release of *Fake*. He chose the French filmmaker François Reichenbach. A couple of reasons prompted this decision. As Reichenbach explained, it would be a collaborative venture of French television and the BBC, which Elmyr greatly respected for their quality work. He also had a history with François, an Oscar recipient for his documentary on the pianist Artur Rubenstein.

On a cool, rainy spring day they arrived from Paris and London to capture Elmyr in his own celluloid portrait. The British producer was Richard Drewett of the BBC. Over a period of about three days, they followed him everywhere but the bathroom. Spider webs of large black cables stretched across the floor of the villa. Blinding arc lights illuminated the interior with sun-surpassing intensity. Elmyr posited his views on art, the art establishment, experts, artists, critics, curators, gallery owners, patrons, culture, society, friends, scoundrels, travel, Ibiza—and himself. One of the first *60 Minutes* news magazine programs excerpted a portion of the ninety-minute exposé titled "Elmyr, The True Picture?" It is one of the most interesting documentaries I have seen, and I remain mystified to this day why, instead of releasing this insightful gem for the public's delight and entertainment, it collects dust in the vault of the BBC's archives.

To illustrate his reluctance to take full credit for his discomforting artistic contributions, he couched his purported authorship of works now passing as authentic Modiglianis in this way. "I don't feel bad for Modigliani, I feel good for me. He worked very little and died very young, so if they add a few Modiglianis here or there, it is not going to destroy his oeuvre. Besides, I never made hundreds of Modigliani's. I made a *few* Modigliani's and they were recognized by Mme. Modigliani and all great experts."

The connection between Elmyr and Reichenbach is also a curious one. Prior to a career switch to filmmaking, François was an art dealer who not only knew Elmyr but also bought artwork from him. As we dined at a local restaurant, François recounted a series of dealings with Elmyr. He had told François that he escaped Hungary after the war with a small portion of his family's art collection, and that, due to some current misfortune, he was obliged to part with some pieces. Would he be interested? To help Elmyr, of course, François bought several drawings by Modigliani, Braque, Picasso, and others. He then told Elmyr that he loved the work of Soutine. Did he have anything by Soutine? Elmyr regretted that he hadn't any. A few days later François received a call from him. Gushing with surprise, Elmyr exclaimed, "François, this is incredible but I was looking through the collection and *I found* a small Soutine portrait!" Thunderous laughter erupted at the table. Drewett then asked Reichenbach, "Did you suspect anything?" François's eyes darted back and forth as though watching a high-speed tennis match. Then with that inimitable Gallic shrug, he said, "I didn't want to know." More laughter ensued. Even Elmyr was visibly amused at the comic retelling of the incident.

I must add here that Reichenbach came from a comfortably bourgeois background and his family possessed an impressive collection of art. They in fact had some important Modigliani paintings. He revealed that one of the sensual reclining nudes (perhaps *Nude on a Cushion*) bothered him somewhat as he thought it needed more pubic and underarm hair, so with boyish impulsiveness, he added some with a crayon. "To this day" he insisted, "the addition remains unchanged." Elmyr always said, "If something hangs in a collection long enough it becomes authentic." François's childhood "improvement" is now an intrinsic part of that work, long accepted as an original feature and indistinguishable from any other intended stroke from the artist's own hand.

This anecdote provides an insight into the relationship between what is real and unreal. Keep in mind that Elmyr's buyers were the supposed cognoscenti, art dealers or museum curators who enjoyed a symbiotic relationship with him. They stood to gain profits or prestige from acquiring his work. The extent to which they openly or knowingly bought something doubtful is questionable. For this to never have occurred during his long career is even more doubtful if Reichenbach's story is to be believed. During my seven-year association with Elmyr, I witnessed enough instances of people's eagerness to profit from his art with no compunction about ethics or legality. While it may have been tempting for Elmyr's clientele to denounce him, anyone coming forward to accuse him of malfeasance also probably risked self-incrimination as well. The taint of guilt by association was a ruinous prospect for many who had dealings with him and, understandably, preferred to stay out of the fray when the scandal finally exposed him. What were they to say? "Oh, I bought several works by him, but I no longer have them as I resold them," for example, or, "Our museum unknowingly procured some fakes and we will no longer be hanging them in our permanent collection."

In that very vein *Time* magazine reported in about 1972 or '73 that the Metropolitan Museum in New York "deaccessioned"—a fancy word for *sold off*—a large Modigliani painting, a portrait of a woman, suspected to be by Elmyr. After demoting it to one of the institution's storerooms, it then resurfaced. London's Marlborough Gallery paid a fire-sale price of $50,000, or between ten to twenty percent of the market value of a bona fide Modigliani. That august institution passed off a work of art they knew was not authentic. Whatever their rationale, it is open to speculation and likely, "no comment" from them. Marlborough, by the way, turned around and promptly sold it to the Japanese for $250,000.

It is precisely this kind of Machiavellian capitalism that abounds in the business world (the art world being very much a part of it) that Elmyr consistently witnessed. Considering his negligible bargaining skills in moments of desperation, he was ill suited to the rough-and-tumble tactics of the marketplace and predictably came out on the short end in his dealings. However, he always made a distinction between selling a work to a private buyer, say, Mrs. Smith from Omaha, and a dealer. The former might have neither the knowledge nor expertise to make an educated decision regarding the purchase of a work of art. The dealer, gallery owner, or museum curator, on the other hand, make it their business to know what they are buying or selling. Elmyr liked to use the analogy that if he walked into Cartier and wanted to sell them a diamond that was actually cut glass—and they thought it *was* a diamond, they have no business being in the gem business. "If they don't know the difference, they should be selling sausage or hosiery in the market instead." He added, "I sold my work uniquely to those who were professionals."

In all fairness, I cannot characterize the wholesale sentiments of an entire class and say with any certainty that the antipathy felt by many toward Elmyr was universal. At this time the wounds were still fresh and largely unhealed. By the mid 1970s, I think everyone seemed to move on. Sales of Elmyr's work à la his repertoire of impressionist and postimpressionist artists cropped up at auctions of Sotheby's and Christie's. As might be expected, fake "Elmyrs" began to surface and have abounded ever since. A friend of Elmyr's, Anthony Hugo, knew him before I appeared on the scene and witnessed much of the turmoil that involved Legros and their circus-like relationship, but without the joy. Tony has a wonderful collection of work by Elmyr, and London's auction houses often seek his opinion when it comes to authenticating Elmyr's work. My point, however, is that he no longer is viewed as a outcast the establishment shuns, but with a little distance and forgiveness they are as happy to make a 15 percent sales commission off his work as indiscriminately as anyone else. They have also voiced their respect for his talent as an artist, and while this posthumous acceptance comes too late for Elmyr to enjoy, the afterglow may be more enduring.

Thankfully for Elmyr, his fame lasted longer than the fifteen minutes allotted to everyone by Andy Warhol. At the same time, hidden from view, his newly conferred celebrity metastasized into something increasingly malignant. No sooner had *Fake* entered the ranks of America's most popular books when Fernand Legros, whose ego, like the universe, was ever-expanding, initiated a lawsuit against the book's publisher, McGraw-Hill, author Cliff Irving, and, of course, Elmyr.

Legros claimed defamation of character and sought damages in the millions, something surpassing the GDP of Guatemala. While the popular book reached a paperback printing, the lawsuit essentially brought a second edition in hardcover to a sinkhole. Predictably, Fernand and his battery of attorneys put everything in a legal headlock. This siege tactic is ancient. Everyone hunkers down for a long war of attrition that assures the litigants of paying the college educations of their attorneys' children and grandchildren. If you have a first-rate lawyer and have deep pockets, the strategy works. O. J. Simpson's case illustrated this point. Also, never mind that the bedrock of the story was factual, according to Elmyr, and that Irving may actually have sanitized or omitted some of the more bizarre and convoluted elements of this saga. Nevertheless, Legros had everyone by the short and curly hairs.

Elmyr, for his part, hired an attorney well known for his list of show business clients, L. Arnold Weissberger, recommended by Howard Sackler. Only because he cut a wide swath in his milieu and was a distinguished man, he warrants mentioning here. Arnold had silver-white hair with an RAF mustache and old-school ethics. He and his partner Milton Goldman were part of New York's Upper East Side elite. In their comfortable and fashionable apartment, quality artwork covered the walls. Both were as charming and personable as could be. Arnold appropriately wore a pinky ring with his initials, L. A. W. Like a great white hunter, he led Elmyr through the legal thickets for the duration of this suit, which dragged out for years. Not surprisingly, it cost him thousands of dollars to defend himself in this case, when he had not made one cent, that I saw, from sales of the book. Such was the price of fame.

If money alone had mitigated his troubles, he would have thrown the coins on the scale with a sense of relief. When they say the wheels of justice move slowly, they often neglect to observe those unfortunates lashed to their spokes. Elmyr paid a high price psychologically as well for his involvement in the book's lawsuit. Legros was in a cross-eyed snit that Elmyr had become a kind of folk hero while HE bore the disgrace of a villain. Therefore, with the unhinged obsession of a stalker, Legros made it his raison d'etre to destroy him—however he could. Using the legal system proved to be an extremely effective instrument of torture and, as single-mindedly driven as he was, with money to boot, it became his preferred tool to use against Elmyr. Like the personal hell of the mythological Sisyphus, Legros represented Elmyr's unrelenting burden that he could never quite overcome.

It would be foolish and misleading to portray Elmyr as an unwitting victim of those who were simply crazy, greedy, or both. At some point he passed the baton of merchant to Fernand Legros, preferring to remain in Ibiza and create his dubious masterpieces in quietude and anonymity. However, he worried that Fernand's dizzying flair for a Marx Brothers' variety of the absurd and slapstick theatrics perpetually threatened the peace of his island sanctuary. Since their hands were simultaneously in each other's pockets, Elmyr's protestations of Legros totally hoodwinking him is in all probability only partially true. Elmyr had a way of looking at you with his soft brown eyes and possessing an inherent gullibility that, when he proclaimed his innocence, you at once wanted to believe him as a parent is inclined to do with a child. There was, however, a disquieting trail of crumbs that led straight from the empty cookie jar to him.

Legros had become used to his Hungarian goose pumping out those golden eggs on demand, and their business arrangement was mutually beneficial. One term Elmyr often used to describe Legros was "diabolically clever." This may have been true, but any shill running a three-shell game on a street corner would have immediately recognized Elmyr's aura of an easy mark. In a way, Legros did no more to Elmyr than does any businessperson who knows how to keep an employee productive and motivated, which was to pay Elmyr a "minimum wage." That assured him of a steady commodity that he could broker, assume the attendant risks, and keep the lion's share of the profits for himself. Because Elmyr was incurably naive, easily manipulated, and removed from the street-level haggling of the marketplace, he may well have believed Legros's understated success at selling his work. Another behind-the-scenes factor was at play here. Elmyr's natural comfort zone was at a societal level where people were titled, wealthy, and privileged. That is where he felt he belonged, and actually having to "work" for a living was an unfortunate fact of life for others, not for him. Even the bourgeois merchant class was a rung farther down the ladder than where he wanted to be. Consequently, it worked out conveniently that he could have the means to be a gentleman artist without the drudgery of being a "commoner." He had already done that, selling his pink poodle paintings door-to-door in Los Angeles, and really didn't much care for it.

The one symbol of his success that he felt was well earned was his villa, La Falaise. Here again, Fernand beguiled him out of the last remnant of common sense when Elmyr elected to put the home in Legros's name. So, offstage the legal tug-of-war over ownership of the house began to rage around the same time Elmyr's star was ascending. The lawsuit over *Fake* was further adding furrows to his brow. It really seemed that for every positive step forward he was taking, there was this wretched riptide pulling him back into a morass of distress that he thought was finally behind him. These disturbing undercurrents, however, were not apparent to anyone outside his intimate circle. As time went on, the tension between the tectonic plates of good versus evil that he appeared to straddle became increasingly sinister and destabilizing.

Elmyr's Madrid Exhibition

An urban crop of trees resembling giant stalks of broccoli sprouted from sidewalks at neat ten-meter intervals. These Gauguin trees with their spindly trunks suggested the city had not entirely divorced itself from nature, though the paltry amount of oxygen they contributed did little to offset the smothering pollution of Madrid's air.

On a hazy, chilled November evening, I accompanied Elmyr and Ursula to his grandest exhibition opening. We left the Hotel Ritz early. It was home when we were in Madrid. Its crystal chandeliers, thick Aubusson rugs, linen sheets, and solicitous concierge epitomized old-world elegance and charm that I now thought was an indispensable and normal part of life. The cab driver stopped in front of a nineteenth-century apartment building. The art gallery was the vision of an enterprising Catalan businessman, Isidro Clot. Before his newest mercantile impulse, he owned a fleet of trawlers and still knew more about wet fish than art. He was wealthy enough to care little about what others thought, but like Elmyr, also knew the importance of appearances. While fine art had more cachet than cod or mackerel, it was simply another vehicle to make money. Deal making was what made his heart beat faster, and I am sure it thumped away merrily that autumn night.

Emerging from our taxi, we stepped under the canopies of those stage-prop trees. A high stone Roman arch centered the building's stucco facade. Above its keystone, an embedded square blue tile with its white numbers, *69*, indicated we had found the gallery's location. We walked through the imperial-looking archway up a few wide stone steps whose surface sagged from frequent use. A Philippine mahogany door with swirling, beveled glass opened to a foyer. Inside, a brass plaque announced the gallery: Second floor, right. "Visitation by appointment only" intoned its exclusionary snob appeal. Directly ahead was an ornate wrought-iron birdcage of an elevator small enough for four slender, well-acquainted people. To the left, two-meter wide white marble steps rose to corner landings between floors, convenient stops for sweaty movers of large Rococo armoires and tassel-fringed sofas.

Elmyr wore a black wool Spanish cape with a generous swath of red velvet lining, suitable for parrying a lunging bull on the loose. Underneath, he donned his signature black velvet jacket, white shirt from his Saville Row tailor, black silk tie, dark trousers, and freshly polished black shoes. A thin gold chain held his monocle between his dress shirt and jacket. Around his left wrist was a postage-stamp-thin wristwatch from Boucheron with his initials, E. H., on its face. The normal glitter of jewelry was subdued on this occasion. He combed his gray hair to the side, precisely parted on the left. His suntanned face was a quick effect that oozed from a tube, although his smile was genuine.

Our footsteps echoed off the stone steps as we ascended the stairs. I pushed the small illuminated button beside the gallery door to announce our arrival. The gleaming wooden door opened. Elmyr and Ursula entered first; I followed them in. The scent of her perfume reminded me of my mother's yellow roses, the ones I carefully uncovered each spring after their long winter hibernation. A staccato of photographers' strobe flashes and clicking camera shutters greeted our entrance. Ursula, still a darling of the paparazzi, assumed her red-carpet persona, radiating her movie-star smile.

Inside the gallery, dark gray velvet drapes hung from its high ceilings to the floor and covered the walls. The space, converted from a private residence, boasted museum-sized salons, illuminated only by picture lights over golden French frames. Strategically placed Louis XVI bergère chairs and an ormolu desk or cabinet punctuated these interior spaces with studied stagecraft. Within his private office at the back of the gallery, Clot and Elmyr frequently set business aside, preferring to talk about anything else at length. As if to remind themselves how much better their lives were now than before, they exchanged war stories—Clot's memories of deprivation during Spain's vicious civil war and Elmyr's survival of torture and prison camp. They shared a mutual admiration for skills the other possessed. Elmyr embodied an artistic ability that awed the calculating entrepreneur, and one could see the marvel in Elmyr's eyes at Clot's unerring financial sleight-of-hand. Each now exhibited the confidence that success brings. Their wealth and hard-earned social status were deserved rewards for their respective talents, tenacity, and surviving crushing hardships.

Over the previous eight years, Elmyr transformed from an itinerant refugee into an object of public curiosity, and was now no longer viewed with disdain by the upper class for the stigma attached to his dubious past. Like the Greek immigrant painter some four hundred years earlier, Domenikos Theotokopoulos, known as El Greco, Elmyr's name now garnered a widespread respect in his adopted and adoptive country. This night's opening lent the most powerful imprimatur of societal acceptance he could desire. It would be his most important exhibition.

The Spanish tabloids twittered, speculating that members of the family of King Juan Carlos would attend the event. Embossed invitations went out to Madrid's glitterati, those who incubated in the hothouse of public attention. By this, I mean all those individuals Elmyr and Clot thought sufficiently titled, wealthy, and famous showed up for an exclusive preview of Elmyr's most recent artwork. A fashion reporter observed that elegantly dressed women represented about every major international designer of haute couture. Their low-cut gowns allowed hefty gem-laden necklaces to drip down to sensuous cleavages, so the simultaneous display of sexuality and wealth beckoned the ogling onlooker. However, prurient thoughts of Saturday night routinely received absolution on Sunday morning.

One of the first lessons I learned at the School of Elmyr was the significance of association. For him, appearances spoke volumes, yet he knew better than most just how deceiving they are. It was, nevertheless, important that people thought well of you, and one sure way of achieving this was being in the company of the right people. That evening his

273

exhibition became his investiture of sorts. The elite of Spanish society came to see Elmyr, and their benediction authenticated him. He now felt vindicated; his sense of self-worth bolstered, as both a person and an artist, by the collective display of adulation, he thought. This law of prestige by association proved correct once again; he radiated pride and self-satisfaction. The whole world would now see him as a person of merit. This perception and acknowledgement were what he craved most.

Elmyr's Madrid exhibition – 1976

Elmyr beamed his irrepressible smile, consuming titles and names as Clot introduced the invitees. He bowed solicitously over the extended hands of the chic women and arched his eyebrows in curiosity at their moneyed spouses. Judging from the shine in his brown eyes, I guessed he was mentally placing people on that heraldic org chart like a child decorating a Christmas tree. Long-stemmed women held fluted crystal glasses of fine French champagne. Their manes of flowing hair and impeccable pedigrees suggested a paddock of bipedal thoroughbreds. There was a prerace excitement in the air. It was long apparent to me that all these people wore their wealth comfortably, as an Olympic champion would his hard-earned olive wreath. However, it was difficult to imagine such people exuding a drop of perspiration for what they had. My perception was skewed, of course, because I knew many, like Clot, actually worked for a living. Their ascent up the social ladder came by virtue of talent and not simply by right of birth.

Whatever their credentials may have been, their presence at the gallery was a paean of respect, and their homage moved him deeply. Perhaps it was the absence of acceptance and love in his childhood that made their attainment an inexorable part of his character. This drive ruled his emotional compass, but its needle often pointed in a direction that was neither true nor advisable. During a fireside chat one evening at La Falaise, when I was still getting to know him, I confused wisdom with intelligence and was too young to know anything about emotional intelligence or the role it played in his life. Now, amid the adulation of those people whose opinions and support he esteemed most, the smoke from the burning wreckage of scandal seemed a distant memory. That's what I thought as I examined the collection of new work unveiled that chilled November night in Madrid.

As for the outcry from museum curators, art dealers, collectors, or experts, their pique had long since subsided. In fact, those with legitimate grievances against him were perhaps the most silent. With the clarity of hindsight and reinflated egos, his critics could claim that *he* never fooled them. In most cases, I suspect, the invective directed his way was probably just on the wrong side of audibility, and protests that he was not as talented as his reputation suggested surfaced a safe distance away from any involvement with him.

A sense of calm replaced the oscillating unpredictability that tethered him to an uncertain existence. His relationship with Clot made financial sense for both, and his need for security in this realm made it a no-brainer for him. It offered none of the complexities of emotionally motivated decisions. When courting Elmyr and proposing a business partnership, Clot made a point of touting his personal and professional success in becoming Salvador Dali's exclusive representative for his sculptures in gold and silver. Clot correctly surmised the lure of being in the company of Dali would prove as irresistible as the scent of quail to a pointer.

Three years earlier in Madrid, Dali had what was the most visually dazzling exhibition of art I have ever seen. Each piece, conceived by his unfathomable and tirelessly fertile imagination, was a construct of precious gems and metals. The hugely successful show not only was a triumph of his unique, surrealistic visions, but also a powerful collaboration with some of Spain's greatest and artistically inventive gold- and silversmiths and jewelers. I recalled the skill and technical virtuosity of Benvenuto Cellini's famous saltcellar or Carl Fabergé's Easter egg collection for Czar Nicolas II.

I believe Clot's being out of his depth in the world of art bothered him little. He wisely left that domain of expertise to the artists his gallery represented. His world was moneymaking, and this real-life talent enabled him to make a seamless transition from selling slippery fish to hawking artwork. Nor could one solely attribute his success to uncanny mercantile instincts. His perception and shrewd ability to read people gave him an edge in his dealings with others. His charm and indulgence toward lavishly entertaining those he wished to impress was simply a tact employed by any effective lobbyist. Elmyr's susceptibility to these overtures was just probably easier to forecast. Their respect for each other, above all else, formed the foundation of their accord. What began ostensibly as a business relationship turned into a friendship that lasted until Elmyr's death.

In Elmyr's finest moment, the presence of his great friend Ursula Andress made the occasion even more luminescent. She had genuine star power, a bona fide celebrity, but whose no-nonsense Swiss pragmatism never allowed her to lose touch with her well-grounded values. She offered him the perfect foil for the event. If anyone could look better in form-fitting clothes than Ursula, it could only be Aphrodite herself. Dressed in black with a plunging neckline, her figure and beauty gathered everyone's attention. Clot seized the opportunity to ask her to wear some of Dali's jewelry. He probably thought it unlikely that anyone else could model it more attractively than her.

Opposite this side illuminated by the incandescent glow of public attention lurked a sinister inverse of Elmyr's principle of prestige by association. Fernand Legros remained living proof and a constant reminder of the notion of guilt by association and personal testimony to Elmyr's unerring ability to make devastatingly poor decisions about people. In today's vernacular, I want to describe him as a "head case" and "stalker" for his unremitting obsession to destroy Elmyr.

There were no outward signs that anything unseemly occurred for those few hours of glory at his exhibition, but a menacing plot was unfolding simultaneously, winding its way through the Spanish courts like poisonous vapors. Legros and his battery of lawyers contrived a means of guaranteeing Elmyr's public disgrace. Fernand's stamina for revenge now was more vigorous than ever and indissolubly linked to his own happiness. Nothing galled him as much as Elmyr's success. The hatred Legros once bore his former lover and expressed in the candid, shocking letter he wrote Elmyr, now paled next to his desire to ruin *him*.

The Spanish government, then known for its capacity to dispense justice harshly and expeditiously, had dealt with the legal issues of Elmyr's case years before. If they had a case against him, it is unlikely they would have demonstrated any compunction against swiftly placing him in prison if found guilty of some punishable crime in connection to his career as an art forger. Fernand tried and failed on two previous attempts to get Spain to extradite Elmyr to France. Each setback only hardened his determination, hoping his third try would be an evil charm. He also learned from his prior mistakes and now constructed charges against Elmyr that would offer the Madrid courts no clear room to escape their new demand. Incidentally, the accusations incriminated Fernand as well. He alleged that Elmyr supplied him with the fake customs stamps used to move works of art from France across international borders. His documented admission and complicity to a criminal act and its ramifications displayed the kind of absence of forethought usually associated with sociopaths and schizophrenics. Self-destructive consequences rarely deter zealots, and Fernand could not see beyond his blind obsession.

The extradition process is neither simple nor easy. It requires the cooperation of a country's Department of State or Foreign Ministry to initiate a demand. Then, the courts determine if the demand conforms to the existing extradition treaty between the two countries. The genesis of this entire scheme was uniquely Legros's idea. If the French government had any substantive grounds for demanding Elmyr's extradition, it would have done so nine years earlier. Rumors long circulated that Legros was blackmailing two French ministers who had connections to him via their reputed homosexuality. Besides, if Elmyr ever testified in French court, it could only lead to more incendiary scandals in the art community that no one desired, except Legros, as any publicity, good or bad, would only fuel his irrepressible megalomania.

Elmyr's feet hardly had time to alight once more, as the euphoria of the Madrid show had overwhelmed him so, when a phone call cast an instant pall over his joyful mood. His lawyer in Ibiza informed him that Madrid received a new demand for his extradition. A hearing scheduled for December 7, 1976, before a tribunal of judges in Palma, Mallorca,

277

would decide his fate. A friend referred him to one of the best attorneys in Palma. Two weeks before the hearing, I accompanied Elmyr to meet with him to discuss the matter. He agreed to defend Elmyr, and together we formulated a strategy that sounded persuasive and provided the despondent artist a ray of hope.

I have a haunting recollection of how time changed during that two-week period. It thrust me into an altered state, like being in a car accident. This is perhaps the closest analogy to what I experienced. The sense of foreboding was palpable, and the other-worldliness so eerie that it still gives me goose bumps when I think of it.

A thick gloom shrouded our lives, and we once more assumed a zombie gait, like in a George Romero movie. Every bit of cheer residing in his body and mind at the zenith of his Madrid show vanished. The cellular memory of that moment gave way to deeper remembrances of his wartime pain and torture; his face wore the mask of tragedy. My paltry attempts at morale boosting were unconvincing; the pervasive sense of doom exposed the worthlessness of my words. We knew the reason why our spirits collapsed.

I no longer recall if the stranger's visit occurred around the time of the first or second extradition demand, although his timing was less consequential than his message. After leaving La Falaise, Elmyr rented a home in the countryside near San Jose. Situated on a hillside with views of terraced groves of almond trees stretching to the sea, it was the picture of pastoral tranquility and beauty. It was also hard to find for anyone unfamiliar with the area. Any unexpected knock at the front door always surprised us, as it did the morning the visitors arrived. Elmyr went to the door to find a man he did not know and a woman with whom he was slightly acquainted. He invited them in, and they went into the sun-filled living room. Their somber demeanors presaged the purpose of their call. The man proceeded to tell Elmyr that he had knowledge of a plot by Fernand Legros directed at him. He told Elmyr, "If you ever go to jail in France, you will be killed. Legros has a contract out on you already." Given our brush with him in Geneva and his attempt to lure Elmyr into that rented house for the phony television interview and the hired thugs, we had every reason to believe this person's claim. No matter how believable his menacing pronouncement was, Elmyr's response was abrupt. "I will not be threatened in my own home," he admonished them, "please leave." It was too late, though; the pathogen of distress instantly found its host—as Legros fully intended with this harbinger of dire news. Against the backdrop of Fernand's tireless efforts to orchestrate Elmyr's demise, it was impossible to expel the grim foresight from our thoughts.

Palma

Elmyr spent enough time with his lawyer to accord him a warm respect that bordered on friendship, given the brevity of their acquaintance. This sentiment was mutual. Every signal one can display to convey this impression evidenced in his voice, eyes, body language, and conviction of opinion. Together these powerful alloys steeled his absolute belief in his client's innocence. Nothing bleeds through the fabric of courtroom rhetoric and ritual as does the unvarnished truth; the canon of Spanish law would be his persuasive artillery. We expected, or hoped, this would be a formidable last line of defense against the relentless Legros.

We arrived the evening of December 6. I had been in Mallorca many times before, but this time there was not a shred of joy connected to the trip. We were both subdued as we dined lightly at our hotel that evening. Neither of us could muster any small talk to distract from the import of the coming day. All I could think of was the constant refrain of FDR's famous words in response to the Japanese attack on Pearl Harbor: "…a day that will live in infamy." Every American school kid knew the date, December 7, 1941, as well as October 12, 1492, Columbus's discovery of the new world. Why did the hearing have to occur on December 7, a historically disastrous day? It was a hugely wretched omen, I thought. I never mentioned it, as I could feel his pain.

The following morning, the hearing lasted about three hours. Elmyr's lawyer laid out a compelling argument, citing obscure passages and precedents of case law that would normally have prevailed if this had been a trial. Unfortunately, it was not. The attorney representing the State succinctly defused the forceful eloquence of Elmyr's defense by reminding the judges three times that "we are not here to discuss the guilt or innocence of Señor de Hory, but *only* determine if the demand for extradition conforms to the treaty that exists between France and Spain." The scope of their decision was so narrow, it would have been easier to suck all those tomes of Spanish law through a straw. Legros counted on the diabolical simplicity of this strategy to achieve his goal.

During the flight back to Ibiza, I did my best to be upbeat and supportive. Elmyr went through an emotional wringer the previous two weeks, sleeping little; the exhaustion in his face and eyes was painfully obvious, and I did not know how to comfort him. A week before, we were at the home of one of his Hungarian friends in Ibiza. They proposed to have a party over the holidays and wanted to know if we would be available. Elmyr calmly replied, "If I am still alive, I will come." His response disarmed everyone, because no one really expected anything to come of this latest legal maneuvering of Legros. It was as though Elmyr had already slipped into a quiet resignation in the way someone terminally ill accepts their fate when all other avenues of recourse are exhausted.

Friday, December 10

Elmyr spent much of the previous two days writing letters to his friends. I knew they were farewell letters. My pep talks must have sounded hollow, yet I could not grasp the calamity at hand. My denial of the looming danger did little to buffer Elmyr from what was looking more like a preordained fate. That prospect was simply outside the realm of possibility, I thought. Elmyr asked me to bring some of his lithographs downstairs to the dining room. As he stood before his sturdy Spanish Renaissance table, he signed them one by one. "I want you to have these," he said, "but if they are not signed they will be worth much less." I witnessed his last artistic testament and felt the blood drain from my veins. No, this could not be happening, I kept telling myself. That afternoon we went to the notary's office in Ibiza town. Here, he signed a simple declaration making me his sole heir. I still refused to see this as an act of surrender, but rather the sort of perfunctory precaution travelers take in opting for flight insurance, thinking the chances of crashing are miniscule.

Saturday, December 11

A good friend of ours, Evelyn Archer, knew personally two of the judges that heard Elmyr's case in Palma. She said she would speak to them and that we should call her Saturday morning. It was a beautiful sunny morning, the kind of morning rich with promise that good weather imparts to the soul. I kept my fingers crossed as I drove over the dusty road to the narrow main highway that ascended to the hilltop village of San Jose. Next to the church, a pay phone stood ready to use. For a long silent moment I sat, trying to collect my thoughts that ricocheted in my head. My usually steady hand held an old envelope with Evelyn's number scribbled in pencil on the back. The paper's edges trembled in my hand, the same way Prosky's auction catalog had in Elmyr's hands long ago. It was time to make that compact with a God I did not believe existed. If the news were good, I would become a believer. If it were bad, it would confirm my atheism. I was open to negotiation, like a good agnostic. A week before I had met John Derek and his not-yet-famous wife, Bo, at the plaza in front of this church. They were going to come for lunch, but Elmyr had to cancel. The extradition matter still lay before him, and he could not muster the

285

enthusiasm to entertain anyone. In my entire life, I have never dreaded making a phone call as much as I did at that moment.

Slowly, I walked to the pay phone, picked up the receiver, and dropped some coins into the slot—then dialed the number on the envelope. Evelyn answered. I said "This is Mark," and asked if she had heard anything. Her voice began to waiver, and then she began to cry. Through her emotional distress, she said the judges expressed their regrets, but could do nothing but accede to the extradition demand. It was beyond their control. Tearfully, I thanked her for giving me the hard news. I never saw or spoke to her again, but there is not one second of that call I will ever forget.

I sat in the car, staring at the sunlit, whitewashed side of the church. It looked like a giant primed canvas awaiting an artist's colored brush, only I knew the canvas would remain untouched. Elmyr waited for me at the house; I had to return, but I would do anything to avoid telling him the news he sensed was coming. It was that feline sense that death is near, that prompts the cat you love to hide because it knows it is vulnerable and about to die. These were the unspoken signs I saw in Elmyr's eyes, gait, and voice. His restless soul was preparing to leave its corporeal world, and I was powerless to intervene. I could only watch, feeling miserably inadequate and confused. Confused because I expected there to be fairness in life where none exists. These were events wildly out of my control and Elmyr's. It had nothing to do with the things he taught me such as social graces and art, things our finite minds could handle— like rules we create for our own artificial reality.

The good weather did not bring a good day, and I had to explain why. I turned the ignition key and listened to the faint hum of the car's engine, then put it in gear as though these were motions completely new to me. On the way back to the house, the slow crunching sound of the tires rolling over small rocks was all I could hear. My delayed return augured what he, anticipating the bleak consequences, already knew. Arriving at the path that led up to the finca, I turned off the car's motor and for a moment listened to the wind, watching it move the green December grass and the branches of nearby trees.

My entire body felt leaden from this burden as I walked to the front door. I found Elmyr in the living room, sitting in his leather easy chair. Dressed in his pajamas and camel-colored cashmere robe I bought for him at Harrod's in London, it was unusual to see him unshaven. Still, he had his customary bowl of tea between his hands. The instant our eyes met, he knew the dismal truth. Collapsing in the chair opposite his, I cried loudly, as I had never cried before. He gestured to me to calm myself, as he did not want his housekeeper to hear my sobbing. Disappearing into the kitchen for a moment, I could hear him speaking to the neighbor woman who eagerly cleaned the house three days a week for the extra income that helped her family and made life a little easier. In his inimitable, faulty Spanish that always made me smile, he informed her in a subdued voice that he would not need her for the rest of the day.

She left the house quietly. When we were alone, we continued to sit in the familiar, comfortable easy chairs, facing one another as we did countless times before, but never in such a dark moment of grave finality. I could see he had transcended that plane of sorrow and regret, now speaking to me in a tone of fatherly concern that denoted the deep caring for a son leaving home. He knew my strengths and weaknesses and focused on what I needed to do in the coming days and weeks, rightfully aware of the void his absence would create in my life. I had to be observant of my obligations, carry out his last wishes, and convey his regrets with the solemn dignity of someone unable to attend an important social function due to unfortunate but unforeseen circumstances.

A stack of sealed letters in their Wedgwood blue envelopes from his favorite Bond Street stationery shop lay on the table between the chairs. Every name on every one evoked a flood of memories. I had to be careful so my tears would not stain any of them. With a note of newfound urgency in his voice, he said, "I must go now." I followed him upstairs to his bedroom. His white terrier, Moody, followed us up. Wherever Elmyr went, his dog was always nearby. He then gave me a small leather bag, telling me that he put his rings, watch, and a few other items in it that I was to keep with me. Tears once more flowed down my face as we embraced each other. Moody jumped onto his bed, wagging his tail, staring at his friend in loving adoration. Elmyr then bent over and kissed the dog's head, stood up, and gestured to me to back up. "Please," he said, "don't make this harder for me than it already is." I left his room. Moody lay at the edge of his bed with his head hanging slightly over its side, ready for his master to come back to bed. His last words echoed in my head, as they *were* the last words I heard him speak. He then took a fatal dose of barbiturates and cognac.

I went back downstairs dazed from grief and disbelief. Elmyr parried all my suggestions to flee the island if the government granted his extradition. He had two counterfeit passports the ex-bookie Talbot had procured for him to use in an emergency. This dilemma met that threshold. "No," he countered, "I will not run to be hunted down by a pack of dogs!" The ignominy of that thought was unbearable to him, especially in the aftermath of his Madrid exhibition. It would be tantamount to spitting on the hard-earned acceptance he struggled to achieve all his life. He preferred a more stoic, honorable end like the Japanese Bushido, orchestrating his own exit from life. He vowed he would not go back to prison, especially facing the prospect of his own murder, as the mysterious visitor prophesized months earlier. The events of the last month, rife with irony, spiraled downward from the summit of his personal success and glory to his tragic and untimely suicide.

In my grief-stricken vigil, I sat in the leather chair, staring at the vacant seat opposite me, knowing he would never occupy it again or share his inexhaustible stories with me. Through large sliding glass doors, I watched the sun move around a tree. The shadow of its trunk became a natural sundial that I never before noticed. I left the house and drove to Ibiza town about twenty-five minutes away, intending to see our dear friend Monique at her real estate office. Of the many great friends we had, she was and remains today one of the people I steadfastly admire and adore. I needed to be with someone and had to tell her what Elmyr had done. I found her and her partner, Henri, at their real estate office and informed them of his intended suicide. She wanted to go the house immediately and I explained his wishes, although she insisted we prevent his death. He adamantly rejected the odium of arrest and the spectacle of being dragged off in handcuffs, yet the thought of losing him was equally unbearable. Her insistence won out, so we ran back to the car and drove back to the house. Henri followed in his vehicle.

We dashed into the house, then upstairs to his bedroom. As I approached his bed, I found him on his side with his face in his pillow. I tried to rouse him gently, saying, "Elmyr...Elmyr!" He then rolled over to see who was disturbing his sleep. As soon as he looked at me, I could see his gaze was vacant, without a glimmer of recognition. Henri and I picked him up and carried him to his car. I cradled him in my arms in the back of his vehicle. He drove with Monique beside him, speeding back to the hospital in Ibiza. When we arrived, I shouted that we needed a doctor. One of the nuns came out, gently picked up his wrist to feel his pulse, and whispered we were too late. He died en route. When he had turned in his bed, I knew his spirit was trying to flee his body, and he was trying mightily to let it go. They placed his body on a gurney and wheeled it into a room. Standing next to him, I picked up his right hand; feeling his cooling fingers, I cried, knowing his life was gone and that hand would never create again. Elmyr shuffled off his mortal coil in the ultimate act of desperation and courage.

I am not sure we can ever fully recover from the loss of a loved one. We become inured to their absence over time, but the emotional pain leaves scar tissue on our souls. The growth rings of our remaining years just cover the disfiguring hurt, but it never completely heals or goes away.

It rained the day of Elmyr's burial, appropriate for the occasion, I thought. The rain also renewed the island this time of year. Wildflowers sprang up everywhere, speckling the countryside as in a Monet painting, reminding one of the cycle of life. That overlooked fact of nature never before conveyed the significance or grief it now possessed. No one close to me had ever died before, so I guess my education on Ibiza was not yet over. I was now at the opposite end of that emotional Rorschach, further away from happiness than I ever knew possible. Can you fully understand or appreciate life without knowing what death is? I asked myself that in my solitude. I imagined a grin on Elmyr's face if I had slid this ontological question into our evening conversations, or, better yet, brought it up during a metaphysical chat with Arlene or Sandy. Before, I had no reason to explore such notions surveying the depth or breadth of sorrow. I thought I careened close enough to sadness in the secondhand tales of Elmyr's hardships and heartaches. In the days following his death, I felt like an alpinist clutching a severed lifeline, falling from the rock's face, jolted awake from a recurring nightmare, except this nightmare was real.

The evening of the day he died police came to the house in the country, placing that yellow plastic tape over the front door as though it were a crime scene. Well, to them that's what it was, suicide being against the law and, more importantly, keeping his soul out of heaven, kind of like the way WASPs used to keep Jews out of country clubs. None of it made any sense to me. Elmyr's good friend Mariano Llobet explained to me that since he took his own life in this arch-Catholic country, we might not get a church-sanctioned service anywhere, and that extended to his being non grata in a cemetery. It looked like Elmyr was heading to the dog graveyard, wherever that was. Mariano had been the prefect of Ibiza for years, so he knew everyone. Years earlier Elmyr had done portraits of him and his wife, Carmen, who died at forty of cancer. Hung side by side, the portraits faced one another like early fifteenth-century Italian renaissance pictures, suggesting love and fidelity. If anyone knew what strings to pull it was Mariano. He arranged for a service at a church in the old city. The only catch was that we had to piggyback with another service of someone else who died more honorably, or at least in accordance with church doctrine.

News of Elmyr's death traveled fast throughout the island and abroad. My brother later told me he read about it in the *L. A. Times*. Peter One sent a telegram of condolence from New York. Isidro Clot came from Madrid. Our longtime friend Jamie Goodbrand flew down from London. Before I arrived, Elmyr fostered Jamie's budding artistic talents. He helped him get an exhibition at Ivan Spence's gallery near the Romanesque cathedral in the old city. Sandy drove out to the house, offering to help me in any way possible. Friends rallied to my support. All the while, Moody, his terrier, stayed close to me.

That night I stayed at the house in a small, attached room but with no door accessing the home's interior. I dragged in a single mattress and blankets from inside before the police sealed the entry. At dusk two uniformed soldiers arrived from the military barracks in town to make sure no one disturbed the house. The soldiers always looked ominous to me because they wore those Nazi helmets, souvenirs of Hitler's support of Franco during the civil war. Their barracks was also just below Los Molinos, the same one the naked girl's car crashed into and caught everything on fire when they released Legros from prison a couple of days early for good behavior. I brought them two rattan chairs I had painted canary yellow when we lived at La Falaise. There was also a pile of firewood outside, so they built a fire to keep themselves warm that night. It was impolite not to ask guests if they wanted something to drink, so I offered them a bottle of wine from a case in Elmyr's studio, even though I had no way to open it. They said, "No, gracias."

I could only cry that night and cuddle with Moody, who curled up by my side. I rose at first light. Heavy dew dripped from everything outside in the cold morning air. The soldiers sat in their chairs near the exhausted fire; their long canvas coats covered them like blankets. Around nine o'clock, the chief of police and a couple of officers arrived. I knew the head of the police department and found him likeable even though he had busted friends of mine for drug possession. He cut the yellow tape. We entered the house. They wanted to see his bedroom. Together we climbed a few steps to a barren room whose purpose was never clear, then up a few more steps to our left to the master bedroom. On Elmyr's night table, a small empty yellow bottle lay on its side. Its contents, barbiturate sleeping pills, were now in Elmyr's stomach, along with much of the Courvoisier from the bottle next to it. One plainclothes officer bent over, picking up a couple of the pills from the pale yellow rug next to the bed. Another man offered a bag for the evidence.

We went downstairs then to the living room. Beside Elmyr's chair lay his *sesta*. It was no longer the hand-woven straw basket with two ropelike shoulder straps. He had one of the local artisans fashion one from smooth mahogany-colored leather. Inside were all the letters in their Wedgwood-blue envelopes. These were his good-byes to his close friends, and, from the authorities' viewpoint, evidence that exonerated me from any criminal implication in his death. It was an inference I never once contemplated. At that moment it first entered my mind that in some way they might view me as—a suspect. What if he had not written those letters, I thought, what then? My mind lurched to the possibility of stepping in my own snare of injustice. I just learned the most lurid lesson about the inadequacy of innocence. That's why it's aptly named "the criminal justice system," that inner voice was telling me.

They looked through every room in the house for any anomalies, I suppose, that might shed light on any details helping their investigation. This is the sort of instance that triggered Elmyr's gag reflex and sweat glands. Now, I felt that queasy anxiety he must have experienced whenever he was near the police. And I hadn't done anything wrong. Wait, how many times did Elmyr tell himself that? The police director then expressed his thanks for my cooperation and regrets about Elmyr's death. "Could you come to see me in a few days?" he asked. "I think I can then return these letters to you," he added, opening the door to leave with the other two men.

Mariano helped make funeral arrangements, contacting the undertaker and paying for a niche in a kind of aboveground honeycomb for the dead. For some reason, Mariano picked out a coffin with a pane of glass on the lid. Perhaps because of this initial exposure to death and funerals, I find any reason possible to excuse myself from these ceremonies. Viewing his lifeless body was the last image I wanted of him in my mind. I don't know if there was any announcement in the local newspaper, but still, many people arrived at the cemetery the day of the burial. Rain pelted opened umbrellas. Tearful friends stood silently. Mariano then approached me, whispered in my ear that the police had just received word from Madrid. The French government wanted his fingerprints. Someone apparently wanted proof that the body in the casket was actually Elmyr—and not someone else. After all, if anyone could fabricate his own death, it would be Elmyr, right?

They moved his coffin inside a small chapel within the walled cemetery. I couldn't witness this last indignation. Mariano, the coroner, and two police officials went inside. Five minutes later they came out, allowing some other men to carry the casket. They climbed a short ladder and lifted it into a niche about six feet high. Before they began mortaring in bricks, I climbed the ladder and kissed the coffin as though I were alone, unafraid to show my grief and my love for him. Learning what it is to lose someone you love must be the hardest thing to learn in this world.

Aftermath

Throughout the weeks following Elmyr's death, I had the support of friends who long before welcomed me into their lives, not for my proximity to him, but for who I was. Together, we reminisced about happier times. Everyone felt his absence. To me it was a sucking chest wound. Moody, now my constant companion and link to Elmyr, came everywhere with me. I was saying my good-byes to my extended family, preparing for the inevitable separation of leaving the island.

In January, within about a month of Elmyr's hearing in Palma, I read an article in *TIME* magazine. French police arrested Abu Daoud, who reputedly masterminded the Munich Olympic massacre. Germany requested his extradition. Instead of sending the terrorist suspect back across the Rhine to stand trial for the atrocities, the French spirited him out of the country aboard a plane to Algeria. Some speculated that the French government simply wanted the politically volatile situation to vanish and not derail a multi-million-dollar deal to sell Egypt Mirage jets and other French-made military equipment. Egypt took delivery of the hardware that very week. While this kind of dollars-and-sense pragmatism commonly disorients the moral compass of elected officials, it is interesting to note how easily French president Giscard d'Estaing's administration cooperated in demanding Elmyr's extradition. The moral imperative to hand over Abu Daoud somehow seemed less clear.

No matter how much I thought about Elmyr's death, it wasn't going to change anything. I had to look ahead. Overnight, all those daily decisions governing the present and future were up to me. He had a contract with Clot, giving his gallery exclusive rights to his work, so I returned to Madrid to take care of unfinished business with Elmyr's estate. Those world-wise skills I had been learning were supposed to ease me into independence. From my first days at La Falaise, Elmyr attempted to give me those tools to empower me, to make me self-sufficient. Still, nothing Elmyr ever imparted to me resembled anything as practical as money management. How could he pass on something that eluded him his entire life? Another irony neither Elmyr nor I saw coming was apparent only after we had been together a few years. It is an awakening that stirs mixed feelings in parents, I imagine, when all one's protection, caring, and guidance culminates in the departure of their offspring. As I matured, he seemed proud and wistful—proud of himself for giving me the education that he wanted me to have, and wistful for completing his mission. His death, however, renewed that sense of disconnectedness and purposelessness that initiated my eight-year sojourn in Europe. Life with Elmyr not only anchored me but also instilled in me the conviction that my future looked promising. The stellar social network with which I had grown comfortable would yield a niche for me, I thought. If I had elected to stay in Spain, I could have continued to work in the Madrid art gallery. Clot, however, knew I wanted to return to the US and suggested I act as their agent, selling Dali's jewelry and gold sculptures. That was my intention.

In the spring of 1977, I flew to New York, where many of my friends from Ibiza were living. There, I sublet an apartment for six weeks in west Greenwich Village. At the time, I couldn't have foreseen that the first few years back in the States would be so awkward. I felt dressed for the cotillion ball, waiting for my date who never arrived. Maybe it was my hairy legs underneath those crinoline petticoats, but there was something wrong with this picture. Anyway, that's the way it seemed. I never dreamed that my carefully tailored education would isolate me from most everyone. It was supposed to be just the opposite. Social etiquette didn't count for much in the drive-thru at a fast-food joint. No one I knew would appreciate puns in French. On those occasions when I encountered Europeans, I went back into the fake hand-kissing mode. Not with men, of course. These customs had their place in Elmyr's world, but that behavior, I began to realize, mostly vanished with the British Empire. To everyone around me it must have looked like an embarrassing ritual of a fraternity hazing. How could I feel so out of place in my own culture, my own country? It reminded me of the saucer-eyed wonderment of my lifelong friends that greeted my first return visit to Minnesota. They patiently waited for this cultured hangover to pass. Slowly, I dropped those affectations that made me, I thought, a sideshow oddity. In many ways, I felt like a monarch who had just abdicated his throne. In my solitude, I reflected on the extraordinary opportunities I had and a love I might never have known, which time can never steal from me.

I know one principal reason why Elmyr and I bonded so strongly. We were both caregivers and generous. That symbiosis worked for us both. Elmyr had no reason to suspect an ordinary gesture of offering Legros his sofa to sleep on would eventually lead to his death. How could he? Even when Legros's psychopathic nature was clear to him, Elmyr's impulse to help others was part of who he was. Those with predatory natures saw this trait as lunch. There seems to be some natural magnetism at work, how givers wed takers. It took me decades to recognize the unhealthy pattern of my inclination to redeem needy people. Until the destructiveness of this do-good inclination was obvious, I had already worked through two failed marriages and other terminal relationships. I believe it mirrored Elmyr's personal life in many respects, and, unfortunately, it was something I could not learn vicariously from his emotional missteps. How strange it is that others' quirky behavior is often immediately evident, while self-awareness is frequently a lifelong quest.

I didn't return to Ibiza for twenty-eight years, until 2005. By that time, I was ready to get some closure around the painful memories associated with Elmyr's death. My wife, Alice, helped me work through these emotional issues and achieve the psychic peace I needed. For years, I felt guilt for not preventing his suicide, even though I could not have deterred him. I also felt I let him down, not living up to his expectations of me. While writing this book, however, I've felt Elmyr's presence and see in my mind's eye his inimitable smile, sense the warmth of his love, and somehow know he approves of what I've done.

Part Three

MY SEARCH FOR THE TRUTH

Humankind cannot bear very much reality.

T. S. Elliot

I often thought that one day I would get a phone call beginning with the words "You don't know me, but…," girding myself for some haunting reminder of things I'd done or said, evidence of past behavior that makes one cringe in shame and would be better left buried under a pile of excuses—like the twin girls I had fathered when I was eighteen and never knew. I left California before I found out my girlfriend was pregnant, and all I knew was that they were put up for adoption after their birth.

That breathtaking declaration of another sort came one morning in March 2010. It was a man's sonorous, radio-quality voice. He said he'd read a newspaper article in the *Minneapolis Star Tribune* about the exhibition at the Hillstrom Museum of Art. The works on display mostly came from my collection, about seventy pieces by Elmyr, the first major showing of his art in almost thirty-five years and largest ever in North America. The initial grip of guilt vanished as he explained the purpose of his call. "...I knew Elmyr in California," he told me. I asked him when that was. "Sixty-four, sixty-five," he said. That time frame didn't gel with the story familiar to me. As far as I knew, Elmyr never returned to the States after going back to Europe in 1959. He had to have his dates wrong. The caller was Jerry Czulewicz, an artist, appraiser, collector, and dealer of fine art, collectibles, books, wines, and maker of friends. "I understand completely the relationship you had with Elmyr," he continued. Jerry was referring to Elmyr's being gay; he was not, but circulated with ease within the gay community, that lifestyle that was unavoidable in Hollywood and particularly the film and art world that brought them together.

"We used to meet at a restaurant called the Matador," Jerry said. "One night I was there with Sasha Brastoff and Howard Shoop. They had a gallery called the Esplanade, with Lee Liberace as a partner. Over dinner one evening, Elmyr asked if they wanted to arrange an exhibition of his work there. Sasha then brought up the rumors of Elmyr's name being connected to art forgery. I could see that he was crushed by this unpleasant news. It caught me by surprise, as this was the first I ever heard anything like that." I'd seen that futureless look in Elmyr's eyes before, his hope exhausted like those awaiting sad but predictable news in hospital lounges. It was not just his rejection but the notion of his illicit past becoming public knowledge that must have alarmed him. He was a marked man with diminishing avenues of escape and means of selling his art to make a living.

Jerry went on to say he thought Elmyr's good friend Count André Esterhazy had helped him reenter the country through Mexico. This would have required a new passport, as the fake Canadian passport Legros had helped procure for his return to Europe had likely expired. The sense of his flight as a fugitive desperate to survive assumed a new reality for me as Jerry's tale unfolded.

All that had fit neatly in place before was now ajar. The tidy facts I'd amassed throughout this chapter in my life just suffered a seismic jolt, toppling some longstanding assumptions, the biggest of which was that I knew everything or nearly everything about Elmyr's life. Jerry and I spoke for about an hour and a half. When our conversation ended I was reeling, my world shaken and leaving me with no doubt about the story Jerry just shared with me.

Around this time I received an e-mail from Scott Richter, an art professor at Cooper Union in New York. He had also learned of the exhibition in Minnesota and possessed a genuine fake Elmyr-Modigliani obtained by his parents in a curious way. According to Scott, Elmyr, who lived in Miami Beach in the mid 1950s, was forced to flee for passing bad checks. He had sold them some small Picasso drawings and wanted to sell them the Modigliani but instead left it behind with them before he fled town. Colette Loll Marvin discovered Scott through a friend and asked if he'd loan his "Modigliani" for the exhibition she was curating for the Museum of Crime and Punishment in Washington DC. Its focus was art crimes, such as fakes, forgeries, and stolen and looted treasures. Colette was director of public and international relations for the Association for Research into Crimes Against Art (ARCA). What was particularly intriguing about the Modigliani ingenue staring from its frame in Richter's collection was the small brass plaque indicating the artist's name: Amedeo Modigliani. It hung for ten years in the University of Miami Art Museum, its originality never questioned until the Richters decided to remove it after its decade-long loan only after Elmyr's story began appearing in the international press and an article in *Look* magazine in 1968.

Prior to this discovery, an old friend from Ibiza, Chris Allaire, took the Jitney (bus running between Manhattan and Long Island) one day. Chris was instrumental in my writing this book, and acquainted with Elmyr for many years when he lived on Ibiza. He began a conversation with the woman seated next to him. She owned an art gallery in the Hamptons, so Elmyr's name soon surfaced. "I know his story," she said. "Do you know Peter Schults?" Peter was a longtime friend of Elmyr's, and although I'd never met him, I knew he would offer a new perspective. Chris got his phone number for me and I contacted him. To my delight, Peter also knew Jean Louis, a character of mythic stature whose name and presence appear frequently in the Elmyr saga. Elmyr mentioned numerous instances of Jean Louis traveling to New York, Hollywood, Rome, Kansas City, Mexico City, Paris, and being aware of Elmyr's fraudulent activities. Thanks to Peter I was able to meet Jean

Louis in Paris in 2011. Colette Marvin, who was living in Paris at this time, accompanied me so I could interview him for this book. Few had as accurate a view of Elmyr's secrets as did Jean Louis.

I possessed a trove of photos of nameless people, though none provided a clue that connected Jean Louis to any of those images. Elmyr said he had dark hair, was thin, attractive, intelligent, and "came from a good family." The "good family" angle was the societal stamp of approval that meant so much to him, the human equivalent to that Underwriter's Laboratories tag on small appliances that guaranteed you would not burst into flames when you used it. I think how much easier Elmyr's life, or all our lives, would be if people came with that little label protecting us from unexpected personal disaster. We then might never read headlines as "Nun Arrested in Shooting Spree."

Jean Louis came from old money, old enough to have infused snobbery and disdain for the likes of the Rothschilds and anyone else hopeful that *new* money would accrue acceptability in a society laden with anti-Semitism and class prejudice. It was that odd bias that stratified the Jewish community, establishing a social pecking order internally that to a lesser degree mirrored the discrimination many non-Jews felt toward them. Some of Jean Louis's family, like many French Jews, could not escape the holocaust, deportation to concentration camps, and methodical extermination during German occupation in World War II. He, however, survived the Nazi plague that infected Europe by fleeing to Spain and ultimately joining the Free French forces that landed at Toulon in 1944 to help liberate his country.

Peter Schults told me he introduced Jean Louis to Elmyr in Los Angeles in the early 1950s. It may have been the universal lure of glamour and ease of the California lifestyle that prompted Jean Louis's west-coast foray. Peter met Elmyr in Hollywood, when Elmyr tried to pick him up. Although Peter rebuffed his overtures, they established a friendship that brought Jean Louis into the picture. Elmyr had already made friends within the film community. Peter recounted a conversation in which Elmyr talked about his friend Rita Hayworth. Jean Louis was starstruck and implored Elmyr to arrange a meeting with the famous actress. Elmyr set up a luncheon. Peter and Elmyr showed up without Jean Louis, who had became distracted by a siren of his preferred gender along Hollywood Boulevard and missed their date. Elmyr never repeated the offer to introduce them.

It is second-hand stories such as these that corroborate the life I knew in Elmyr's company and give credibility to the extraordinary events and people that entwine this tale. While I don't recall Elmyr ever telling me this anecdote, there were countless others laced with celebrity name-dropping. Herein is the challenge. It was in Elmyr's nature to appropriate descriptive detail and thought any narrative worthy of one's attention would sound better if it resembled the lushness of a Raymond Chandler novel. He felt obliged to make it memorable and a little artistic license was just fine. That these stories wavered on occasion in their retelling, I cannot write off as deliberate deceit. Dr. Charles V. Ford, in his insightful book *Lies! Lies! Lies!: The Psychology of Deceit*, explains memories this way:

Our memories of past events are *not* like computer files but are highly malleable, fluid in time and space, and reflective of our recent needs. Memories are being continuously reconstructed; the past is not fixed in memory. Rather, we remember the past in terms of our current emotions, experiences, and prejudices (Swartz 1984).

PARIS

It was 2011, early March in Paris. The air was cold, but not enough to impede the crocuses and daffodils from blooming in the sunlit Luxembourg Gardens. Colette, my wife Alice, and I stood before the unadorned facade of an art deco apartment building with its smooth stucco curves and industrial glass block. Colette pressed the buzzer opposite Jean Louis's name. A moment later a voice crackled in French, asking who was there. We announced ourselves and heard the electronic latch click on the wrought-iron-grilled glass door. Traversing an inner courtyard, I looked up to see the side of a landlocked ocean liner. Round porthole windows and sleek tubular steel balconies allowed the ship's passengers inward views of its timeless simplicity in this marriage of techno-minimalism and stackable living.

Jean Louis greeted us, holding the apartment door open. His great-nephew Philippe was there to help translate if we needed. Jean Louis's slightly curly dark hair had a hint of gray, far less than mine, though he was over thirty years older. Dressed in charcoal trousers, open-collared shirt, and camel sweater, he welcomed us in deliberate but perfect English. "Please…come in." He gestured to the sofa. We sat down. I told him how much I appreciated his sharing his time, allowing us to pry a little into the past. I said I knew he and Elmyr had a long friendship, shared many experiences throughout the years, and that I thought of him in almost legendary terms, as Elmyr talked about him so much. "Peter gave you an early draft of the book I've been working on about Elmyr and my life with him," I said, "and I believe it would add so much to the story to get your perspective on his life." He was ninety-two, a declaration that came up more than once during our meeting. It was offered more by way of disclaimer than source of pride. I asked him questions specific to what he knew about Elmyr and when he knew it. I could see the despair and frustration in his eyes as answers eluded his grasp—like the fisherman whose line slackens as the trophy catch frees itself just short of his fingertips. His distress was visible each time he considered my questions but had to say, "I don't remember." I felt more compassion over his struggle to recapture things he once knew than disappointment at my dashed hopes for his valuable recollections. If his small living room were a courtroom, he revealed nothing incriminating, only to say that Elmyr always knew interesting people and "I enjoyed his company." Nor did he see anything particularly disturbing about Elmyr's art crimes, but seemed more amused that he was privy to his secrets than alarmed by them. His nonjudgmental sentiment seemed odd in view of a story Peter Schults shared with me.

Jean Louis, according to Peter, traveled with two small Renoir paintings, dear to him as souvenirs from his family and for the colorful charm of the impressionist's works. Once, when Jean Louis and Elmyr were together in New York, Elmyr took the two Renoirs and sold them to the art dealer Paul Rosenberg. Later, he confessed his perfidy to Jean Louis. Contrite and tearful, Elmyr begged forgiveness for this act of betrayal, insisting he would redeem the paintings. He never did. Jean Louis told me he had to buy them back with the dealer's mark-up included. Surprisingly, this did not ruin their friendship. Jean Louis sighed, "Elmyr *always* had money problems." Indeed, a mystery to Jean Louis, who *never* had *any*. They managed to overcome this breach of trust, and their relationship thrived for another twenty years. A remarkable testimony to the marrow of both men, especially as it would be understandable if Jean Louis had immediately jettisoned Elmyr for stealing from a friend. Yet, I could see a wistful glimmer in his eyes when Jean Louis looked at me that Parisian afternoon, giving a slight shrug, and relegating this story to those facts of life one must simply accept and then move on. This does, however, reveal a side of Elmyr he would never have volunteered or probably admitted to me. It also shows that he was careful to keep those unpalatable truths from staining the self-image he constantly curated.

Our conversation wasn't yielding all I had hoped for in our allotted time before fatigue overwhelmed him. Jean Louis could not add any insight into Elmyr's family, only to say that our recent discoveries were all new to him, and he couldn't recall Elmyr talking about his family. Given their years of association, and Elmyr's fixation with who was connected to whom and how, this seems unlikely. Even though Elmyr could drop some affectations because his deepest secret was revealed, it remained important to him that his self-spun history appeared convincing, especially to those with legitimate social pedigrees like Jean Louis. Thus establishing *some* element of believability in the persona he carefully crafted was essential to his own self-esteem. It once more amounted to camouflage, manufacturing the appearance of gentility to mitigate a brutal law of nature that stalked him relentlessly, that made him predator or prey in a world where he only knew one way to survive, although it made him a criminal. And that was at odds with the standards of the propriety he aspired to and had faith in. It was as though every ploy of trickery and dishonesty were capsulated in some tumor, living, feeding off its host with only a thin membrane keeping this disreputable activity from infecting the healthy image he wanted others to see, segregating his illusory self from reality. Selective ethics afforded him the means of nourishing his psychic health as well. This process of creating his own "personal myth" is described here in Dr. Charles Ford's book:

We also present ourselves to others duplicitously, playing certain roles and providing selective information about ourselves. Responses from others confirm and help mold the resultant myth. Each person's personal myth is unique and serves to mediate between the internal world of illusions and the external material world; the myth conditions the way we transact our business in the external world (Swartz, 1984).

Even if Elmyr's life and identity were riddled with invention and colored by self-deception, I wanted to replace much of the standard storyline with facts. It was sadly evident that Jean Louis was not the font of behind-the-scenes truths that would chip away the mythology that had become dogma these past forty years.

For a moment we all seemed lost in a labyrinth without exit when the doorbell rang. A man strolled in, an old friend named Pierre. We stood and introduced ourselves. Pierre's round, tanned face, beaming smile, and stocky body gave him a physical presence one could not ignore. He and Jean Louis went back decades. "Pierre is my godfather," Philippe explained. Jean Louis mentioned my longtime relationship with Elmyr. Raising his arms as though finding a long-lost friend, Pierre sparkled. "I knew Elmyr! I went with him to the flea markets when he was looking for old paintings to use for his fakes." Laughter erupted with this surprising admission, affirming once more that Elmyr's secret life was accruing a larger audience familiar with his criminal career. However perilous this inside knowledge may have been, and loaded with potential disaster for Elmyr, he still enjoyed an immunity that defies logic. I have the impression that many of those who were privy to the reality of his activities simply did not care or may have thought they weren't grave enough to land him in hell. Anyway, it seems deceit did not grate on Gallic sensibilities, or not to the degree that tightens sphincter muscles of some with Puritan ancestry. Pierre transported us though sweeping gestures, his constant grin and amused eyes, how Elmyr would pick up an old canvas he found, run his fingertips across the fabric back. "'This is from Anvers (Antwerp).' He knew just by the feel if the canvas was from Antwerp, Brusselles, or Paris." Pierre then gestured how Elmyr would scrape away the old surface oil paint down to the white lead primer coat, prepping it for its rebirth as a modern masterpiece, albeit a beautiful bastard. He leaned forward in his chair, savoring the shameless pleasure of imparting old secrets and deeming our celestial trajectory the perfect planetary alignment to do so.

As if this fresh anecdotal insight weren't delightful enough, Pierre also offered his own background. He too was an artist who had worked in the employ of another Hungarian painter, the op-artist Victor Vasarely.

Pierre said Vasarely had an atelier and staff of four to six artists who worked for him. Each would submit a "maquette," a scale model of a painting done in his style. If he approved, each assistant would produce a larger version of the work, which Vasarely signed when finished. His admission enthralled us. Philippe then added, "I've known you my whole life, and I never knew that about you." Pierre's joy in sharing this pearl lapsed into mime as he zipped his lips, as if to say, "Everyone has secrets." Some are just more closely guarded than others. Pierre's face reanimated as he declared, "Elmyr made original fakes, and I made fake originals!" Our laughter likely disturbed the neighbors. Given Colette's dedication to detecting art crimes, our afternoon chat may have begun resembling a smokeless corner of a men's club where members exude an esprit de corps and share intimacies with an understood discretion.

The Research Trail

These various witnesses provide testimonies that paint a different picture of Elmyr, and are at odds with the "official story" dictated to Clifford Irving in Elmyr's 1969 biography and that also cast doubt on elements of Irving's account. Many of the new findings made since the Hillstrom exhibition I owe to the serious historical investigation led by Colette Marvin. In May of 2010, she arranged for translators to review documents and personal correspondence I had saved from Elmyr. Several letters in Hungarian between Elmyr and his brother Istvan revealed secrets kept from me and most everyone. The small script on onionskin paper tell of the complicity between them in manufacturing fake birth certificates using Elmyr's alleged family name, Hory. We also located records listing Elmyr's brother and mother as holocaust survivors, learning also that his mother had not divorced Elmyr's father as he claimed (when Elmyr was sixteen), and that she survived until the 1960s. There remained some mystery about the fate of Elmyr's father, as we were uncertain of his first name, although we knew their real family name was Hoffmann. Elmyr's mother's maiden name was Irene Tenner, and she was Jewish. Elmyr told me his father was Catholic, but for the moment we could not verify that. We also had addresses where the family lived at in Budapest, and these, we thought, might provide a glimpse into the socioeconomic status of the family, a surer indication than stories subject to the embroidery of an expert storyteller.

Budapest Sock Exchange, Liberty Square (1907) copy

At the time of Elmyr's birth in 1906, the family lived in Budapest's fifth district at Sétatér 2. What the family would have seen from their apartment was a construction site that would soon become the Budapest Stock Exchange at Liberty Square, an imposing Beaux Arts style building with manicured gardens. It was what the British refer to as a "good address." This suggests the family enjoyed some bourgeois comfort and was upwardly mobile, having moved from a more working-class district after his brother was born in 1901. Andrea Megyes, a Hungarian art historian and scholar, also pointed out that it was not uncommon for apartment dwellers of varying income levels to live in the same building. If this was indeed the case with Elmyr's family, she posited that the models for his class ambitions could have begun here in close quarters with wealthier, perhaps titled neighbors. Nevertheless, the savoir faire with which Elmyr carried himself in the company of genuine aristocrats always appeared natural to me, as though this was a behavior learned early in his life.

Elmyr, with his mother and aunt – circa 1916

Mary Doering, professor of costume design at Smithsonian Associates, examined the family photo of Elmyr, his mother, and his aunt, taken at his grandparent's home in Billéd, Hungary. She wrote, "the clothing looks fashionable, solidly middle class or perhaps upper-middle class." However, she dismissed the notion that their dress would suggest an aristocratic status.

The "De Laszlo" Portrait

One of the most intriguing questions we hoped to answer was the origin of the mysterious family portrait left to me when Elmyr died. It was a painting of Elmyr and his brother. In the lower right-hand corner of the canvas, it bore the signature "P.A. de Laszlo." This picture alone, if authentic, could be viewed as unimpeachable evidence supporting Elmyr's claim to membership in Europe's landed gentry. When John Singer Sargent stopped accepting commissions in 1907, Philip de Laszlo became the preferred portraitist of kings, presidents, and mavens of the social elite. The sweep of his brushwork and ease of execution made him as prolific as he was popular. According to the De Laszlo Archive Trust in London, his body of work numbers in the thousands, many of which have been lost over time.

Elmyr exhibited his art at a London art gallery in the early 1970s, and at that time we became acquainted with Sandra de Laszlo and her husband, who is the artist's grandson. They purchased a number of works by Elmyr from his show. We later dined together at a London hotel. It was a lively, engaged evening. Elmyr was in rapture while the conversation percolated about art, social connectivity, and exchanging thoughts with those who knew his world, and he knew theirs. In January 2010, I

purported P. A. de Laszlo portrait of Elmyr and his older brother, Istvan

contacted Sandra and refreshed her memory of our meeting. I told her about the de Laszlo portrait of Elmyr and asked if she would be kind enough to examine an enlarged photo I would e-mail her. She wrote back that she thought it strange that Elmyr didn't mention it, and this curious omission was supported by her husband's recollection. My memory was somewhat different, that Elmyr did mention the portrait, but in a throwaway nonchalance that invited no follow-up discussion. That itself seemed odd, given this nexus of common legacy and substantial reason for cultivating this noteworthy Hungarian connection.

I remember the day the portrait arrived, shipped to his villa on Ibiza. It was rolled in a cardboard tube. Another small oil painting on a stretcher, a portrait of his mother, signed HORY in the upper right-hand corner, arrived at the same time, along with a cache of family photos from—a *cousin,* Elmyr said. How a cousin came to possess these items garnered a glancing question mark, only to be quickly displaced by some other momentary distraction requiring less thought, I'm sure. At twenty-one, it was not my habit of exercising any critical thinking about what Elmyr told me. I was wholly under his influence. My life was akin to a lottery winner's metamorphosis, abandoning my working-class roots altogether and adopting the virtues of the newly rich. I was fully invested in the world he created around me, the perfect acolyte in this new world order, dedicated and versed in the Gospel according to Elmyr.

I watched Elmyr remove the painting from its container, attentive, like working an archeological site. He knelt on the white wool rug in the foyer, leaned over, and unrolled the canvas on the floor. He asked me to hold one end that wanted to recoil from years of maintaining its curl. Holding the bottom edge, we could see through brownish, cracked varnish a young Elmyr, about four to six years old, leaning into his seated brother, a few years older. Both bore slight smiles and wore identical sailor suits. Although the almost-life-size double portrait conveyed an image of insular class wealth, a reprise of those early twentieth-century films documenting the similarly dressed children of Czar Nicolas and Czarina at the close of an age of innocence, the picture appeared ravaged by time, the surface paint missing along asymmetrical folds, identifying a derelict past. The paint-free areas revealed an underlying fabric, dark as though soaked in black tea.

After examining the photo, Sandra asked if there were any distinguishing markings or gallery labels on the stretcher that could provide specific information tying it to de Laszlo. Then she asked what year it might have been painted. Approximating Elmyr's age would put it around 1910 to 1912. Sandra replied that was a timeframe when he was painting the Spanish royal family in Madrid and other *important* commissions. Without making her doubt explicit, the improbability of the double-portrait being a product of the great painter was the implication. A friend of Colette's, Alexandra Tice, a Washington, DC, area restorer, had done restoration work on some de Laszlos. After examining a photo, she said the Elmyr portrait's likelihood of being authentic was "not even close." This epitaph opens another door. If the de Laszlo portrait is a fake, then who painted it? Despite its fuzzy origin, it remains a high-caliber painting. When the picture arrived in Ibiza, it wasn't long before Elmyr initiated some cleaning of the canvas and some superficial over-painting in spots in need of restoring. Its authorship presents an intriguing mystery, and while it would be easy for me to say "I can see his brushwork in it." that would be premature. However, if Elmyr actually created it, it would add years, maybe another decade onto his illicit twenty-year career, stretching it to thirty years (although his longevity would not earn him a gold watch and testimonial dinner). Until the painting can undergo a more thorough analysis, this will remain an inviting uncertainty.

Inching my way along this path of discovery of who Elmyr really was felt oddly surreal and something I never imagined doing—like looking for a toehold on an ice-glazed cliff face while wearing red six-inch

313

stiletto pumps. Well, that image might not be sufficiently bizarre in conveying how strange this reevaluation process seemed. In a way, it was like asking a Christian fundamentalist to burn a Bible. The notion of pulling out by the roots things I held to be true was exactly the prospect I faced. That I bought Elmyr's version of the truth may smack of the delusional mother of a serial killer insisting "He was always a good boy!"— suggesting a kaleidoscopic perception that fractures reality, especially in defense of what we elect to believe. Still, the nature of Elmyr's deceit is something I understand, and that his lies never harmed me, nor eroded the emotional bond between us. His storytelling may well have been the product of wish fulfillment, burnishing his self-image, rewriting a personal history to salve flaws or failures that only wounded his self-esteem and tethered him to secrets in his past and whose revelations served no beneficial purpose. The fictionalized account of his life, however, intertwines with elements that awe and amaze, and are, incidentally, true. I witnessed astonishing things, met astounding people through him, and my life with him corroborates what Peter Schults said to me: "Anywhere Elmyr went, he knew everyone worth knowing." He was a "connector" that Malcolm Gladwell describes in *The Tipping Point* (Little Brown and Company, 2000); a networker by disposition, and it was this natural inclination that allowed him to collect friends and acquaintances in abundance.

In March of 2011, I traveled to Budapest to lecture on Elmyr and hoped to uncover the longstanding mystery of his true identity. Among the boxes of his personal effects, the most remarkable may be the letter from Edith Tenner written to Elmyr in the mid 1970s. She married Elmyr's first cousin, and to my surprise was alive and residing in Germany. We used the postal address to find her, and luckily for us, she hadn't moved in thirty-five years. Colette and two friends from Budapest—Dr. Jeff Taylor, an expert on art and the Hungarian art market, and his wife Andrea Megyes went to interview her in April 2011. She could provide new insight into Elmyr's background. Did he come from a family of means, minor aristocracy? She would know these things. Andrea described her as a slight woman with well-coiffed gray hair, wearing a simple sweater with beaded embroidery, a strand of pearls, and pants with matching jacket. Her misgivings over the purpose of their visit dissipated over afternoon tea and recapitulated memories of her life, husband, and hardships. Jeff characterized her initial suspicions as a by-product of living in a communist police state where it was safer not to ask questions "and keep one's eyes on the ground." She and Fritzy married after the war, after her harrowing survival at Auschwitz, after the loss of her entire family in the Jewish extermination camps. On her small apartment wall, she pointed out a rare and unique souvenir, a childhood pastel landscape done by Elmyr, one from Fritzy and Elmyr's grandparent's home in Billéd, Hungary. It was one of the early works Elmyr reminisced about in the 1970 BBC documentary. Here was proof of that story.

I possessed a draft of a letter to Fritzy and Edith; it bore the hotel letterhead from San Sabastián in northern Spain, where Elmyr and I stayed during the film festival in 1973 for the debut of Orson Welles's film *F for Fake*. Elmyr wrote of the glamour that surrounded the event, a world far removed from his cousin and his wife. They both knew Fritzy's recent diagnosis of cancer was bleak without access to western hospitals. Elmyr promised he'd help them and arranged for Fritzy to be treated in Vienna. He later flew to Vienna to meet his cousin for the first time in over thirty years. This was also the first and only time he met Edith. According to her, Elmyr paid for all Fritzy's medical care, and when he died months later, Elmyr also paid the funeral expenses. In recounting this painful episode in 2011, Andrea said Edith was near tears. I was used to Elmyr acting in this way, always keen to serve the needy when he was in a position to do so. Never mind that his bank account could show a negative balance a few weeks hence. Forethought or caution never trumped impulse when he heard a cry for help.

What makes this encounter with Edith Tenner more than extraordinary, beyond her longevity and good fortune to have survived the Holocaust, is the meager size of Elmyr's family. Contrary to turn-of-the-century customs of having large families, it turns out that Elmyr's mother had just one brother, who had just one son, Fritzy, Elmyr's only cousin on his mother's side. We're unsure of the genealogy of Elmyr's father. However, the roots of this family tree began to look certain for us when we found marriage and birth records at the Association of Jewish Communities in Budapest. Colette Marvin and Andrea Megyes entered through a metal detector, then a series of locked, tall wooden doors led by a matron, admitted into this inner sanctum by special permission of

Rabbi Zoltan Radnoti. They asked their guide if anyone had ever asked to see the records regarding the infamous painter. "No, never," she said. She then brought out a coffee-table-size book dated 1906. They leafed through pages, big like sails, until they found an entry opposite April 14, 1906. There was Elmyr's family name. He was born Elemér Albert Hoffmann. Colette Marvin and Andrea Megyes finally cracked the code after more than forty years of uncertainty that surrounded his true identity. Not Clifford Irving, not the Norwegian documentary crew, *no one* before had found the elusive truth of *who* Elmyr really was—until now. It was that flesh-tingling moment that gives researchers a natural high few other things can replicate.

The leather-bound tome also indicated that his father, Adolf Hofmann, contrary to Elmyr's insistence that he was Catholic, we now know for certain was Jewish, as was his mother, Irene Tenner. His father's occupation was listed as "wholesaler of handcrafted goods." He was not a diplomat, as Elmyr claimed. His brother, Istvan's, birth was duly noted in 1901, a five-year difference in age, but perhaps a world apart in temperaments.

In 1975 I met his brother Istvan when he came to visit Elmyr in Ibiza, although he was also assigned a role to play in Elmyr's charade. I was told years before that he was Elmyr's cousin. I discovered their true relationship only after Elmyr died. Elmyr had been sending him money regularly through a Hungarian banker friend who had a house on the island, and he phoned Istvan, informing him of Elmyr's suicide, saying he was sorry to have to tell him of his cousin's death. Istvan replied, "He wasn't my cousin, he was my brother." This was the first revelation that began unraveling Elmyr's fabric of lies, but also left more questions than answers.

Istvan was slightly taller than Elmyr, quieter, subdued by ill heath, and with eyes that suggested a melancholy lurking behind them. From what little Elmyr allowed me to know, Istvan endured the postwar deprivations like all other victims of a totalitarian regime that robbed its citizens of basic freedoms, while extolling the virtues of life free from western excess and depravity. Elmyr may not have been a rabid democrat, but his hatred of the communists was clear, so I was curious and wanted to learn more about him, his life in an "iron curtain" country. Unfortunately, I couldn't speak Hungarian or his second language, German, so I became the deaf mute at the table during their exchanges in Hungarian, an audible mime deciphered by their tone and body language only. They hadn't seen each other in at least thirty years too, perhaps longer. One translated letter from Istvan mentioned how their mother kept a photo of Elmyr when he was sixteen, and how much she desired to see him again. When I began living with Elmyr, he told me he had no living family members left, that they perished before or during the war, that his brother died in motor racing accident in Tripoli (in a Bugatti), his father in Auschwitz, his mother shot by a Russian soldier for not surrendering her fur coat to him in the depth of winter. Every reference to family and descriptive detail dripped with pathos meant to tear the listener's eyes, but it was just effective sentimental subterfuge. None of this was true. The tenor of the letter where Istvan mentions their mother's longing to see Elmyr again, however, strongly suggests her desire to reconnect with her son, yet nothing pointed to Elmyr's preexisting awareness of her overture or anything that would explain why he had rewritten his personal history that expunged any connection to family members who were still living long after the war, especially his mother.

During Istvan's week-long visit, I sensed a tension between them, at least evident in Elmyr's face, on which no emotion or thought could hide. I never asked the reason for this impression, although I knew Elmyr had taken on more of the financial burden of caring for his aging brother, and having helped his cousin Fritzy. Besides the collusion between them in cooking up Elmyr's phony birth certificates, Istvan's letters revealed a destitute existence in Budapest, not having enough money to buy a sorely needed winter coat, and having to still work at a low-paying government job despite being well past retirement age. At the same time, Elmyr constantly juggled his own finances with predictable disregard for future planning that prevented him from becoming the polished schemer that Legros was, and who was once more on the warpath concocting an extradition demand for Elmyr. All these stress factors were probably dancing through his mind. Or, perhaps Istvan reminded Elmyr of the mythology he'd constructed about himself, and his brother's presence in some way threatened the self-deception he'd grown comfortable with. Edith Tenner provided a provocative glimpse into Elmyr's past, a possible foreshadowing of a life and legend that was preordained.

Elmyr with his brother Istvan on the Left-1975

Her husband Fritzy knew Elmyr from childhood on and spent time with him as their families vacationed together. His recollections, according to Edith, portrayed a young boy who was "deferred to" in the small town where their grandfather lived, the owner of a brick factory who was respected and viewed as an important figure in the community. Fritzy thought his grandfather's prestige may have fostered Elmyr's sense of self-importance, or an inclination to put on airs. Furthermore, he depicted young Elmyr as a spinner of yarns, the product of a precocious imagination. While the etiology of this adolescent behavior is intriguing, its exact origin is open to conjecture and may never be known in Elmyr's case. What we do know for certain is that the manufacture of his stories preceded his criminal career but was integral to his mastery at deception and role-playing. It was a skill he honed early in his life, and I can only believe it yielded what he wanted, an image that suited his needs. Dr. Charles V. Ford says: "The results of this type of behavior are not particularly malignant, especially when compared to the wide spectrum of human misconduct...Patterns in the types of lies told and the circumstances in which each person is inclined to lie point to the use of lying and self-deception as coping mechanisms. The lies are responses made to deal with the stresses produced by both the external and internal worlds." Psychoanalyst and theorist Otto Fenichel opined, "If it is possible to make someone believe that untrue things are true, then it is also possible that true things, the memory of which threatens me, are untrue." These insights may come closest to explaining the workings of Elmyr's mind, the self-deluding, lacey arabesques of deceit he constructed that made legend a far more appealing alternative to the truth. My attempt to examine the invention that has become knotted with his story may not fill all the voids. Efforts to get a clear picture of Elmyr's psyche is a challenge still and might well remain open to speculation among experts, although we have some facts now that update our knowledge base.

It would be hard for anyone with a shred of empathy not to succumb to Elmyr's stories of personal tragedy that left him without family. I suspect he well understood the seduction of heartrending tales that instantly makes one sympathize with someone hurt or harmed. It at once earned him converts of those who might otherwise be more suspicious and probably prevented any further unwelcome shaking of his family tree.

When Elmyr sold his fakes to buyers, I know for a fact that they were not limited to professionals or the cognoscenti, as he always insisted. In some cases they were friends or acquaintances who may not have been knowledgeable enough to detect the scam he was running. What I believe *is* accurate is that his offerings were often made in moments of financial desperation, a demonstrable plea for help. Neuroeconomist Dr. Paul Zak explains the psychology of a con man's strategy to earn one's confidence this way: "Conmen ply their trade by appearing fragile or needing help, by seeming vulnerable. Because of oxytocin and its effect on other parts of the brain, we feel good when we help others—this is the basis for attachment to family and friends and cooperation with strangers. 'I need your help' is a potent stimulus for action."

While friends may have responded sympathetically, Elmyr likely looked like prey to his target audience, art merchants. His standard ploy was to explain that he was a refugee who had escaped Hungary before the Russians arrived, managing to flee with a few family treasures, and was reluctantly willing to sell his artwork at an attractive price because he needed the money. It is unsurprising if his buyers saw their opportunism as charitable acts. Their profiteering from someone else's position of weakness may have seemed too insignificant to thwart their altruism in most instances.

Elmyr's oft-repeated mantra is key to understanding his view that *he* was the one being exploited by others, which thereby justified what he did: "What I sold, I sold very miserably, and the big money was not made by me but the dealers and the people who resold them." I also know that he thought this explanation somehow mollified his life of crime, so his subsequent self-forgiveness was a medicinal remedy for a sense of remorse attached to his actions. While his rationalization was psychologically soothing, it was essential to allaying the feelings of guilt that I suspect lurked in his subconscious. Nevertheless, how others viewed him, what they thought of him, was hugely important to Elmyr. Why this was the case begs clarity, although the answers to this may be lost with the passage of time. However, the fact that this external validation defined his self-image suggests an absence of a sociopathic lack of conscience and disregard of others' opinions. So, he knew precisely the difference between right and wrong, ethical and unethical behavior, and only the exigencies he thought threatened his survival permitted changing the rules of the game. It was only these moments of self-preservation, as he perceived his crimes to be, that emancipated him from the normally high standards of integrity and honesty he thought he upheld and expected of others. He'd placed the bar higher for me than for himself, but then, he saw only a life ahead of me full of potential and expectations, that his tutelage might spare me the missteps in his own life. It was unabashedly a parental instinct he never tried to hide and showed his misplaced trust in the notion that we can learn vicariously.

Being ordained as Elmyr's friend conferred on me all the rights, privileges, and obligations of a club member, and that meant my fiduciary duties to him trumped everything else. It was like a blood oath, and there wasn't a hint of doubt in his voice that left room for questioning his expectations of me or my fidelity to him. Elmyr would on occasion posture himself, leaning into his audience like an orator full of moment in his forthcoming pronouncement. "Right or wrong," he'd say, "friends stand by one another." It showed the depth of his commitment to friendship. It was the "right or wrong" part I found troubling. The implication, of course, was that there was an unbreakable allegiance friends shared, insulated from any constraints whatsoever. Free from any moral, ethical, or legal considerations? It reminded me of that distinction between a friend and a good friend: A friend will help you move. A good friend will help you move a body. This was contradictory to all those rules of social etiquette that tempered my education, and important, he insisted. But then, wasn't the lesson of Elmyr's story that we should not so easily be influenced by appearances, blindly accepting what reinforces our own interests over the need for critical analysis? When it came to personal relationships, he expected unquestioning support. Moreover, this code of behavior was not only rigid, it also showed your mettle.

I suppose I had observed enough inconsistencies in his "do as I say, not as I do" history, while remembrances of his artistic piracy seemed far from his thoughts when judging the actions of others. The lack of equivocation on his part I can only attribute to an esprit de corps, that willful and unassailable unity that neatly defines an us-versus-them mentality. I recall a scene in the film *Full Metal Jacket*, when the drill instructor discusses the assassination of President John Kennedy and revels in the fact that Lee Harvey Oswald learned his marksmanship as a Marine, suggesting that above all, Oswald was a Marine. And the Marine Corps motto is semper fidelis —always faithful. This just illustrates how values can be molded to abide any perversion, endure any assault by reason, and dismiss any challenge to what we choose to believe. This is how Elmyr could gloss over the serious crimes of defrauding the art world. He often became disoriented when crossing that marshland of ethics and the law, relying instead on his personal interests as his compass. After all, what speaks more eloquently to us than that which suits our needs? This is how we uncomplicate the complicated.

When I first met Elmyr, his celebrity was growing, and he wore the mantel of the talented scoundrel with some reluctance. His admirers seemed more intrigued by his exploits for duping the experts than concerned by the damage done to institutions, reputations, or artists' oeuvres. Indeed, press coverage was more favorable than disdainful of Elmyr's expertise at deception, and he in turn confused their fascination with expiation of his sins. As far as I could see, the court of public opinion gave him no incentive to exhibit any remorse for past actions. If fame or power aggrandizes one's ego, it is easy to understand how this unexpected approval distorted his view of himself and his crimes.

If others were forgiving, then why shouldn't he be as generous? There is something captivating in those stories about dethroning the rich and powerful that makes the underclass cheer, and he heard only their cheering. Then again, Elmyr possessed a disarming charm that was the social lubricant for his talent. Both traits lend authority to any confidence man, and personal charisma sways perception beyond the mere weight of facts. Politicians are frequently masters of feel-good rhetoric and the appearance of credibility. In tandem, these are powerfully persuasive, especially when Elmyr targeted those who were already predisposed to influence by covetousness and self-interest. When our emotionality sweeps aside rationality, investing trust in the conman is a comfortable consequence—and they know it.

Han van Meegeren's tale was one example Elmyr cited of an art forger becoming a folk hero, and I sensed Elmyr felt a kinship with him on that level. Van Meegeren's deception earned him public applause when he sold his spurious Vermeers to Hermann Goering. In the aftermath of the war, the Dutch were eager to overlook his criminal activity and blatant self-enrichment, instead reveling in his hoodwinking Germany's number-two Nazi. Never mind that van Meegeren was an enthusiastic Nazi supporter himself. This normally unpalatable fact would have earned him the enmity of any other enemy sympathizer in post-war Holland, but the artist's sting operation proved more valuable in boosting national pride in his clever ruse of the foppish art thief Goering.

Elmyr was committing crimes when he sold his wares to dealers, curators, or privates, and he knew it. What he was able to appreciate only after his "outing" was the landslide approval of the general public, who appeared more enthralled than upset by his curious life and adventures. That sentiment, though, was not universal, particularly from those left holding Elmyr's art once thought legitimate and later discredited, along with the wisdom of his victims. What, then, would explain the backslapping approbation Elmyr enjoyed after he was identified as "the greatest art forger of the twentieth century?" It seems counterintuitive that activities that generally earn perpetrators a prison sentence elicit favorable public opinion. That contradictory response may stem from some subconscious attraction of those who defy authority, and against the odds, win. Thus the appeal and romanticized view of rule-breakers like Elmyr. Dr. Charles Ford offers this provocative insight:

"...and there really seems to be little doubt—we live in a world that thrives on deception..." Further adding "...the importance of deception and detection is so great that it was a major influence in the evolution of progressively greater cognitive powers in humans and in the structural evolution of the prefrontal lobes of the human brain."

So, we are not only socially accustomed to lying, we are hardwired, physiologically predisposed through evolution to be able practitioners of deceit. Nor should it be surprising that we strategize by deception whenever rivalry exits between people, resorting to deceit as a standard practice to increase our chances of success in the selection process or basic survival. The pervasiveness of lying would then explain the loss of shock-value among everyone beyond Elmyr's victims. Ford's research paints a picture of a society inured to the culture of deception, and thereby explains the whimper of protest and condemnation of Elmyr's crimes. It may also stem from a common misperception that his brand of art crime was a victimless crime, which was not the case.

Elmyr's story bears a common thread with other fakers or forgers. Their careers often began as a result of rejection, an inability to earn critical or financial success, and their spurned efforts served as a justification to show the disbelievers their true merit. It's a convenient rationalization, though disingenuous, and one that eased Elmyr's conscience. For all those who feel a sense of injustice in their lives, a lack of fairness or opportunity, their empathy, I suppose, resonates with those who earn some retribution through unconventional or even illegal tactics. Desperation is a game-changer, and those marginalized by social breakdown such as war will often abandon legal or moral constraints that reflect their value systems, and once emancipated from limitations, the nature of personal responsibility changes. The advent of child soldiers used in campaigns of genocide illustrates how debased human behavior can become when we detach from those mechanisms that keep society civil and law-abiding.

I believe Elmyr allowed self-interest (if not self-preservation) to derail any feeling of regret for the deceit that became an inseparable part of his life. His talent at convincing others something was what it was not, in essence, became his most reliable survival skill, and at some point, I suspect, self-deception made his version of truth more palatable and more memorable. He found comfort in a favorite aphorism. Slightly tilting his head back, as though getting in the last word in a dispute, he said in French: *"Qui s'excuse s'accuse."* (He who excuses himself accuses himself.) This perfectly suited his disinclination to incriminate himself; it was at once a clever exoneration of his guilt while making apologies unnecessary. What is language for, if it can't be self-serving?

The paradox I have yet to fully understand is how Elmyr, who had spent a good portion of his life convincingly deceiving others, exercised negligible awareness in detecting cons perpetrated against him. His longtime dealer Fernand Legros was a case in point. Although I cannot offer observations with the confidence of proximity and familiarity I enjoyed with Elmyr, I can say with surety that there was much about Legros's personality that invited psychoanalysis. His hatred and obsession with Elmyr's destruction are a matter of record. An in-depth psychological profile of their tortured relationship is better left to medical professionals, the entertainment value of the craziness notwithstanding.

The indictments against Elmyr are many, and criticisms of him in some instances reflect one's nearness to the damage he did to the art establishment. The farther away from the epicenter one was, the more benign his fakery appeared, in much the same way as someone who owns no stocks may feel detached from the vicissitudes of the market. It also bears remembering the time frame in which Elmyr's crimes were exposed. It was in the 1960s, a decade wrought with social unrest, rebellion against authority, and a wholesale questioning of tradition and conventional values. Against that backdrop it was easier to cast Elmyr in the maverick mold, and he seized that convenient swell of public sentiment, interpreting the mood of contemporary history as implied support of his criminal exploits.

For those reexamining his place in history today, a common question is: If he had any real talent, why couldn't he earn any recognition? Another complaint is: He was a follower, not an innovator, and showed no originality. These deserve a response, though I can offer my viewpoint only in this way: First, there are few strikingly original thinkers. Most of us are followers, as was Elmyr. He explained to me how throughout the history of western art there are occasionally beacons that illuminate new paths and progenitors of change. Among the legions of artists, some names stand out, such as Giotto, Masaccio, della Francesca, Caravaggio, Turner to Picasso. Others are left in their wake and benefit from theses seers and teachers. Elmyr never once claimed to be an originator, and would have dismissed any such notion. His respect for these geniuses bordered on the reverential, and he would not have placed himself on such a pedestal.

A comparison of Elmyr to his contemporaries or near-contemporaries is, however, valid. Elmyr, in much the same manner of these artists, learned from a teaching tradition following established tenets of figurative art for five hundred years. This apples-to-apples assessment supports an objective evaluation, and it is on this basis that his merit can be best judged. In this regard, I can only defer to his track record of his fakes passing muster with those who were often poised to make those crucial decisions. Self-interest aside, there were plenty of experts, curators, and dealers with suitable training and experience to offer a discerning judgment and evaluation of his bogus masterpieces that could well have halted Elmyr's career earlier if they were less convincing.

So why was he unable to make his own mark in the art world? Malcolm Gladwell's research for his book *Outliers* (Little Brown and Company, 2008) turned up some remarkable findings that may help answer this question. A group of geniuses born between 1903 and 1917 were studied to see how they fulfilled their potential. Those in the first half, born between 1903 and 1911, were more likely to be failures because they came of age around the beginning of the Great Depression. They lacked opportunities. "To have been born before 1911 is to have been demographically unlucky. The most devastating events of the twentieth century hit you at exactly the wrong time." Also, "The sense of possibility so necessary for success comes not just from inside us or from our parents. It comes from our time: from the particular opportunities that our particular place in history presents us with…Some cannot escape the limitations of their generation." Elmyr was born in 1906.

Along with the missed opportunities of ill timing, but having all the talent required for success, his art possessed the freshness of a bygone era. Fauvism, expressionism, and cubism came and went before Elmyr began his art studies and education that by then looked increasingly out of step with the artistic revolt that swept through Europe in the first two decades of the twentieth century. The train of public taste departed, leaving him dismayed, eyeing his chances for recognition disappearing from sight.

What Elmyr never grasped was the other side of that disappointment. If, for example, the trajectory of his talent had intersected with the art movements that formed the basis of his training, he may have gained the accolades he longed for. It's hard to tell if that would have been the outcome. Clearly, that was his lifelong wish. Circumstances instead took his career in another direction. What he never realized was that that disappointment may have been a blessing in disguise. Elmyr turned that rejection into a triumph of a different sort by becoming the most prolific and successful art forger of modern times. Maybe it was a crown of thorns. Whether he was perceived as a pariah or folk hero may have troubled him less than providing the world *no* reason to remember him. He thrived on clever repartee, and a favorite quote from Oscar Wilde was, "The only thing worse than being talked about was not being talked about." Even if he should be remembered as a rogue, he would prefer that to being forgotten, although until his spurious artistic contributions are ultimately segregated from the realm of authentic works, it is likely that Elmyr's ghost will continue to haunt the art world. I continue to see him and his passage through the history of twentieth-century art as colorful as the fauve-period paintings he mimicked so well.

Another question relevant to Elmyr's legacy is inescapable. Is it possible for the forger or faker to survive the odium that infects public perception of their crimes? I suspect every practitioner of these dark arts would argue on behalf of an impartial hearing, inviting judgment based on skill, untainted by reputation. I know Elmyr lobbied hard for a reevaluation of his art in the aftermath of scandal and lawlessness. He remained steadfast, confident that his talent warranted recognition, while realizing the rewards of public acceptance and success were often a contrivance of gamesmanship and a rising art market that increasingly treated art as an "investment." Elmyr knew the role dealers played in manipulating prices of art and their power as kingmakers. It was the only way he could explain the otherwise mystifying ascent in values attached to Jackson Pollock's art and others'. Certainly by the mid twentieth century, purveyors of art had a firm grip on Madison Avenue's bag of tricks, the notion of branding and image building. Elmyr insisted that the rise in popularity of abstract expressionism, or conceptual art, had as much, if not more to do with a diminishing pool of accessibly priced old-master, impressionist, or postimpressionist works. Because of their scarcity and values that restricted buyers to institutions or the ultra rich, art merchants helped develop a new reservoir of art and a new audience for it. It was, in his view, the only way to explain the newfound virtues of Pollack's wet-paint drippings, the incomprehensible black swaths on white canvas of Robert Motherwell, or others a world away from Elmyr's frame of reference. This may have looked like Kabuki to Elmyr, an exaggerated reality and product of stagecraft, but one that redirected interest and buyers away from anything that might bear his name.

These new trends stranded him in a futureless no-man's land, making his own art appear even more obsolete than before, while this "anarchism," as he saw it, assaulted every definition of what fine art was supposed to be. Even art forgers have principles that are inviolable, it seems. He thought this phenomenon was mostly commercial hucksterism, a passing flavor of the day, and whose value would have no real staying power. Even more disturbing to him was the Big Money people paid for these works when in almost every instance his own art was greeted with robust disinterest. I'm not surprised that his bile level was dangerously high due to his growing disrespect for those who jumped aboard the bandwagon of enthusiasts for this new art, but could not recognize "real" art—meaning his.

I must add that Elmyr did not wholly dismiss modern art. When I first entered his home, abstract or semi-abstract art was abundant, mostly works representing Ibiza's sizeable colony of artists whom he supported through his purchases from local galleries or directly from them. However, he distinguished figurative from non-figurative art this way. He said, "The appeal of abstract art depends on the viewer, whether one likes it or doesn't like it." So, some he liked, some he didn't. It was a fairly vague and forgiving criterion to gauge its merit. At the same time, he ran through a litany of standard criteria universally used to judge the quality of figurative art, from which abstract art was mostly liberated.

That said, he still maintained that the vocal champions of these new and "facile" art movements were too often financially invested in their advancement. Modern art museums gathered momentum; their existence predicated on artistic integrity of their collections and the wisdom of those boards, directors, and contributors whose interests were substantial. As the price tags of their art rose into the millions, Elmyr wondered when the curtain would be pulled back and the hoax exposed. The mutated market for abstract art probably made Elmyr not feel so bad about selling his fakes. His buyers were at least getting a bigger bang for their buck, he believed. He also thought many of the "qualities" of contemporary art extolled by its defenders were often the product of smooth-talking snake oil pitchmen and mass hypnosis. He remained unconvinced in the face of this sway on public consciousness, insisting it, like the fashionable academic painters of the late nineteenth century, as the once-great but now obscure Meissonier, may not endure the test of time. He knew too well the fickleness of taste, having himself been a victim of its whims.

Whether Elmyr deserves notice beyond being a footnote in the history of twentieth-century art is a more complicated issue and a source of some debate. His artistic legacy, however muddled by his fakery, in all likelihood defies a catalogue raisonné. Where his authorship is clear, those works invite an honest evaluation, and in these instances their merit can be examined and compared to others, exponents of the School of Paris like himself. It is wholly fitting and appropriate, a comparison Elmyr would welcome. As for his fakes, his name will forever be linked to his illicit career that is unlikely to be matched ever again. I suspect it is here where his impact is felt most. In the wake of his long spree of deception, the art market has been quicker to discover and interdict fakers and forgers through improved laboratory analysis, a process that did not thwart Elmyr's sales efforts in his day. Decisions by dealers or curators then relied more on a connoisseurship largely influenced by personal knowledge and opinion. In the post-Elmyr era, both institutions and individuals appear more gun-shy in authenticating works of art without a preponderance of proof supporting the provenance of a piece, and more often than not err on the side of caution, thereby avoiding any backdraft of scandal. While he could not be defined as a whistle-blower, his story illuminated much about the world of art that is neither refined nor praiseworthy, but rather a realm governed by profit motive, and frequently abject greed. Elmyr used the "system" and its weaknesses to his advantage, and in turn was used by it. I therefore view him more as a player than a villain in this theater piece. As someone pointed out, "Corporations are amoral…they operate without regard to morality." If this is true, then ethics are not imperatives or constraints defining how corporations operate or safeguard public well-being. This loophole might then explain how Elmyr shed a sense of guilt attached to his crimes.

Don Myers, the director of the Hillstrom Museum of Art, offers an intriguing view of the forger's role in art in his director's notes for the exhibition *Elmyr de Hory, Artist and Faker*, in 2010:

Many of the most famous forgers, including de Hory, were very intelligent and knowledgeable about art and in general, in addition to being talented artists capable of producing admired artwork.

Infrequently, that admiration remains even after revelation of forgery, as when the purchasers of Giovanni Bastianini's bust of *Lucrezia Donati* discovered that it was not a Renaissance work as they had been told, declaring nevertheless pleasure in knowing that a talented artist such as Bastianini was still alive; or in the case of collectors who learned from their dealer that their Modigliani was actually a de Hory fake, then electing not to return it, noting that they bought it not because they thought it was by a certain artist but because they loved and admired it. Such admiration, however, more often completely dissolves away after forgery has been revealed, and one of the most fascinating questions in considering fakes is how experts—sometimes the same people who had previously prized the works—later instead see them as quite poor works of art. As David M. Wilson states in the introduction to the exhibition catalogue of *Fake? The Art of Deception*, held at the British Museum in London in 1990, when Wilson was its director, "the final question is the one that appears to be unanswerable, although psychologists have tried to explain it: why does an object which is declared a fake lose virtue immediately? This question, which concerns the eye and mind of the beholder, should be pondered by all who read this book or visit the exhibition which it records."

That question—of why the very same drawing or painting can appear beautiful when it is believed to be a genuine work by Matisse but, after it has been revealed as a fake by Elmyr de Hory, is perceived as unaccomplished, dead, and despicable—likely has much to do with the manner in which the human brain perceives. Aesthetic purists embrace the idea of the unaffected, pure eye, and hold that an artwork can and should be judged only by its appearance, without regard to anything outside of the purely visual operation, an attitude termed "aesthetic empiricism." The relatively new field of neuroesthetics, however, has shown that vision is not just in the eye, but is conditioned and affected by the brain. Furthermore, neuroesthetic scientists such as Semir Zeki, professor of neurobiology at University College, London, have suggested that it is likely that a connoisseurship system exists in the brain and probably can soon be located—as was noted in an article by Ann Landi titled "Is Beauty in the Brain of the Beholder?" in *ARTnews* in January 2010. Thus the brain is equipped with an area that assesses, categorizes, and groups artworks seen by the eyes, and also, using its collected data, intermediates in how those artworks are perceived. Some of the disdain for a newly revealed fake artwork comes from the brain shifting its functioning toward the object with the added knowledge about its nature. In other words, the brain, based on the new information it has acquired, changes what is actually seen. This is, effectively, a more scientific basis or explanation for observations made by art historian and perceptual psychologist Rudolf Arnheim (1904–2007), whose *Art and Visual Perception: A Psychology of the Creative Eye* (1954) remains a fundamental study on the perception of art. Arnheim has noted, in his essay "On Duplication," in *The Forger's Art: Forgery and the Philosophy of Art* (Denis Dutton, ed., 1983), that "perception is not a mechanical absorption of stimuli but a search for structure," continuing by stating that the "same painting, considered...a forgery, is not only judged differently but actually seen as a different painting." He further noted, "Once a work is suspected of being a fake, it becomes a different perceptual object."

The point is that, in some significant, physiological way, a fake artwork is not seen in the same way as when it was believed to be genuine. Gertrude Stein famously claimed that "a rose is a rose is a rose is a rose," but the brain, armed with newly acquired facts, is capable of changing a rose into a weed, a beautiful artwork into a despised and ugly fake. Thus a drawing by Elmyr de Hory that was accepted as a fine example of the draftsmanship of Henri Matisse or Amedeo Modigliani can suddenly, when its true genesis is uncovered, look far less accomplished—perhaps especially to those who have been embarrassed or harmed by the trick. But to those who are removed from the situation, as is the case with most viewers of de Hory's artwork today, it is possible to appreciate the evident abilities of the artist, and to perhaps regret that his talent was diverted from what might have been.

So, while public perception of the faker and his art is now better understood by recent research into brain function, he still stands naked before public judgment, unable to shed his mug-shot image and burden of criminality. However, once more this invites a closer look into the strangely symbiotic relationship of the faker or forger within the largest unregulated market in the world—the art market.

The vertical rise in popularity of online auction sites, most notably eBay, or television broadcasts of *Antiques Roadshow*, give witness to how pervasive public interest has become and how these formats are an instant source of reference for any artwork or collectible the world over. Fascination with art has never been greater, its audience larger, or the challenges of the fertile market this activity has created been more substantial. Its genesis has its roots in the mid-twentieth-century art boom that rode a postwar economic wave of prosperity, and Elmyr was in the right place at the right time to take full advantage of this gold-rush fever and satisfy his buyer's desire for his believable and always-affordable fakes.

He recognized the roles of his enablers and how often mutual interests intersected at the bottom line, whether that meant profit or prestige. And it is this common ground, where morality is brushed aside by willing participants that renders laws ineffective inhibitors to art crimes. The lessons learned from this forger's tale, I suspect, may well arm the art world with knowledge to avoid being duped by future artists gone to the dark side, but will do little to thwart the indomitable self-interest and mercantile survival-of-the-fittest instinct that prevails in the art world. Furthermore, as this return to social Darwinism gains traction, the notion that business (any business) should be tempered with a modicum of fair play (morality), which lends civility and benefits a society, is then discarded and has no place in laissez-faire capitalism. If greed then is the engine that drives our economy, it is unsurprising that this is the same rule by which criminals play. In addition, "regulation" is not a welcome remedy, but rather a dirty word to the free-market slaves. They consistently insist that measures meant to police business practices are hostile to free enterprise, thus creating the loopholes and havens for unethical or illegal activity. The steady ascent of prices attached to art continues to provide the greatest incentive to make art crime a growth industry in a bleak landscape of economic disparity. According to *The Journal of Art Crime* in 2010, "The annual dollar value of art and cultural property theft is exceeded only by trafficking in illicit narcotics and arms." Elmyr's saga may then become a how-to book rather than a cautionary parable to the would-be forger.

Profit-motive is what art dealers and Elmyr had in common, and in this respect, they were cut from the same cloth. This reality is what obscures the line that separates Elmyr from his victims. Law-and-order enthusiasts see less gray than black and white here, and that allows their condemnation of Elmyr and others like him to be unequivocal. This moral superiority, in my view, is disingenuous in light of a culture that discourages stricter regulation of this business. The laws that now exist governing the art trade are as unsettling as they are ineffectual. A dealer cannot be prosecuted for fraud unless he "knowingly" traffics in inauthentic or stolen works of art. "Plausible deniability" is a time-honored escape mechanism for those fleeing accountability. Even though establishing provenance of an artwork is an important part of the due-diligence process in buying or selling, it too often gets short shrift, as witnessed by numerous instances of reputable auction houses selling works either stolen or looted. Nor do they accept any responsibility for determining authenticity, as that is not part of their business. They are merchants with deep pockets and worldwide influence who work tirelessly to maximize profits. Yet, I expect they too would disavow engaging in any "illegal" activity.

The *New York Times* featured an article in February, 2012, about a "little known art dealer" who sold—repeatedly—to Ann Freedman, president of Knoedler & Company, New York's oldest gallery, a passel of modern masters, including works by Motherwell, Rothko, and Pollack. Their authenticity became a firestorm of contentious lawsuits that coincided with the demise of the 160-year-old gallery. Only after huge sums of money changed hand did paint analysis indicate the presence of pigments not contemporary to those used in the purportedly genuine works. That these transactions occurred without *any* prelimi-nary testing, is only slightly less astounding than the fact that the source of the art preferred to remain anonymous—and that raised no red flags. While the lack of due diligence in establishing the bona fides of prov-enance is mystifying, it suggests a mind-set prone to engage in risky business little changed from the halcyon days of Elmyr's fakery. As long as the business practices of the art world bend to the bad habits of self-interest or greed, a fruitful future is assured for forgers and fak-ers. This inertia guarantees a paradigm impeding the forces of change. As *Atlantic* writer Megan McArdle points out, "Even a dysfunctional culture, once well established, is astonishingly efficient at reproducing itself." (*the Atlantic*, March, 2012). Here again, fine art has a cachet, a public perception, warranted or not, that dealers of such refinements and the cultural elite who make up their clientele enjoy a trustworthiness implied by economic or social status.

Democratic Senator George Washington Plunkett was famous for his alacrity to engage in "honest graft." In this regard he said, "I seen my opportunity and I took it." Elmyr just did the same. In totality, when viewing the very serious damage done by nefarious but legal Wall Street traders, speculators, bankers, junk-bond brokers, and insurance, phar-maceutical, petroleum, medical, and food industry giants and their paid-off political cronies, Elmyr's crimes amounted to chump change. For these reasons, Elmyr's exploits raise no sense of outrage in me, nor does he deserve an afterlife of perdition. And, while I am mindful not to excuse his criminality, but better understand it, I would argue that he actually provided something beautiful at fire-sale prices, and never pauperized his victims in the process.

Elmyr not only understood the murky ethics of these institutions and the powerful art dealers' cartel, but also seamlessly fit in among the champagne-sipping society, the patrons of this world whose thirst for his fakes seemed unquenchable. Over time, as his own works were consistently rejected, his bitterness replaced remaining vestiges of guilt attached to his art crimes. After all, value, public esteem and commer-cial success were kept at bay only by a *signature* that appeared in the lower corner of his art, whereas the demand for his art was vigorous under the names of Picasso, Matisse, Modigliani, and other established artists. The question that persisted was "If my fakes earn respect and acceptance, and my own work is grounded in the same ability, then why can't I too earn the acclaim given others?" Moreover, he thought his talent was equal to or greater than some of those he emulated. Elmyr liked to ask, "Would you prefer a bad original to a good fake?" It drew attention to how we value art and how much is based on intrinsic merit.

I suppose the foremost lesson Elmyr imparted to me was that we should not immediately look to the signature on an artwork to seek validation, nor to the price attached to it. He also rejected the notion of art as an investment and thought if these became the benchmarks to determine the worth of art, then for those whose judgment was based on these ephemeral criteria, he had little sympathy. Why? Because, if we put stock in the signature alone, we don't understand art. If we view it as a commodity, we are courting disappointment. If we think of art as an investment vehicle, we disconnect it from its cultural significance. Furthermore, Elmyr knew these distorted motives put him and his art on an uneven playing field. In a way, he also knew that he was powerless to change a system that panders to artifice, and in the end, he too realized that his celebrity and eventual commercial success was built on that artifice. People became enchanted by owning an Elmyr. I could see in his eyes his mixed emotions that the onetime rebel could only go with the flow. So, he resigned himself to this irony. Still, it was better than going unrecognized. That recognition meant that people knew his name—and if they knew him, they could love him.

For my part, these new discoveries of Elmyr's past, gaining a clearer view of a man's life consumed by deception and the realization that even I was a victim of his lies, oddly do little to change my feelings about him. As Dr. Ford once more eloquently states:

Trust is not destroyed by deceit but rather by a loss of confidence that the offending party does not have our best interests at heart.

Elmyr never once gave me pause to doubt his affection or loyalty to me, and nothing assails my love for him. My friendship with him was a blessing, and I will feel endlessly indebted to him for allowing me into his life, being a witness to an extraordinary man and time, and enabling me to now share that unique perspective. I'm lucky to have known him and loved him. I'm also confident that there are people out there enjoying his art—no matter whose name is on it.

Elmyr's self-portrait – oil

*bronze bust of Elmyr de Hory by
James Goodbrand*

Acknowledgements

This book's completion is largely due to the help, patience, and better judgment of friends, scholars, editors, and others kind enough to read or listen to rough drafts or excerpts, and who exercised more diplomacy than I could ever display.

First, I want to thank my friends, Jeff Oppenheim and Chris Allaire for giving me the inspiration to attempt writing this story. Their conviction that it merited a feature film treatment inaugurated this journey. It has not only allowed me to pay my respect to my dear friend Elmyr, it has turned me into a writer, for better or worse.

My advisors and friends, Ian Graham Leask, Lauren Coss, Susan King, Nancy Adam, and Scott Ross have provided valuable advice during this project, which leaves me in their debt. My principal editor Jennifer Lynn took on the daunting task of dusting and cleaning these pages in a way that made sense of it all. My special thanks also to Sharon Stevenson for her splendid book cover design. Most of all, it is my wife, Alice Doll, who deserves full credit for her relentless support and love she has shown me throughout these past years.

My good friend Colette Loll Marvin brought a depth of research and detail to this story that continues to amaze me. Dr. Jeff Taylor and Andrea Megyes helped enormously in gaining access to Elmyr's family records in Budapest, and interviewing Edith Tenner, Elmyr's last surviving family member.

Made in the USA
Charleston, SC
06 March 2013